SAMUEL WHITBREAD

D1209087

Also by Roger Fulford

ROYAL DUKES
GEORGE THE FOURTH
THE RIGHT HONOURABLE GENTLEMAN
THE PRINCE CONSORT
QUEEN VICTORIA
GLYN'S, 1753–1953
VOTES FOR WOMEN
THE LIBERAL CASE
HANOVER TO WINDSOR

Edited by Roger Fulford

THE GREVILLE MEMOIRS
(*With Lytton Strachey*)
THE AUTOBIOGRAPHY OF MISS KNIGHT
DEAREST CHILD: LETTERS BETWEEN QUEEN VICTORIA
AND THE PRINCESS ROYAL

SAMUEL WHITBREAD AS A YOUNG MAN

By Thomas Gainsborough

Samuel Whitbread

1764–1815

A STUDY IN OPPOSITION

ROGER FULFORD

MACMILLAN

LONDON · MELBOURNE · TORONTO

1967

Universitas
BIBLIOTHECA
Ottaviensis

© Roger Fulford 1967

MACMILLAN AND COMPANY LIMITED
Little Essex Street London WC2
also Bombay Calcutta Madras Melbourne

THE MACMILLAN COMPANY OF CANADA LIMITED
70 Bond Street Toronto 2

PRINTED IN GREAT BRITAIN

DA
522
.W45-F8
1967

Contents

List of Illustrations

Preface

O F the parliamentarians who immediately followed Fox and
Pitt the most renowned was Samuel Whitbread. For a decade
after the death of those two great men he dominated the House
of Commons. Although his speeches were seldom oratorical and
never elegant they convinced all who heard them by the sincerity
and compassion with which they were spoken. He was the
invariable champion of any victim of injustice or oppression. A
famous editor of *The Times* could refer to him without seeming
to exaggerate as 'England's greatest and most useful citizen'.

He started in politics with an advantage. He was made
completely independent by a private fortune. It is true that this
was, in one particular, a disadvantage to him, because his
wealth — or rather the source of it — prevented his being
considered for the higher Cabinet offices. He was greatly
chagrined and disappointed by this exclusion. But if his circumstances were a barrier to one side of a parliamentary career, they
were an immense advantage to him as a Member of the House
of Commons. He was never obliged — as could be said of some
of his contemporaries — to adjust his beliefs to fit what was
popular; it was never necessary for him to angle for the rewards
and security of office. This was especially fortunate since caution
and prudence were not in his character; an unpopular cause
never made him flinch — rather its unpopularity was, for him, a
clarion call to action. Such men may make themselves immediately tiresome to their fellow Members of the House of
Commons, but their indifference to the current fashions of
opinion almost invariably wins the respect of the country. In
parliamentary history Whitbread's importance lies in his being

one of the earliest Members of Parliament who were approach-
able by the obscure and unknown outside. They might have no
claim on him as acquaintances, private friends or even as
constituents but they turned to him knowing that their troubles
would be heard. If a complaint or a petition reached him he
would lay it before the House of Commons explaining to the
person concerned that he was ventilating the subject though not
necessarily endorsing the complaint. Nothing more surely
roused him than cases of indignity to human beings. There was
an example of this in 1807 when Captain Lake of the Royal
Navy was annoyed by the behaviour of a seaman on his ship and
landed him, for a punishment, on the desert island of Sombrero
in the West Indies, and then sailed away. Whitbread took up
the matter with zeal at the Admiralty and it could be said that as
a result of his exertions Lake was dismissed : Whitbread was
throughout in close correspondence with the seaman's family,
who lived in Polperro. If we were to transpose to his day a
fashionable word from the present decade, he was a parliamentary ombudsman — perhaps the earliest example known to
English political history. Parliament was his first, but not his
only preoccupation. For his life was not bounded by the House
of Commons as might possibly have been said of his contemporary, William Wilberforce, or his successful rival, George
Canning. A large part of his mortal existence was given to
Bedfordshire, to the human problems of country life and — as
was illustrated by his services to the theatre at Drury Lane and
by a multiplicity of acts of generosity — to proving that he was
conscious of the obligations of wealth.

Posterity may well be surprised that no biography of
Whitbread has ever been attempted. I am glad to have had the
opportunity to rescue from oblivion a personality who, during
the struggle with Napoleon, served the nation in the realm of
ideas. Since no account of him is readily available, except the
excellent article about him in the *Dictionary of National Biography*, he is perhaps largely remembered today for two reasons
which hardly do him justice. The first is that his circumstances

contradicted his opinions — he was rich and he was a Radical. His wealth was based on beer, and there is perhaps a further contradiction here because members of the liquor trade — though they may have influenced political opinions have seldom formed them. He is also remembered because he was one of three distinguished public men — Castlereagh and Romilly are the others — who committed suicide after Waterloo. But, as often happens in human affairs, the things most easily remembered are seldom the most important and in Whitbread's case they certainly do not explain why he was called 'England's greatest and most useful citizen'.

There are two particular reasons why the more serious side of Whitbread's life is scarcely noticed today. The curtain falls abruptly on any man who dies in mid-career. Whitbread was 51. His possible achievement in the maturity of his powers is only guess-work. We might perhaps hazard the guess — and justify it — that if Whitbread had lived we should have been speaking of Whitbread of the Reform Bill rather than applying that term to his brother-in-law, Grey. So it is that since his party was in opposition for virtually all the time that he was prominent in Parliament, the historian will search in vain for any positive achievement to attach to his name. The other particular reason which kept the curtain firmly down on his career was the nature of his death. Suicide was still regarded by many people with almost medieval horror. We should therefore be justified in supposing — though there is no proof for this — that his family felt that a biography would only arouse speculation about his death, and since he had many critics on account of his opinions they probably felt that the matter was best left alone. So completely was he overlooked that a sound twentieth-century historian could lament that all his papers had disappeared.

The facts about his collection of papers were quite otherwise. When their disappearance was lamented more than 6,000 letters and documents were in the custody of his great-grandson, Mr. Howard Whitbread. Samuel Whitbread had in fact kept his

correspondence with the meticulous care of a filing clerk in a
government department. He not only kept the letters which
were written to him, but in early days rough-copied all his
answers. Later he employed a secretary to do this, and also gave
the task of copying to his young children. The history of the
collection is curious. After Whitbread's death, his neighbour
and business friend, William Wilshere of the Frythe, with Grey,
went through them. We know that they destroyed a great many
but there is no indication what they were or why they were
burned. No doubt everything bearing on the suicide went; it is
also likely that anything revealing the quarrels with Grey and
the official Whig leaders likewise went. Letters thought to be of
especial interest — such as those from the Duke of Wellington
and those of family concern — were handed over to Whitbread's
eldest daughter, who three years earlier had married Captain
William Waldegrave, R.N. After this destruction and distribution the remainder lay at Whitbread's house in Bedfordshire
(Southill) guarded but unarranged. All looking through the
collection have reason to be grateful to Mr. Howard Whitbread,
who arranged to have them catalogued and sorted by Major
Montagu Duberly. Anyone working on the collection would
wish to acknowledge their indebtedness to Major Duberly's
careful work and to the extremely helpful index which he compiled. After the Second World War Major Simon Whitbread
handed over the papers to the safe-keeping of the Bedfordshire
County Record Office. Miss Ethel Hampson, a distinguished
economic historian, had been invited to write a biography of
Whitbread from these papers. Unhappily she died during the
progress of the work, and it is only possible to lament that she
did not live to complete it. Her book, dealing closely with the
great economic and public issues of the time, would have been
more than a biography and would have been of great service to
historical learning. For the more limited and personal study
which I have attempted, the collection at Bedford was possibly
of less value than it would have been to one writing a more
strictly historical and less biographical study. As would be true

of the correspondence of a twentieth-century Member of Parliament it is more revealing of the topics of the day than of the character of the recipient. They are not so much the papers of an individual as the storehouse of a champion of human rights.

I should like to thank Major Whitbread most warmly for making these papers available for me. Miss Godber — the Bedfordshire County Archivist — has helped me in countless ways with her knowledge and experience so that I have come to regard her headquarters above the Ouse as a place where problems and difficulties are almost magically solved. Mr. and Mrs. Sam Whitbread have allowed me to enjoy the architectural beauties of Southill and to take note of the books and personal possessions of their predecessor to be seen there. Mr. Humphrey Whitbread, who lives at Cardington and has unrivalled knowledge of the family and of the treasures at Southill, has helped and encouraged me from the start. The chairman and directors of the Brewery, and in particular Mr. Raymond Seymour, have done everything possible to ease my path. I have been lucky in their choice of Mr. Dennis Cole as the collaborator with me over the collection of material, and he has journeyed from library to museum in response to suggestions or requests from me, and I have been the gainer from his hard work and ordered mind. Mr. P. R. Wright, a member of the accounting staff at the Brewery, has helped me by shedding a clear light on the finances of Whitbread which were hidden (however hard I tried to master them) in impenetrable fog. Mr. H. Douglas Thomson and Mr. Martineau have guided me with their knowledge of the history of the Brewery, and saved me from many pitfalls.

Lord and Lady Waldegrave unwearyingly entertained me, and allowed me to make the fullest use of the important Whitbread papers in their possession. Mr. Blackett Ord has generously allowed me to see the unpublished typescripts of the Creevey letters at Whitfield, and Mr. and Mrs. James Blackett Ord made it possible for me to do this at their home at Helbeck. What I saw of these papers encouraged my belief that Creevey is a more considerable politician than is sometimes supposed.

Mr. Quentin Skinner of Christ's College, Cambridge, allowed
me to see some valuable conclusions which he formed when
working on the Whitbread manuscripts, especially about Drury
Lane and the details of Whitbread's enclosure of Cardington in
1812. The Librarian at Eton College took much trouble on my
behalf over the career of the Reverend William Langford, D.D.
Mr. J. E. Fagg, Reader in Palaeography at Durham allowed me
to use letters from Whitbread to Lord Grey, which are de-
posited in the Prior's Kitchen under an arrangement between
the university and the dean and chapter. Lady Howick gave me
much helpful family information. The Oxford University Press
gave me permission to see an advance copy of the important
edition of Sheridan's letters, edited by Mr. Cecil Price. Lady
Bonham-Carter, who is descended from Whitbread's younger
daughter, and the archivist of the Hampshire County Record
Office, provided me with copies of material in their possession.
The British Museum, the Public Record Office and University
College, London, which possesses the papers of Lord Brougham,
have been extremely helpful. The reader will notice that in some
of the footnotes I have referred to these manuscript collections,
and I have done so by the place where they are kept. As always
I have availed myself of the ungrudging service of the Librarian
and staff of the London Library. For all this help I should like to
express my deep obligation and my sincere thanks. Mr. R. W.
Ketton-Cremer most generously spared the time to read the
book in typescript, and gave me the benefit of his deep understanding of the period. Mr. Richard Garnett, with infinite
patience and kindness, has saved me from countless mistakes
and errors of taste. Those that remain are mine, not his.

A final word. Although there is in existence a large body of
manuscript material and many printed allusions about Whitbread, little of it runs below the surface of his personality. Like
many another biographer I have been left lamenting that the
subject of my book was happily married. He and Lady Elizabeth
were always together. After they married, the letters between
them could be counted by the pawns on a chess-board. More-

over, though Whitbread was a large letter-writer he was a
guarded one. He confined himself to the point and had little time
for those trifles about himself which reveal character. Perhaps it
would have been possible to amplify the picture of the man by
psychology — to trace back the disaster of his death to influences
in his mature and early life. But I have preferred to leave my
readers to judge the matter for themselves and to see the man
as he appears in his letters and speeches, as he looked to those
who lived in the world with him and above all as he emerges
from the fairly detailed background to his life which I have
attempted to recapture. And perhaps only those who have stood
out against public opinion in a time of national danger can fully
appreciate the sweep of mind and braveness of spirit which were
the companions of Whitbread along his often solitary path.
Such qualities deserve to be rescued from oblivion.

ROGER FULFORD

June 1966

MAP OF BEDFORDSHIRE

From The New British Traveller, *published by* **G. A. Walpoole** *and others, London, 1784*

CHAPTER ONE

Family Background

BEDFORDSHIRE is certainly not an arresting county for the headlong sightseer, since it is neither distinguished by dramatic scenery, nor studded with antique, architectural fragments. A slip of a county, about thirty-five miles long and twenty miles wide, it is an area of movement traversed by Watling Street — the great highway from London to the north-west, by the Great North Road to Scotland and by the Icknield Way which led the traveller on from the civilisation of the Thames Valley to the sterner realities of existence in East Anglia. The fens which begin to the north-east of Bedfordshire prepare the unwary for the great monotony which stretches ahead of him. Into the same corner the Ouse flows down from Bedford; before Bedford it swings from the Buckinghamshire border north-east and roughly divides the shire into two.

In the eighteenth century before the brussels sprout with a host of minor trades transformed the scene, Bedfordshire was a purely agricultural county — mainly arable but with some sheep especially westwards. There were — it is true — gleams of a more varied day in the straw-plaiters of the southern villages, the pillow-lace makers of the north and west towards the Buckinghamshire border and the growers of garden-vegetables in that girdle of sand which ran in an easy loop eastwards from the great house at Woburn to the Cambridgeshire boundary. But the vale of Bedford was all golden corn, and to the north of it the fields were largely wheat and barley : the southern part of the county below the turn of the Ouse was largely dairy farms, whence carts of Bedfordshire butter slowly travelled towards London. Bedfordshire people enjoyed a less enviable diet than butter : their slow-moving rivers produced an abundance of vast

pike, gudgeon and black, fine eels. The residents were duly
thankful for anything so satisfying as these coarse fish, for
among the fields and the rivers poverty was general and
conspicuous. A Scotsman, travelling through the county in the
1780's, and familiar with the frugal habits of his native land,
noticed that the people of Bedfordshire were glad to burn cow-
dung in their homes, standing it on end as the Scotsman stood
up his sweeter divots of peat.[1]*

But for all its drawbacks Bedfordshire had one solid, emphatic
advantage. It was healthy. The air was brisk — without the
enervations of Oxford to the west or the too bracing, liverish
buffetings of Cambridge to the east. And in those distant days
before agricultural machinery, railways, ladies' hats and motor-
ways, there was a charm about the Bedfordshire landscape —
perhaps inconspicuous to the rattling tourist, but patent and
satisfying to the perceptive, unhurried visitor. Certainly it was a
quiet scene, broken by nothing more dramatic than the steeples
of churches and made beautiful and fruitful by 'the fantastic
windings' of the Ouse. Edward FitzGerald, who loved and knew
every inch of the country round Bedford, every turn in the Ouse,
every country pot-house and the quality of its ale, summed it up
for us who can never know it as it was, never catch the silence
behind the roar of industry — 'it's all deuced pleasant'.[2]
Unquestionably it was.

One characteristic of English life the county lacked. The
absence of an aristocracy was remarked in Bedfordshire by a
shrewd observer — 'Hungry time hath made a glutton's meal
on this catalogue of gentry, and hath left but a little morsel for
manners remaining'.[3] It is true that the great family of Russell,
housed like princes to the west of Bedford, was a fairly substantial and enduring morsel, but for the rest the feudal families
of Bedfordshire had dwindled to a few political lords, with
shadowy pedigrees going back to the days of the fighting
kings — the Edwards and Henrys — and just a few proud
squires, mouldering close to some starving village and im-

* The figure [1] indicates an entry in the References on p. 318.

prisoned for the winter by roads along which even the stoutest horse could scarcely flounder. The gentry were reinforced by a flow of London merchants and notabilities. But if the clay soil and clear air of Bedfordshire proved fatal to the feudal aristocracy, it combined to produce a sterner breed of famous sons. Bunyan and John Howard — the prison reformer — lend illustrious names to the county and they are supported by a stalwart company of men — less renowned but famous in their generation for deep and enlightened feelings. Among them was Samuel Whitbread, father of the subject of this biography.

Samuel Whitbread, known as Samuel Whitbread I to distinguish him from his son and from the proliferation of Samuel Whitbreads which was to follow through many generations, was born under King George I at Cardington in Bedfordshire. Cardington is an attractive village, some two miles to the south-east of Bedford, with a simple charm which is characteristic of the countryside approaching the Ouse. In a modest Bedfordshire style the Whitbreads, through many generations, had lived in a house on the approaches to Cardington called The Barns — an agreeable name with its suggestion of threshing and owls in the rafters. Samuel Whitbread I's grandfather had fought for Cromwell, distinguishing himself when Newport Pagnell was besieged by Prince Rupert. He would seem to have bequeathed to his descendants a certain ineradicable defiance of established authority.

The first Samuel Whitbread's father, Henry, was Receiver-General of the Taxes for Bedfordshire; he was twice married, and the boy — as one of eight children — had to look beyond the Ouse and the cornfields for his prospects in life. When he was 16 he was apprenticed to a London brewer, John Wightman, for what was then the large fee of £300. Six years later he opened up a small brewery with two partners in Old Street in the City of London, starting eight years later the Brewery in Chiswell Street, which was to prosper amazingly and spread his name to the four corners of England and to the world beyond the seas.* To an

* I am not concerned in this biography — except incidentally — with the

B

extent Whitbread was lucky : he entered the brewing trade at a prosperous moment. In the first place home-brewing was passing out of fashion at the same time as the hefty men of England — those, for example, who had to shift heavy loads in the London produce markets — were acquiring a taste for something rather stronger than the light ales. This demand was met by porter, deriving its name from the brawny drinkers who were supposed to have a particular relish for it. Another popular name for it was 'entire'. Stout and porter were the only beers brewed by Whitbread. This kind of beer was peculiarly suitable for large-scale, commercial brewing and the demand for it — not capable of a rational explanation but dependent on fashion, which in the same way ordained that stout was to become popular in the nineteenth century — became a highly popular venture and led to the great brewing fortunes which became apparent through the eighteenth century. Pre-eminent among these fortunes was that of Whitbread, and an envious comment on the size of Whitbread's riches came to the ears of Horace Walpole through one of his favourite correspondents living not far from Bedford. Replying, Walpole alluded to Whitbread's 'insolent wealth'. He did not know Samuel Whitbread, and the adjective was unfair.

No doubt Whitbread launched his venture at the right moment : the tide of popularity for porter was flowing strongly and steadily with him through all the middle and later decades of the eighteenth century : he could hardly have failed to move forward prosperously but it was the extent of his success which was phenomenal. (It was admired and envied by his competitors as those familiar with Mrs. Thrale and Dr. Johnson will remember. Indeed did not Thrale in an effort to surpass Whitbread 'overbrew' himself?) The Chiswell Street Brewery was one of the wonders of business London among the multi-

history of the Brewery. It is, of course, a distinguished one, and it has been well told in *The Story of Whitbread's* (1964), to which the reader is referred. Against a wider background Peter Mathias's book *The Brewing Industry in England* (*1700–1800*) (1959) is invaluable. I have borrowed some information from this important book.

plication of riches which marked the Augustan age. Part of the explanation for the astonishing success of Whitbread's Brewery was that the owner had that kind of open, expansive mind which is always ready to experiment. In Chiswell Street new machinery, and ingeniously designed premises were the secrets of a success which was triumphant. Steam-powered machinery was introduced in 1785.

But what the fates gave with one hand they took from him with the other. In private life he was singularly unfortunate. He married, when he was in the late thirties, Harriet Hayton, the daughter of a London lawyer, with territorial connexions at Ivinghoe in Buckinghamshire and with a distant family link with the aristocratic house of Duncombe.* They were married in 1758, and she bore him two daughters before giving birth, on 17 January 1764, to an only son — the subject of this book.† Six weeks later she died.

The year following his wife's death he bought Bedwell, a fine property, close to Hatfield and less than twenty miles from Chiswell Street. Although this property was in Hertfordshire he maintained his family connexion with Bedfordshire through the ownership of The Barns at Cardington and his political connexion as Member for the town of Bedford. Bedwell, a massive structure standing today, testifies to the well-lined pockets and to the stylish, up-to-date taste in country-house life which influenced the family which bought it. ‡ When Whitbread lived there the house was old, ramshackle and set in one of those blazing Hertfordshire gardens which delight the eye and surprise the visitor to that sombre countryside. After a day in the Brewery in the summer, Whitbread used to drive down to Bedwell — a journey of perhaps two and a half hours — and

* This explains why she is sometimes (though incorrectly) described as descended from the great Parliamentarian Pym.

† His birth is given as 1758 in all the books of reference. I had accepted this though puzzled why he had seemingly gone so late to school and the university. I am very grateful to Mr. Quentin Skinner, of Christ's College, Cambridge, for pointing out the correct date, which is confirmed by the Cardington register at the time of his burial.

‡ Whitbread sold it to Sir Culling Smith.

one of his daughters has recalled the house as she remembered it — 'the age of the house, its pointed roof, old staircase and window, old yew and fir trees hanging over it as you drove in at the gate, through a double avenue of oak, on a summer evening from London had most captivating charm'.[4]

He also owned a house in Westminster, later moving to Portman Square. Five years after his wife's death he married again — into a family which was, on this occasion influential. He married Lady Mary Cornwallis, sister to the celebrated general who is remembered for his surrender to the American insurgents at Yorktown, but should likewise be remembered for a highly distinguished career in India and Ireland. She was niece to the Archbishop of Canterbury. But this powerful connexion did not dazzle the brewer and in August 1769 he wrote to the brother of his first wife : 'It is both my wish and intention to keep up the connexion that has subsisted between our families ever since my first marriage. Lady Mary is particularly desirous it may be continued, and I will answer for her behaving in all respects accordingly.'[5] But the fates were to give her little chance to behave as her husband wished, for she died in December 1770 giving birth to a daughter who, in the years ahead, was to marry into the Grey family and become the great-grandmother of Lord Grey of Fallodon.

Faced by these tribulations Whitbread met them with the fortitude of a devout churchman and by preoccupying himself with his business and with public affairs. He was elected Member of Parliament for Bedford Town in 1768 and continued to represent it for nearly a quarter of a century. In politics he increasingly adhered to the side opposed to change, becoming in the 1780's one of the most faithful of Pitt's followers. He signed his first election address 'your affectionate countryman and neighbour'.[6] Many years after this, two Members of Parliament were walking home after listening to Whitbread's son in the House of Commons and one turned to the other and said of the father : 'he was an exceedingly odd man'.[7] Judged from the conventional outlook of the landed aristocracy he must have seemed so. He had no background of the classics : his mind had not been broadened by foreign travel : his characteristics were rather practical and patriarchal and marked by success and independence from the fashionable opinions of his contemporaries. He seemed odd because, as his descendants recognised, he was uneducated but yet possessed a mind endowed with great resources. He was the personal friend of Pitt and acquainted with Dr. Johnson — two men with whom the conventional parvenu would have had little enough in common. They both highly valued his originality and common sense. Though his character was strong he had a certain playfulness of mind which he liked to indulge with a long glance at posterity. He erected a summer-house at Cardington, and years later when his descendants pulled it down they found a parchment, describing a little ceremony of laying the foundation stone 'in the presence of Mr. Samuel Whitbread and of Ann Cromwell, great-great-great granddaughter of Oliver Cromwell of glorious memory'. In somewhat the same way he set down for his descendants the reason why Cardington was the first place where he bought land 'because it was the place of my birth and inheritance of my fathers and as it has pleased God to bless us with good abundance who went out, as Jacob said "with my staff only" '.*

He would also have seemed odd to the realistic Englishmen of his generation because he was devout and unashamedly so. Among his books there has survived a copy of Dr. Johnson's *Prayers and Meditations* which were published in 1785. This was obviously in daily use by the brewer and had scores of annotations and reminders about the season when each prayer was appropriate. In his younger days when benevolence had not become the fashionable quality which it was to become at the end of the century, he never hardened his heart to those in distress, and he was always mindful of those who had helped him to build up the Brewery. Here is a touching prayer which he wrote on 31

* 'I am not worthy of the least of all the mercies, and of all the truth, which thou hast showed unto thy servant: for with my staff I passed over this Jordan.' (Genesis xxxii.) These particulars are at Bedford.

August 1791 — his 71st birthday. After recollecting his sins and God's mercy he says :

I bless thee O God for all thy goodness to all my dear dear dear dear children. . . . Oh may I never forget my God, beware of covetousness and be mindful of the wants of others and never turn my face from any poor man that the face of God may never be turned from me. . . . I pray for opportunity to take leave of my dear children and recommend them to the mercy and favour of God and advise them against waste of time especially in bed as incompatible with duty to God and man.[8]

No doubt in the censorious twentieth century we smile at the simplicity of the supplication, at the reason which he offers for giving to the poor and the last and totally unexpected advice to his children. But we can understand how it was that twenty years after his death he was alluded to in the House of Commons as 'that good man'. Good men, however, are not necessarily the best of fathers.

His son's upbringing was severe, as was customary for one of his generation, sombre, as was perhaps inevitable for a motherless child, and marked by a certain joylessness which, in those days, was an inevitable accompaniment of the religious mind. Samuel Whitbread the younger was largely brought up by his mother's mother and by her unmarried daughter.* They were devoted ladies who gladly included in the little family the motherless half-sister after Lady Mary's death. One letter only from Mrs. Hayton has survived, a letter which she wrote when Whitbread became engaged : 'I am thankful to God I have lived to hear it. . . . I can only hope that you will both accept the blessing of a grandmother who is grateful for all your goodness to her.'[9] But family life in the eighteenth century — at any rate among the conventional classes — was strangely stiff and formal. The only letter, written by his aunt, which has survived, begins 'My dear Sir' and ends 'I am, dear sir, yours most affectionately'.[10] And always, in the background, was the formal and frosty presence of his step-grandmother, Lady Cornwallis.

* Hereafter 'Whitbread' without prefix or suffix means the younger Samuel, the subject of this biography.

This is the letter which she wrote to his father when he told her of the engagement of his younger daughter.* The point of the letter is that the elder daughter† was yet unmarried.

Corke Street Aug ye 14 1780

I beg you would assist me in making my congratulations to Miss Emma. Would Miss Whitbread excuse me if, with compliments to her, I added, she would oblige me very much if she would give me an opportunity of writing just such a letter on her account. These easterlies prevent all news.‡ I am, Dear Sir,

Your humble servant
E. CORNWALLIS[11]

Although in childhood and boyhood Whitbread was seldom with his father, the precepts and morality which that good man loved must have been often ringing in his ears. In the great closing speech which he made on the impeachment of Lord Melville, Whitbread referred to something which he must surely have acquired from contact with his father :

In the early tales of infancy some golden dreams have amused my imagination, and I have heard of a mountain, at the summit of which a great treasure was to be obtained that many had undertaken to acquire, but so many obstacles have been successively presented to them, that their hopes were disappointed. If they waited to listen or indulge themselves with the view of the flashing objects, they were turned into stone : they were to be alarmed by no threats, fatigued under no trials, and to pursue their objects straight onwards until they had accomplished of their noble ambition.§

Severity and melancholy were blended in Whitbread's origins. When his father lost one of his sisters, he decked his infant children in mourning, and added 'it seems theirs as well as my livery'.[12] But the temper of the child did not match the

* Emma, probably born in 1762. She married the twelfth Lord St. John of Bletso at Bedwell in 1780 and died in 1825. They had four daughters.

† Harriot, born 1758. She married James Gordon of Stocks in 1789. He was M.P. for Stockbridge, Truro and Clitheroe. She was living in 1829.

‡ i.e. from America, where her son the general was campaigning.

§ *The Arabian Nights' Entertainments* — possibly a rather unexpected children's book in the Whitbread home.

livery. 'Sammy is as usual easy and happy' was his father's comment on him in infancy. Perhaps school was less of a contrast than it would have been for his more tenderly-fostered, aristocratic contemporaries and as he would seem to have gone away to school when he was only five this may have been as well. His father, though insular in his own habits, had an implicit faith in foreign travel, and the boy was only nine when he was first taken abroad, through the Low Countries, to Spa.

The great liberating influence in the boy's life was unquestionably Eton, and it is likely that Lady Cornwallis, who had married into one of the renowned Eton families, was responsible for the choice of school.* He went there when he was 11 to a private tutor, Heath, who was presumably the subsequent headmaster Benjamin Heath. He was in the sixth form when he was 15. One of the friends he made there — Charles Grey, the future Prime Minister, who was known at school as 'Lanky',[13] — was a constant influence over his life until his dying day; another, William Lambton, father of the celebrated Lord Durham, was to prove an intimate not only at school but at Cambridge and in public life until his untimely death in 1797.† Also in the same circle was Richard Wellesley, afterwards a distinguished Governor-General of India. Although no information has come down to us of Whitbread's time as a schoolboy, we are perhaps justified in drawing two conclusions about it.

First and unlike his father he was an educated man — in fact extremely well educated. So much is clear from his speeches in public life into which were woven a diversity of allusions to the classics and to the literature of his native land. These interests are also clear from his personal collection of books at Southill. (As early as 1797 Charles Grey was urging him to buy the poems of Coleridge and Southey — perhaps the tragedy about Robespierre.) He was obviously a clever boy, but some of the

---

* In the Eton College Register he is described as her grandson.

† Whitbread was one of the trustees of his will, and just survived to see the election to the House of Commons of his distinguished son.

credit for his educated tastes must belong to the school where they were formed.

Eton can also fairly be given the credit (or the blame) for the political principles which he absorbed with his friends Lambton and Grey. The later 1770's revealed a mood in England which was not so much dissatisfaction with political parties or with political leaders as with the whole system which could provoke — and continue the attempt to overwhelm — the colonists in America. In that distant land lay the cause of freedom, and many enlightened people felt that the attempt to subdue America, which was accepted by the conventional and easy-going, was comparable with the attacks on freedom associated, in the previous century, with our Stuart sovereigns. Lafayette in drawing his sword for Washington reflected the spirit of the chivalry of Europe, the fight for liberty against tyranny. This feeling that freedom's battle was being fought out in the uninteresting countryside inland from New York is shown over and over again in the pages of Horace Walpole; it could make him say when the rift between the two English-speaking peoples was complete 'If England is free, and America free, though disunited, the whole earth will not be in vassalage'.[14] No doubt it is a natural but dangerous mistake for political mankind to interpret the present by the precepts of the immediate past: no doubt there is a case to be argued for King George III and Lord North, and no doubt they had little enough in common with the tyrants and despots of the seventeenth century. But the point was that people felt that Great Britain had been guilty of more than a mistake in policy: rather it was a betrayal of those enlightened principles, won amid the tribulations of the seventeenth century, which shone out from the island through a dark world. So it seemed, at least, to the young. When one of the young princes of the blood was supposed to have shouted outside his father's door 'Keppel for ever' (Keppel was the popular anti-Government candidate for Windsor) he was not so much mocking his father as acting as spokesman for his generation. Opinions which penetrated to the young within the stone walls of Windsor

Castle were likewise felt within the mellow bricks of Eton.

Whitbread's university career was curious, as it embraced a spell at both the ancient seats of learning. A letter from his father, dated 13 October 1781 says: 'I left Bedwell this morning and went to Eton to set off Sam to Oxford'.[15] He was young (17) though not so young as William Pitt the younger, who was alleged to have arrived at Cambridge with both a tutor and a nurse. His contemporaries Wellesley and Grey went to the university when they were older, and it is possible that his father, anxious for his help in Chiswell Street, was forcing him on. The next we hear of him is being comfortably installed as a fellow-commoner at St. John's College, Cambridge, in 1782, and we can only guess that he may have had some kind of illness at Christ Church since neither disorderly behaviour nor intractability were among his characteristics. Those who know Whitbread's future might be tempted to argue that there was an essential disharmony between his opinions and those of Church and King which dominated the common-rooms of Oxford, and especially Christ Church: it was only a generation before Whitbread's day that the university rang with shouts of 'redeat' — a veiled allusion to a Stuart restoration. But youthful undergraduates, easy in their own companionship, are apt not to heed the encrustments of the senior members of the University. The mystery of his change of university remains.

At the end of the eighteenth century St. John's and Trinity were the pre-eminent colleges at Cambridge with perhaps the former leading by a canvas. Together they filled one-third of the places in the Senate (the governing body of the university) and their combined force of undergraduates dominated Cambridge in reading, boisterousness and rank. Here in Cambridge the three Eton friends were reunited — Whitbread at St. John's and Grey and Lambton at Trinity. They were high-spirited, though a certain gravity tempered their spirits: Grey, in reply to a correspondent asking how he was enjoying Cambridge, wrote 'My only objection to it is that I think the study too confined. If a man is not a mathematician he is nobody.'[16] The friends read a little, worried their heads over the way the world was turning but yet contrived to enjoy themselves.

From these undergraduate days began the most extraordinary but the most constant of Whitbread's private friendships. The three friends formed part of the circle of one of those odd characters who, in every generation, are to be found haunting our universities. Tom Adkin was six years older than Whitbread and had been born at Downham Market in Norfolk. He was extravagant, open-handed, conversational, extremely witty, enjoying the sallies of youth and watching with relish the play of dawning powers on argument and reason. Reputedly rich, he spent his patrimony in a wild burst at Cambridge.* He was a member of Corpus, and took his B.A. degree in 1782. Although such examples of his wit as have survived seem to raise no smile after nearly two centuries, there was an inconsequence and absurdity about his conversation which smoothed the frowns of the authorities of his college and entranced his younger friends. He thought that he might have made an excellent Irish bishop; chiefly because he could never pass the simplest examination in theology. He was offered a sinecure post by Grey, but when he found that this involved a journey to Jamaica he, perhaps wisely, declined it. He lived opposite Trinity at the White Bear Inn which became known for many years as Adkin College. His dinners were frequent and invariably riotous : when the proctors, attracted by the noise, demanded what was going on they were always told that Squire Adkin was entertaining a few hunting friends. This was possibly not an unfair disguise for Lambton and Whitbread since both were keen followers to hounds.[17] Tom Adkin and Whitbread's father were not calculated to understand one another : they were divided by that difference which distinguishes the producer of a commodity from its user. In 1785 Whitbread received this letter from his father 'I have received a letter from Mr. Atkins [sic] of Downham. I dislike this man's

---

* I doubt his riches since his father seems to have been only the curate at Downham. I am grateful to the present rector there for finding this and other particulars about him.

character'. Then after saying that his son has been helping this
reprobate with money he ends 'he is a man of a loose character,
not fit for your acquaintance. I wish you would Explain how
you left that money'.[18] Young Whitbread was not persuaded to
drop his friend : when he married, Tom became a part of the
establishment — a jester and greatly at his ease among the
mahogany and the glass.

CHAPTER TWO

Abroad with the Archdeacon

CAMBRIDGE drew to an end for Whitbread with the spring of 1784, and in February the father, in his crabbed and fastidious hand was writing 'Many speak well of you at Coll: so pray make a good finish'.[1] In those days there was a mixed examination for the B.A. degree — a little divinity, mathematics, logic, algebra, Euclid and the classics. The verdict was 'pass' or 'fail'; there was no grading by classes. Whitbread passed. But in college examinations at St. John's, held throughout an undergraduate's time of residence, there was a grading by classes and some record of these has survived. In June 1782, the record goes :

Had it been usual to compare those who was examined for the first time with the others Lambe [William Lambe] and Whitbread would have been classed very superior ... December 1782. First Year. The first class consisted of Mr. Whitbread and ... [names of eight others]. [As a fellow-commoner Whitbread was correctly given the courteous prefix.] June 1783 First year. First class. [other names] and Mr. Whitbread. All very good and have prizes. December 1783. The third class consists of Mr. Whitbread and [three others].*

The slight falling off in pre-eminence no doubt explains Whitbread's father's comment and was perhaps a consequence of the gay hospitality of Adkin College.

Whitbread's father was essentially restless — an energetic nomad hurrying to Brighton or Margate to bathe, to Bath to sip the waters or to Wales to gaze on mountains. Foreign travel (though he had himself no time to spare for this indulgence) was for him a natural specific for youth. He shared with his generation a belief that the mind was broadened by being brought into

* I am very grateful to the Keeper of the Records at St. John's College for this information.

contact with capitals and glaciers. In the case of Whitbread he
was determined that his son should not make the universally
fashionable tour down France and along the leg of Italy to
Rome, but decided that he should travel east and north, rounding
off the tour with a rapid excursion to Italy. Today such a
journey might be called a tour of the northern capitals : in the
eighteenth century it was rather a visit to the domains of those
extremely alarming potentates — Frederick the Great of
Prussia, Catherine the Great of Russia, Stanislaus of Poland,
Gustavus III of Sweden and Christian VII of Denmark. Lord
Chesterfield once called the sovereign of one of these nations
'that northern brute'. They all perhaps in varying degree
merited that description : they were all certainly far removed
from the sultry, effete personages to be met in Venice or Rome.
Whitbread's tour was designed to strengthen character rather
than to polish it.

The problem for the father was to find a companion-tutor who
would be congenial but firm. Eventually he chose William Coxe,
the future Archdeacon of Wiltshire, a voluminous writer, and
still a standard authority on such edifying topics as the Bourbon
kings of Spain and the members of the imperial family of Austria.
Northern Europe he knew well as he had travelled there with
Lord Pembroke's heir, Lord Herbert, and had collected facts
about prison-life in Muscovy — a fairly grisly undertaking —
for John Howard, the great humanitarian and prison-reformer,
who was descended from an aunt of Samuel Whitbread and was
a strong and abiding influence over him. But the elder Whitbread left nothing to chance. He first consulted his brother-in-
law, Cornwallis, and reported back to his son 'My Lord thought
Coxe unexceptionable.'[2] And when the tour was fairly under
way he was able to send his son an endorsement of the choice
which was decisive. On 25 June 1784 he wrote :

I this day paid a visit to Dr. Johnson, who is indeed in a bad state of
health.* I told him where you was and your plans and who was your
friend and fellow-traveller — he knew Mr. Coxe perfectly well and

* This was three days after Johnson dined for the last time at The Club.

said many exceedingly handsome things of him . . . surely you had the person with you of whom for the purpose there was not, he thought, any other so proper or so equal in the kingdom.[3]

With complacency Whitbread added his own encomium on Coxe 'In him you have the classick — historian — Friend — and Gentleman.'[4]

But perhaps as the east wind blew over northern Europe, and the youth and forty-year-old divine forged manfully onwards other qualities were necessary than a knowledge of Cicero or of the capabilities and charms of King Carlos III of Spain. These additional qualities Coxe had in abundance; short and stocky, the future archdeacon was an admirable companion on a journey; he was not only full of topographical knowledge but, as Lord Herbert said, 'he was a hardy, stout traveller'. But a question mark hangs over one side of his character, and the reader is left wondering whether his private life was quite up to the gaiters he was to assume, and the encomiums of Johnson. His visit to St. Petersburg with Lord Herbert and an officer in the Army, seven years before he went with Whitbread, must have been decidedly gay — or unseemly as the reader prefers. This is clear from a letter which Lord Herbert wrote to him when he arrived at St. Petersburg with Whitbread, asking for news of some of their friends. The letter went like this 'I suppose the Narishkin girls are married ere this and f-k-g about Petersburg like rabbits. There was one *handsome*, not unlike a *horse*. The Neledinski with her wrinkled temples, still alive? . . . And the great, fat, beastly Zuphoff (I believe was her name) is she still breathing? My comps. to them all, if you please, and do not tell them I say they may all go and be damned.' And complimenting his old tutor on the gift of a diamond-studded snuff-box from their Russian friends the expressive peer adds, 'Ye gods and buttered fish'. From Cambridge the clergyman had written to Lord Herbert, lamenting that, in the monkish life of Cambridge, he had seen 'hardly any other women than his bed-maker'.* This correspon-

* These particulars are to be found in the delightful *Pembroke Papers 1780–94*, edited by Lord Herbert (1950).

dence seems somewhat removed from Johnson's verdict that
Coxe was the most proper person in the kingdom for the care of
the young, but such gaieties are unlikely to have been indulged
by Whitbread who, through life, showed no partiality for them.
No hint or whisper of such things was ever attached to him.

Lord Herbert's father, Lord Pembroke, was in Italy when
Coxe and Whitbread arrived there at the beginning of 1786 and
wrote: 'Cox is here and *vous dit mille choses*. He has £800 per
annum for travelling with a rich young brewer Whitbread, who,
entre nous, will not learn either modesty or *bon ton* from him.'⁵
Lord Pembroke, with the edge to what he said which marked
the eighteenth-century aristocrat, has put his finger on the real
point. He had always found Coxe rather tiresome and lively —
he liked his clergy to be quiet, gouty personages — and he was
perhaps right to hint that he was deficient in gentility. Whitbread was a young man of high spirits and vanity to whom
modesty was something of a stranger: to the superficial
conventions of the *bon ton* he was all his life antipathetic. He was
likely to be swayed in such propensities by a man like Coxe,
whom he greatly admired. If Lord Pembroke's verdict on Coxe
was correct and so far as it was a part of Coxe's duties to give
the character of the young man an aristocratic polish he could
not be counted a completely wise choice.

In the 1780s Europe, somewhat like a small craft which lies
uneasily in the seeming calm of the trough between two gigantic
waves, had left behind the long drawn-out struggle of the
Seven Years War and was preparing to encounter the towering
danger of the Revolution in France. Those are the picturesque
episodes of Europe's history — vivid, easily remembered, and a
delight for the investigation of historians. But the development
of the lives of the peoples of Europe between these two spectacular events of history was possibly of more lasting
consequence than the battles of Frederick or the massacres of
Robespierre. A great liberal writer, H. A. L. Fisher, has
pointed out that before ever the people of Europe plunged into
the wars of the Revolution there were 'faint signals of the

SAMUEL WHITBREAD THE ELDER

By Sir William Beechey

THE SOUTH YARD OF THE BREWERY AT CHISWELL STREET, c. 1792

From an engraving by W. Ward after a painting by G. Garrard

coming industrial democracy which were already visible in the sky'. The industrial development of England was proving contagious.[6] Possibly for this reason the father was anxious for his son to go east and north rather than to the languors of the peasant south, and to mark the signs of industrial change in countries other than his own.

Coxe and Whitbread left in June 1784 and travelled to Hamburg with several servants and their own chaise. Travelling through north Germany and Schleswig-Holstein they reached Copenhagen on 14 July and entered Sweden six days later. Here they were received with distinction. The King — Gustavus III — was one of the ablest and most arresting of the benevolent despots. Gifted with an amazing memory — he could come home from the theatre and repeat the principal speeches of the play — he shared with his uncle, Frederick the Great, a taste for the arts. He was a clever, capricious man bored by politics and fighting, and consequently classed 'a play-boy' by those who think superficially on the nature of human beings. Among his rather easy-going and uncompetitive subjects he kept up a regal splendour which owed much to Versailles. A few weeks before the English visitors reached Stockholm, the King had returned from a long tour in Europe, and on 8 August he held a court which was attended by the clergyman and the young brewer. They had to cross from Stockholm to the Queen's Palace (Drottningholm) on Lake Malar. They were in full dress; for the layman this meant sword, knee-breeches and powdered hair : they travelled in the Foreign Minister's barge but as the weather was squally the experience was disagreeable. At the palace they were amazed by the apparel of members of the court, which was blue silk and satin, lined with white, for both sexes. King Gustavus was wearing what Coxe described as 'a fancy dress of purplish silk, much embroidered with gold'. Whitbread and Coxe were presented to the King, and he told them that Sweden had few paintings or statues 'but we can show you the works of Trollhätta, Karlskrona and Sveaborg'. This was an allusion to the docks (commercial and naval), the building of

c

which were the glory of the King's reign. Later the two
Englishmen were presented to the Prince Royal, who went
through the forms of the drawing-room with wonderful ease
and address. He was six years old.[7]

When they left Sweden they travelled through Finland and
entered Russia, reaching St. Petersburg on 2 November and
staying there until the beginning of April. The architectural
glories of the city belong to a time just after Whitbread's visit;
when he knew it, St. Petersburg was an open, spacious city the
political and social capital of Catherine the Great's vast Empire.
It was a little patch of civilisation — polished, urbane and
Frenchified — in the midst of a great and barbarous waste.
There were considerable settlements of foreigners drawn there
by Russia's export trade of which it was the centre, and though
the society was gay and the court brilliant they were both
dimmed by the languor of the Russian temperament. But life
was agreeably arranged : at the end of the 1770's the Foreign
Minister never found it necessary to work for more than an hour
a day. When an Englishman had occasion to complain of a
robbery he found the Chief of Police, at seven in the morning,
playing a game of *la grande patience* by himself with a filthy
pack of cards. The English Minister at St. Petersburg summed
up the feel of the place and its inhabitants some six years before
Whitbread arrived there 'The friendship of this country
partakes of its climate, — a clear, brilliant sky with a cold
freezing atmosphere : all words and no deeds : empty professions, and shuffling evasions.'[8]

We do not know to what extent Whitbread entered into the
social life of St. Petersburg. He was probably present at one of
the court functions of Catherine the Great. His father, who
always wanted him to mix with foreigners, would have been
vexed to know that in St. Petersburg his companions were
found among the English community. On leaving Russia he
confessed that he had been very glad to see it but emphasised
the magnificence, filth, knavery and vice, 'from which Good
Lord deliver me. My stay at Petersburg, however, will be

remembered by me with delight, from the pleasure I had in the company of a select half dozen, who I am proud of calling my friends.'⁹

The most constant of these friends was an English business man — J. Browne.* They corresponded frequently and Browne, who had the *Morning Chronicle* sent out to him, 'to be sure it does not come damp to breakfast every morning but in the lump weekly' congratulated Whitbread only two years after he was elected to the House of Commons 'on being so conspicuous there'.¹⁰ Another friend was Joseph Billings, the companion of Captain Cook in 1779, who was commissioned by the Empress to explore the Eastern Ocean (the North Pacific) and described his experiences in a letter with many messages to Whitbread. A third friend was called Sutherland and he wrote to Whitbread fifteen years later that he well remembered Whitbread's words when he was in Russia viz. that he feared 'my father's riches were mere ropes of sand'.¹¹ That was a curious remark — perhaps engendered by the easy-come, easy-go fortunes of St. Petersburg, but revealing an indifference to wealth, which marked Whitbread's character, and also perhaps a certain insensitiveness to his father who was striving to make the ropes of sand.

He left St. Petersburg and his English friends in April 1785. At Riga they dined with the Count de Browne, who had been born when William III was king, and like other Irish jacobites put his sword at the service of the Russian Empire. He was governor of Livonia for the last thirty years of his long life. From Memel they travelled along the narrow strip of sandy beach, the Kurische Nehrung, never able to progress at more than three miles in the hour. They travelled at this snail's pace for forty hours, the travellers getting out from their carriage to walk along the sea-shore and pick up pieces of amber. They reached Königsberg and then cut down south for Warsaw — as

* Keats's friend, Charles Armitage Brown, had an elder brother, John, who was ruined by the collapse of his business in St. Petersburg in 1810. Despite the difference in spelling he may be the same J. Browne.

Coxe puts it, 'we quitted the Black Eagle of Prussia, and recognised the White Eagle of Poland'. The white eagle had not many years left to soar over Eastern Europe and had already suffered loss by partition from the savagery of its black and double-headed brethren in neighbouring eyries. At Warsaw the travellers were 'benignly' received by King Stanislaus Augustus.[12] In his brilliant youth this sovereign had drawn to himself the lascivious eye of Catherine the Great and in return she had engineered him on to the vacant throne of Poland. Surrounded by a camarilla of ladies including a favourite sultana, who was the widow of an upholsterer, King Stanislaus reigned ingloriously for three decades. In addition to the information that they were benignly received we should have liked to know the exact feelings of the straightforward young Englishmen towards this ageing roué.

From Warsaw they moved west to Berlin, still under the sway of Frederick the Great, and Whitbread would remember his father's request, 'I wish for some picture of that old man'. But he was able to send his father something more personal than a picture, for he and Coxe had a short interview with the formidable sovereign himself. Alarming, quizzical, unhappy, the King, who had kept all Europe in turmoil, faced the handsome young Englishman. Within a few months Frederick the Great would be no more, and it might not be fanciful to see in that chance encounter the meeting of two civilisations — the mannered but ruthless European typifying the eighteenth century and the generous-hearted young Englishman already revealing something of the humanitarianism of the age which was to follow. Whitbread noticed the ill-kempt clothes 'nastied with snuff' and the absence of front teeth 'which breaks his voice and prevents him from playing the flute'. The conversation started rather stickily with the King asking Whitbread 'whether I was related to Mr. Pitt. I answered "no". He repeated the question with surprise and on my second denial he changed the subject.' The King had been told that Whitbread's father was a friend of Pitt and he had evidently confused the words

in translation. They then talked easily — largely about Russia.[13]
Leaving Prussia they travelled through Munich to Switzerland. Here, no doubt through Coxe, they met M. de Bonstettin,
who had aroused a romantic passion in the poet Gray at
Cambridge — 'an old friend at Cambridge of our poet Gray has
been very civil to us here' Whitbread wrote.[14] They met two
English brothers, Roman Catholics, Thomas Clifford and his
brother, afterwards Lord Clifford : together they clambered up
the approaches to Mont Blanc, and reached a heap of stones
known as 'le bon homme' overlooking the valley of Chamonix.
They made two heaps, six feet in height and ceremoniously
styled them 'Le monument de quatre Anglais'. They stayed on the
St. Gotthard pass at the celebrated hospice as the guests of Friar
Francis. No doubt this was on the way down to Florence, and
they must have stayed there on the way back because in 1787,
when Whitbread was in Switzerland again and stayed there, he
refers to it as his third visit.[15] Despite the presence of his
Roman Catholic friends it is reasonable to wonder if Whitbread
had any of the feelings experienced by Matthew Arnold in the
Grand Chartreuse :

> Wandering between two worlds, one dead,
> The other powerless to be born.

Whether or no he was conscious of this wider conflict he was
certainly acutely conscious of a conflict between his own
intentions and the views of his father. To begin with the old
gentleman (as Whitbread called him) was anxious that the tour
should cover a great area of Europe and that it should not
include English companions. 'As you don't mention them, I
hope you see no English' he wrote in the first weeks of Whitbread's absence.[16] He would not have approved of the
convivialities at St. Petersburg with Messrs. Browne and
Sutherland, nor of the sojourn at the hospice with the two Mr.
Cliffords. For the father the tour was intended to make a brewer.
He had in large part rebuilt the Brewery in the summer of 1784
and wrote off to his son with a triumphant description of the new

structure : 'I have since been in town to see how the Brewhouse affairs go on which is very rapidly — the walls to the yard are got up and look very handsome. The coppers are setting and there will be a very noble stage for the mash tuns. The whole place will be very capital when finished and bespeaks you for a master.'[17] We can picture Whitbread folding the letter and placing it in a portfolio — perhaps sighing as he thought of the hopeful expression for the future with which the letter closed. For had not his education and his travels and the opportunity to see something of foreign statesmen at first hand widened his horizon far beyond the Brewery and Chiswell Street, beyond the world of business to the world of affairs, beyond the society of the Trumans, the Perkinses, the Thrales, the Allsopps, and the Calverts, to the company of men concerned not so much with their own fortunes as with the fortunes of their country? And in justice to the father it should be said that although he naturally hoped that his life's work would be continued by his son he was understanding of Whitbread's reluctance to be a brewer. The following letter which he wrote to his son shows that this was the case :

Portman Square Jan. 25 1785

. . . the reasons you give for being serious and thoughtful at times are proper and you express yourself handsomely and feelingly on the subject of Trade. But pray don't make a burthen of it to hurt your spirits, for it is a matter that you and myself can part with and I have studied the mode of doing of it if occasion [arise] and written my thoughts on it for your inspection and guide. And you would have two good reasons to give; one that it would take too much of your time from other employment in life that you are from education more inclined to yourself. The second is that you have as much affluence as can make a reasonable man happy. . . .[18]

And here one point must be made. Some writers — including his own family — have suggested that Whitbread was a man without friends. That is certainly not true of him in youth. He plainly held the affection of those he met. Twenty years after their jaunt on Mont Blanc, Thomas Clifford wrote to him explaining that he and his brother — they were both married —

never came to London because 'as things are, a Roman Catholic gentleman can have no business there but pleasure'. He adds how he would have enjoyed seeing Whitbread 'how happy I should have been in other circumstances to have improved the advantage which a kind fortune had thrown in my way'.[19]

CHAPTER THREE

Elizabeth Grey

O N getting back to England in the autumn of 1785 Whitbread no doubt settled down to help his father in Chiswell Street — though reluctantly. The reader would be mistaken in supposing that Whitbread's aristocratic friends from Cambridge somehow led him astray from Chiswell Street and dimmed the delights of brewing. This has often been suggested but it reveals a slender knowledge of the subtleties of English social life. Though they may not have been a part of the aristocracy, the Whitbreads were accepted by it; at Portman Square and at Bedwell the old gentleman entertained a very stylish circle of friends. In September 1784 he wrote to his son describing an 'illumination' which his daughter gave at Woolmers, the small property adjoining Bedwell. 'Your sister took infinite pains and altho' it was sudden as possible yet there was no want of company, for all the neighbourhood was there of all sorts — the Hatfield family, the Exeters, the Clarendons and others. . . . I think there were about fifty of our principal company. They danced till two in the morning.'[1] There was no lack of aristocratic company round Whitbread's home, and the old gentleman hoped that his son would bring home as his bride — Lady Charlotte Bertie, the daughter of Lord Abingdon,[2] with whose family the Whitbreads were friendly. It was not that Whitbread moved in aristocratic society (which would not have markedly distinguished him from his father) but it was that he joined a particular, political coterie of the aristocracy, and it was this, coupled with his own inclinations, which led him away from Chiswell Street. He was introduced to this circle through his friend Charles Grey, though it is just to add that Whitbread's wealth, his charm of manner and his appearance, which had won him friends abroad, made him an acceptable guest in the great Whig houses and in particular at Devonshire House. Perhaps women never enjoyed a more decided political influence in this country (even after they achieved the right to vote) than did the celebrated hostesses on the Whig side at the end of the eighteenth century. Among these sharp-witted ladies the Duchess of Devonshire was pre-eminent. The duke (though a shrewd and warm party-man) was very solemn: his was, in fact, a somewhat thunderous personality, adding little by way of lightness or gaiety to the brilliant entertainments arranged by his wife. His character is well caught by the remark which he is supposed to have made when his wife fainted in a crowded room. Being told what had happened he simply commented 'I thought the disturbance came from the women'. The duchess was 30 when Whitbread returned from his tour and was at the height of her fame and loveliness. She was not only full of grace and beauty but gifted with wit and a mind of great capacity. Perhaps her only conspicuous failing was a certain recklessness which did not restrain her from living in a curious *ménage à trois* with her husband's lover, Lady Elizabeth Foster, and from making appreciable inroads into the Cavendish fortune by an irresistible passion for gambling. She won the undying devotion of the Prince of Wales, of Fox and of Sheridan. Many loved her. The duchess's most sympathetic biographer tells us that of her lovers she really loved only one in return — Charles Grey.[3] Remembering Grey as the resolute Prime Minister of the Reform Government, with his faithful wife and swarming tribe of children, we have difficulty in seeing him, as he once was, ardent, handsome and gay. So he seemed in that brilliant summer of 1786, and both Georgiana, Duchess of Devonshire and Fox saw in him a lively recruit for the social and political beliefs on which Devonshire House rested. What began as a love-affair — the Duchess bore a child by Grey (familiar to social gossips as Eliza Courtney) — ended with honourable admission to the ark of the Whig Party. The affair, apart from these bare facts, is

completely obscure, shrouded in the mists of history and
safeguarded by the loyal reticence of those who knew. In the
admirable biography of Grey by G. M. Trevelyan there is no
shadow of the story — not even the slightest hint of it.*
Unquestionably both Whitbread and Lambton moved at the
heels of the lover and, though not sharing the favours of the
duchess, were welcomed with open arms to the very heart of the
Whig cause. Long years afterwards Whitbread, towards the end
of his life, received a letter from the third member of the *ménage
à trois* at Devonshire House, who had married the duke after
Georgiana's death. The letter is only dated 'Wednesday night',
but it was written some time after 1811, when the duke died.

'Dear Mr. Whitbread, in a large parcel of papers wh I took
with me from D. House, but wh I never had courage till now to
examine, I found some letters of yours wh I now return you —
pray believe me very sincerely yours E.Devonshire.' It is of
course possible that the letters were merely political and that
with the good feeling of the day the duchess was returning them
to the writer lest they should fall under the scrutiny of some
political journaliser. But if that is so it is strange that they have
not survived with the rest of Whitbread's political correspondence. And it is possibly significant that Grey went through
Whitbread's papers after his death and is known to have
destroyed a large number of them.

And the friendship with Grey bore fruit of a different variety.
During that summer Whitbread fell irresistibly in love with
Grey's sister Elizabeth. Perhaps it would not be discourteous to
a distinguished family to define the Greys in the eighteenth
century as a provincial aristocracy. And if that were true it is
right to remember that the provinces, north of the Trent, lent
to the families living there a lustre — derived from long lineage
and wide acres — which distinguished them from similar
families living in the south. There park-wall jostled park-wall :

---

* 'I know little of my father's life, when not attending his parliamentary duties,
before his marriage' (General Charles Grey, *Life and Opinions of Charles, 2nd Earl
Grey* (1861).

in the north the range of property seemed to stretch as far as the proudest eye could see. The Greys had a family connexion with the illustrious houses of Tankerville and Grey of Werke: distant and shadowy this relationship may have been, but it is sufficiently established to provide, no doubt, many a happy afternoon for a genealogist in the College of Arms.

The medieval connexions of the Greys lay buried in the violence of Border life and through the eighteenth century they were preparing to emerge from northern eminence to metropolitan fame. Some of their prosperity, which made possible this descent on London, came from a tactical but happy marriage with an heiress of the Woods of Fallodon. Whitbread, like many a writer after him and many a patient scanner of proofs, was to write to his future wife — 'Is Fallodon or Falladon correct?' The house was built of red-brick with stone facings in the year of Blenheim: it was of moderate size — three windows on either side of the front door — standing in a neat, though not spectacular, countryside with gardens famous for fruit. 'You can never eat too much fruit' once observed Edward Grey — the most celebrated occupant of Fallodon. To the west lay the Cheviots, hiding Fallodon and sheltering it from Scotland, while two miles on the east were the shallow breakers of the North Sea. Although the family at this time owned Howick that property boasted of no house but only an old tower by the sea, so that the Greys made Fallodon their centre. Charles was the eldest of a vigorous and delightful family of five sons and two daughters. They loved the Queen Anne house and its surroundings. What for Whitbread began in the London summer of 1786 was completed in the autumn at Fallodon against a background of family gaiety and northern sport. The father, another Charles, was a tough, north-country general — possibly a trifle surprised to have produced this good-looking and talented family of children. He fought at Minden in 1759, where he was wounded, and thereafter won distinction in battles across the Atlantic. He won an important victory over the Colonists in the American War of Independence — partly

owing to a surprise attack which he brought off by ordering his
men to remove the flints from their muskets, thereby avoiding
the risk of impetuous fire. He was known thereafter in military
circles, as 'no-flint Grey'.

His final command was in the West Indies after his daughter's
marriage to Whitbread. In the 1790's the sugar islands —
divided between the French and English — were for each
nation one of the chief sources of their national wealth. Engrossed in the heart of Europe the French had to leave their
extremities, and Grey mopped up the French islands with the
ease of a knight on the chess-board prancing among the pawns.
But Grande Terre (Guadeloupe) eluded him, and he was
languishing in the West Indies pouring out his misfortunes (in
somewhat unsoldierly fashion) to Whitbread. 'Every friend I
brought out dead . . . reinforcements only sent out to fill the
hospitals and die . . . all my servants dead except for one little
black . . . I am nearly done for.'[4]

He was to live for twelve more years, being made a peer, as
Lord Howick, in 1801 and advanced to an earldom in 1806.
Their politics did not coincide, and Charles Grey said of his
father 'the stuff he writes me about politics quite makes me
sweat'.[5] But those versed in the history of the peerage have
hinted that he was only honoured out of respect to his distinguished son.* The father was in reality a fine, strong-charactered
general whose forthright temper and impatience of opposition
were reflected in his children and lent their distinctive strength
to the family qualities.

His eldest daughter, Bess, was like Emma Woodhouse
handsome and clever and had lived in the world for rather more
than twenty years with very little to distress or vex her. She
was well-read, not particularly sociable but shared the self-
centredness which marked her distinguished brother. She was,

---

* This is absolutely untrue. When the peerage was announced in 1801 Fox wrote
to Charles Grey : 'I am very much concerned indeed to hear of your father's
peerage, more especially as I understand that it vexes you very much. It is
undoubtedly a provoking event.' (C. J. Fox, *Memorials and Correspondence*, (1853)
iii, 340.)

in short, outwardly an appropriate wife for Whitbread. Unlike Emma Woodhouse she was not rich but in the circumstances that was neither here nor there. Consequently it is difficult to say why Whitbread's father objected to the marriage, though it is possible that he was instinctively apprehensive of the political allies of Charles Grey — Fox and the Devonshire House circle. Though she may have lacked the aristocratic splendour of Lady Charlotte Bertie his objection can scarcely have rested on the delicate issue of quarterings. We also know that there was nothing personal. 'He told me that he liked the match much better than the intended match with Lady Charlotte Bertie.'[6] There is also no evidence that he disliked Charles Grey; we hear of Grey staying at Bedwell, listening to Miss Harriot Whitbread playing 'My Lodging' on the organ and letting out a great horse-laugh at the conclusion of that performance. We must therefore conclude that the marriage was not sufficiently brilliant to overcome the natural prejudices against marriage of the father, who was looking forward to Whitbread's concentrated help with the Brewery in Chiswell Street. But object he did.

After his stay at Fallodon in the autumn of 1786 Whitbread was eager to get married, but his father insisted that he should go abroad for a few months — possibly with the hope of shaking his son's intention and certainly with the reasonable object of giving him time for reflection. Loud and constant were the son's complaints about his father. He described what he endured as 'the agony and tears he has cost me'. And as he landed at Calais in May 1787 he wrote imploring his father to let him come back. But there was no relenting even though it meant that Whitbread had to miss the celebrated visit of King George III, Queen Charlotte and some of the princesses to Chiswell Street, which took place in June, on the King's birthday. Peter Pindar wrote a highly diverting poem on this visit displaying for the benefit of his readers all the components of the Brewery from bungs and water-pumps down to the number of nails in each hoop: the characteristics of the Brewer himself are well caught including his habit of cajoling the voters of

Bedford with prayer-books and copies of Bunyan, rather than with the more conventional dressing of gold and beer.[7] And the poem included the scandalous allegation that Whitbread always enjoyed a calf's head on each anniversary of the execution of King Charles I. The King was supposed to have offered the 'man of malt' a knighthood and to have received the reply that he was 'too old'. Whitbread's eldest sister Harriot was there and according to Pindar, the King said:

> Hae? what? Miss Whitbread's still a maid, a maid?
> What what's the matter with the men?

The poet also pictured the King, writing in a memorandum-book, the facts and figures which struck him. Rather cruelly he was supposed to have added:

> To remember to forget to ask
> Old Whitbread to my house one day

For his part, Whitbread was delighted and wrote to his son that the day had gone much to the satisfaction of the visitors and the visited. With the easy wit of youth Whitbread, writing to Elizabeth Grey, said that he would have called it a visitation. Harriot was not his favourite sister and he makes no reference to her: he was devoted to his young half-sister and was always amused by her failure to manage her 'r's' — 'Mary was pwesented, and was monstwously fwightened'. He goes on to say that the enquiries about him from the King and Queen had been numerous and particular. He added 'an old lady from Berkeley Square attended and was not the least inquisitive of the party'.[8] This was Lady Harcourt who had a distant family connexion with Lady Charlotte Bertie: no doubt there was curiosity among that then small world of coronets about the reason for Whitbread's absence on such an historic occasion — curiosity tinged with regret that his great fortune was doomed to go elsewhere than within their narrow, gilded circle.

Unhappily Whitbread pursued his summer journey through France. He was accompanied by two friends — a north-countryman called Nesfield, who was reading for the Bar, and had to leave the party in Paris so as to eat his dinners in the Temple. His other companion was Tom Monson, the younger son of Lord Monson and in the future for many years Rector of Bedale. After lingering in Paris, seemingly unconscious of the march of change, for it was only a few weeks after the Englishmen left that those memorable if ominous words were spoken : 'it is not *états de finance* [statements of account] that we want : it is *états généraux*', they went west to Bordeaux. The highlight of adventure on this trip was their decision to abandon their carriage and travel on horseback. From Bordeaux a hogshead of claret was sent to the 'old gentleman' and also to Sir Charles Grey at Fallodon. Finding it almost unbearably hot they turned once more to the mountains and glaciers, and Whitbread again sojourned with the monks on the St. Gotthard pass and landed safely in England towards the end of September.

The journey could not be called pleasure : it was discipline. And perhaps the sensitive reader will feel most deeply for the future Rector of Bedale with this sighing companion at his heels. Monson must have been a delightful and sensible young man, because in spite of everything the two travellers seem to have got on excellently — there are few grumbles, except about his *esprit railleur*, against him in Whitbread's letters to Miss Grey — and, when the vagaries of the French postal service failed to disgorge a letter from Fallodon, Monson changed Sam — 'that ugly monosyllable' as Whitbread himself described it — to Sad. For sad he certainly was. There were three separate causes of disagreement with his father. The paramount one was marriage, but his father evidently wished him to settle down at the Brewery and disapproved of Whitbread's political stirrings. Such things were beyond the comprehension of the father who once wrote 'The Brewery is always in my thoughts'. From France, Whitbread wrote to his father that if he had to stay abroad till Michaelmas he would not be able to settle down in Chiswell Street because his mind and time would be occupied in the arrangements for his marriage. Then he went on : 'The General Election will probably come off before the next winter

is completed,* and there will probably arise another very
material source of distraction, and a lasting one for business,
before I shall have made myself master of it' (i.e. the Brewhouse). That sentence is of singular importance to an
understanding of Whitbread's life. Could an active career in
politics go together with the management of Chiswell Street?
His father thought not. And the clash between politics and
business was to prove a perpetual 'pull baker — pull devil'
throughout his life. His phrase that politics might prove a
lasting source of distraction from the Brewhouse could have
been a threat to further his main objective — marriage. It was
also a prophecy. All these things were heavy anxieties for the
young man and if it is true that he had had some kind of
breakdown at Oxford there is perhaps significance in his saying
that if his father would let him come back 'it would rid my mind
of a burthen it is almost unable to support'.

And it is fair to try to see matters from the father's side.
Whitbread could be not only very obstinate but too outspoken
and too blunt in his choice of language. Whitbread wrote, on
receiving his son's first letter from France on 17 May 1787 :

My Dear Dear Son, I had much pleasure in receiving your favour
from Calais, as I think it an affectionate one, and in the style in which
you was used to write to me. . . .
   The present excursion is rational and intended to amuse yourself in
a pleasing variety of objects and country and to clear your mind from
very fixed and stern ideas — such as of late I have seen lay hold of
you.† I thank God and am very happy to think what a companion‡
you will have in every view — therefore I beg you to return his
civilities and show yourself a man, be calm, live temperately or else if
your spirits are bad and ruffled will make you more subject to fever
disorders.
   Both of us [i.e. father and son] earnestly aim at your happiness in
domestic life — for all the possessions of this world will not avail

---

   * Parliament had been elected in 1784 and no election, under the Septennial Act,
need have been held till 1791. Whitbread presumably followed the prevailing Whig
opinion that Pitt's government was too shaky to run its full course.
   † Politics.
   ‡ Monson.

SAMUEL WHITBREAD ON LEAVING ETON

By George Romney

LADY ELIZABETH WHITBREAD

By John Hoppner

without peace *here*. . . . Be cheerful, write to me often, give me your plans, take care of your health, do not be miserable — you have no reason to be so.[9]

The father's ideas on travel were those of a modern citizen of the United States : the son's were more seemly. From Switzerland at the end of the tour Whitbread wrote to his father 'We should not do well to travel together, our principles on this head are so very different. Yours is "see all you can"; mine "that it is better to see one thing well than ten imperfectly merely for the sake of saying that one has seen them."' After explaining that he has always carried out his father's wishes over travel he adds 'so that if ever I should come in company with the man who says "I have seen more *kings* and *postilions* than any person in Europe" I shall desire him to count with me — and probably beat him'. And whether this was the intended consequence of travel in the father's eyes or not, the journeys had the effect of making Whitbread something of a John Bull — not in contempt for foreigners and their politics but in the sense that he loved England and the English character, and both in his outlook and his utterances reflected that honourable partiality. 'Yes I do glory in that attachment to my own country which characterises a travelled man.'[10]

Through his own words in a letter to his father, written at this time, we can see Whitbread as he was to strike the House of Commons during his twenty-five years as member. 'My intentions I find irreproachable'. Such a sentiment may fall somewhat bleakly on a modern ear : it sounded complacent to his opponents but at least it showed that he was prepared to submit his actions to some sort of judgment : even if he himself was the judge. 'My disposition — I am sensible of it — is faulty and warm'. That was absolutely true. But this distinction is important. Whitbread, though quick-tempered, was seldom one to take personal offence : he was not given to that most odious of human weaknesses — taking umbrage. His temper and warmth were reserved for causes rather than people; for principles rather than enemies. He went on 'I am long before I

D

do speak and then probably do it with too much vehemence'. The hesitation in speaking he was quick to shake off, and the vehemence grew with the years.

In the last letter from abroad he assured his father that he remained perfectly steady in his attachment.

Passion has no share in my present feelings. I have a reasoning;

> And on reason built resolve
> That column of true majesty in man.'[11]

His love letters show him to have been a thoughtful lover — persistent rather than ardent. He wrote in much the vein that millions of men have written before his day and since. He was filled with alarm because he fancied the terms in the letters of Lady Elizabeth, were not so warm as he had expected : he was terrified that she might turn against him in consequence of the vagaries of the old gentleman. He tried to be loyal to his father and described him as 'really good *au fond*, and although the *fond* is sometimes a great way off one is sure to find it at last.'[12] Then there was the common anxieties of lovers — what men was she seeing and who would partner the Regina of Northumberland (the phrase was Monson's) at the great assize ball in Newcastle. And then the gossip and innuendoes which he had to endure. He met an elderly Lady Glyn, when he got home, in a London shop. The conversation went as follows : *Lady Glyn* : 'I last heard of you in Northumberland.' *Whitbread* : I came back about a month ago.' *Lady Glyn* : 'Pray, was Lord Erroll there when you were ?' *Whitbread* : 'I had seen him; he is now at Fallodon.' *Lady Glyn* : '*And do you return ?*' But Lord Erroll, who later committed suicide for betraying an official secret entrusted to him by Pitt, did not seem a very serious rival. Whitbread, recounting the episode to Elizabeth Grey, merely added 'I hope his stay at Fallodon will be protracted to see you and me married.'

Looking through this collection of letters (all treasured by the recipient) the reader feels that mixture of sound sense, kindliness and good feeling which marked the writer. Such qualities always seem in control : their power over him is never dethroned by passion. He emerges as respectably ordinary, not adventurous but always warm-hearted and considerate. In short a son-in-law whom all the world might envy. Though the letter might seem too dramatic for all tastes, he wrote, on setting out for France, urging Elizabeth Grey not to forget him but to marry another if he should have the misfortune to die abroad.

Here and there glimpses of him appear from the letters. He had had since infancy a lock of white hair over his left temple. He confesses to a taste for horses and hunting which he well knew that Elizabeth Grey neither shared nor approved. In spite of his father's injunction that he should avoid English people he and Monson had a spirited encounter with some young bloods — Mr. Askey and Sir Francis Sykes's son. 'Lord Belgrave and Lord Paget etc etc make up the tribe'.* These worthies organised a horse race and 'the whole town turned out to see the gentlemen in their Caps and Jackets. . . . You will suppose that where horses were in any way concerned I was one of the first in the affray'. He goes on that this was not the case because he was as unconcerned a spectator as any watchmaker in the town. He adds 'I am Boy eno' and Fool eno' to like riding a race most exceedingly. . . . I have been stript to my orange jacket very often'. But the reason he gave for taking no part in this contest was that everything got back to the English papers which were 'set for my name', and would have liked nothing better than to publish a paragraph that 'young W— is ruining himself on the continent by horse-racing'. He might not have minded so much if he had not known that the paragraphs would find their way to the censorious eyes of his father and his confidants, in Chiswell Street. Moreover the father would not have approved the lingering in Switzerland which he described as a country, like Scotland, 'to be trotted into' at any time from England.[13]

There is one other scrap of evidence to suggest that, though naturally serious, he had a lighter side. A few days before Christmas 1787 he dined with two friends in London. One was

* Other escapades of 'the tribe' are amusingly described in Lord Anglesey's *One Leg* (1961).

Lee Antonie — a Bedfordshire sportsman, who was a lifelong friend of Whitbread's and was to share with him the representation of Bedford. The other is simply alluded to as 'Punch' : though there is no evidence for this it is likely that Punch was the old reprobate Tom Adkin, and that the 'old gentleman' would have shivered if he had known of that convivial, December dinner. The friends parted at 2.30 a.m. 'we were by no means beasts only elated' Whitbread wrote to Bess. Just as they were parting Whitbread's two friends suddenly called the watch and charged Whitbread with an attempted murder. He, possibly wisely, took to his heels : the watch followed in hot pursuit. With his rattle blaring he attracted numerous other members of the watch who joined in crying 'Stop the murderer!' Whitbread was chased down Piccadilly and was only able to escape by dashing into his hotel in Albemarle Street.[14]

But the time for these bachelor gaieties grew shorter. On the last day of the year his old friend Lambton, who had been Whig member for Durham since the previous February, wrote 'what a fortunate dog to marry the woman you love'.[15] As an unattached member of the family he spent his last Christmas at Bedwell and commented a little impatiently on the truly patriarchal style of his father's Christmas — 'mince pies and prayers'. A fortnight later he was writing of the house in Wimpole Street which he had taken and of the arrangements which he had made for the comfort of the Regina of Northumberland. 'Your establishment is complete', he wrote. 'Mr. Duc* at the head. Two footmen — a coachman — a House-keeper — a Housemaid — a Laundry-maid — a Cook — a Kitchen-maid a pair of horses and all awaiting your orders.'

They were married at Fallodon on 26 January 1788. It was a civilised wedding. No fashionable Northumbrians crowded the church : the bride and bridegroom were almost alone — solitary and conspicuous in the church. No members of Whitbread's family were present — the distance made that prohibitive. The

---

* M. Duc or le Duc had been abroad with Whitbread in charge of all the travelling arrangements. He was presumably butler in Wimpole Street.

only concession to the old gentleman's sense of occasion was a visit by father and son to Lambeth — presumably for a special licence. Archbishop Moore, who was more attentive to his own family when preferment offered than was altogether seemly, gave the young man his blessing. The comfortable, easy-going habits of the eighteenth century and the sterner outlook of the nineteenth touched for a moment as archbishop and brewer met on that January day in Lambeth Palace. On the day before the wedding he wrote to his father, apologising for any harsh things he may have said and ending, 'I remain your sincerely, affectionate and dutiful son and friend, S.Whitbread'. In the letter he had also said '*All* cause of dispute between us is now removed'. But that, alas, was not correct.

CHAPTER FOUR

A Recruit for Fox

'THE situation has become confused'. Those puzzling words have often proved the comfortable refuge of a military commentator compelled to describe a defeat. They could justly be applied to the Whig Party as Whitbread was approaching maturity. Broadly speaking that famous party had governed England for seventy years: it was a government, at its best, which guided the nation to great triumphs and at its worst a government, which was not infamous but soothed by indolence and spiced by corruption. The whole structure of that system of government and each root from which it drew its strength have been examined with microscopic attention by modern writers of renown. No doubt their labours are essential for an understanding of the causes which brought about the collapse of the Whigs in the years when Whitbread was enjoying life at Cambridge, but — as is generally true of youth — he was concerned with the panorama of events rather than with the ingenious manipulation on which the device rested.

The end of Whig Party government was not unlike the final curtain of some brilliant spectacle on the stage : the light is at its most brilliant, the music at its gayest, and the performers come dancing on changing partners or taking their places in the *contre danse*. Old favourites are identified as they come twirling by. We see Lord Rockingham the Prime Minister in 1782, doomed to die from summer influenza, sedate and dignified and applaud, in the words of Burke, 'the firmness of that noble person'. After him comes the dreaded but affable figure of Lord Shelburne 'the Jesuit of Berkeley Square' moving with the unconscious grace of the Reverend Walker skating, as depicted for us by Raeburn. And then comes the astonishing spectacle of the slightly bewildered Duke of Portland with the ponderous North moving heavily on one arm and on the other the dazzling Charles James Fox. And then as the curtain falls a wondrous *pas seul* by the younger Pitt. Between March 1782 and December 1783 there were four prime ministers, four separate combinations of ministers, confronting the great issues of the time — peace with America, Burke's blow at corruption in his Economic Reform Bill and Fox's India Bill aimed to end the misgovernment associated with the East India Company. Can we marvel if the ordinary Member of Parliament found the changes and combinations baffling so that he scarcely knew if he were an old Rockingham Whig, a tool of the Jesuit or a coalition Whig supporting Fox and North or even a supporter of the beardless boy Pitt, whose government, under the hammer of events, was to be driven into the blue mists of Toryism? To us (though not to them) one thing was as clear as a church tower in the Fens — the Whig dominance was ended, the Whig Party was in dissolution. To them their misfortunes were temporary — symptoms of the machinations of King and Lords against them over India and of the adroit manipulation of the House of Commons by Pitt. But it was a defeat not a reverse. As Peel in 1846 and Gladstone in 1894 so Fox in 1784 stands in history as a leader who led his forces to disaster.

It was the means by which they had been overthrown which rankled. Here is Fox himself at the time: 'we are beat in the House of Lords by such treachery on the part of the King and such meanness on the part of his friends in the House of Lords as one could not expect either from him or them'.[1] The Whigs turned on the usurpers, as they regarded Pitt's government, with a savagery which displayed their talents but won no votes either in Westminster or beyond. The defeat of those long in power is, in English political history, often followed by an almost hysterical violence as they assail those who have taken their place. The Tories in 1830 and the Conservatives in 1906 as well as the Whigs in 1784 remind us of this truth. Pitt and his

followers had to face the playful but indignant wit of Sheridan,
the torrential violence of Burke and the barbed oratory of Fox.
But Pitt's strength was not diminished: rather otherwise. And
one fact made the cleavage between the two more bitter; the
differences between Fox and Pitt, at this stage, were less
political than personal.[2] Had not Pitt, a member of the Whig
Party, crept into office under the ermine of the King, of George
III the traditional enemy of the Whigs? But indignation and
vituperation are seldom the high roads to Downing Street. The
more violent Fox became the calmer and more assured seemed
Pitt by contrast.

Yet unquestionably adversity had its rewards. It welded Fox
and his entourage into a party, firmly based on loyalty to tradition and devotion to a man. In 1794 when the prospects for the
Whigs had become more conspicuously dismal than they had
been in the 1780's Fox, almost thinking aloud, gave some
reasons for his belief in party. Public men, he thought, were
inevitably more or less influenced by their own interests of fortune or ambition: if in isolation, they were vulnerable to such
pressures, partly because many men were incapable of clear
decisions on public matters. For the average man whose
comprehensive understanding of affairs was limited and whose
public virtue was likewise limited, party spirit was the only
solution.

In the waning fortunes of the Whig Party the adherence of
the three young men — Grey, Lambton and Whitbread — was
a stimulating encouragement to Fox. In those days when, as
Fox hinted in the remarks about party which have been
previously quoted, office rather than the propagation of
policy was the object of a political life — their decision to join
Fox was a courageous one. Possibly, like their school-fellows
by the Thames, they lived for the moment and were undeterred
by visions of the long years in the wilderness. 'No sense have
they of ills to come'. Death was to spare Lambton the grinding
years of opposition, with all the bitter disappointments of the
other two friends and — worst of all — the personal feuds

between them. These tribulations lay in the future: for the present they were happy enough to respond with ardour and eagerness to the battle-cry of Fox. 'The tinkling of empty words such as "freedom" and "the people" were always heard when he rose to address the House', complained a twentieth-century writer.[3] Over the years and through constant repetition such words may have lost the stir and swell with which they struck those who heard them at the time. They drew the generous-hearted Whitbread inexorably to the side of Fox. For family reasons the choice was not easy and it showed courage. At that period constituencies were often regarded as a perquisite to be kept within the family; not unlike a pipe of port which the owner had become too enfeebled to enjoy, a seat in Parliament could be handed down from father to son. For example in 1787, Lambton's father who had sat for many years for Durham City as a Whig applied for the Chiltern Hundreds. Immediately his constituents chose his son, Whitbread's friend, in his place. In Bedford, on the other hand, the choice of the son, in similar circumstances, would have given no gratification to the father.

Whitbread's father starting political life as an orthodox Whig became an ardent Pittite. When the son was presented to Frederick the Great, it may be remembered that his father was described as the friend of Pitt; since Pitt had then only been Prime Minister for a few months we are justified in thinking that the father was not only a constant supporter of Pitt but an original one.

But there were dangers in this adherence to Pitt for one who was fighting elections almost within sight of Woburn Abbey, which sheltered the very heart of aristocratic Whiggery. Moreover the electoral arrangements at Bedford, though comfortable for the Dukes of Bedford at Woburn, were strangely unorthodox even in those days of weird political contests. There was no need for the Duke of Bedford to tempt the electors with the beverage which was produced in Chiswell Street or even with the works of Bunyan for, if the day seemed to be turning against him, he simply created extra voters. By a decision of the

House of Commons at the end of the seventeenth century the
right of election at Bedford was limited to inhabitants being
householders and to burgesses and freemen. This was taken to
mean that burgesses and freemen need not be inhabitants, and
it meant that the corporation of the town, which could be at will
recruited by freemen from outside, controlled elections. The
Duke was hereditary Recorder of Bedford and he could therefore
control the corporation and consequently the election. During
most of the time that the elder Whitbread sat for Bedford, the
Woburn influence was quiet because the duke was a minor; but
in 1787 the duke, who was then 22, took his seat in the House of
Lords. Francis, Duke of Bedford was a strange man. When he
was 17 he looked not unlike some product of the modern world
'with long, lank, black hair covering his face, shoulders, back and
neck.'* He was extremely nervous of speaking for fear of
expressing himself in faulty English, but he fought to overcome
his deficiencies being inspired by hereditary attachment to the
Whigs and by devotion to their leader, Fox; he won in return
the deep devotion and ungrudging admiration of that generous
man. Some years later he was summoned to a meeting of
Whig potentates who were caballing against Fox. On arriving
in the hall of the house he asked if Fox was there: on being
told 'no' he picked up his hat and walked straight out of the
house saying 'Then this is no place for me'. Again in the
future he was to draw on himself the splendid invective of Burke
— 'Poor rich man' and 'I was not like his grace of Bedford
swaddled and rocked and dandled into a legislator'.⁴ Yet Burke
was not exactly right, for if the background to the duke's life
was splendid there was — and this was historically true of his
family — a marked and frugal simplicity about the man himself.
He was the reverse of a *grand seigneur*. A visitor to Woburn in
1789 found forty horses in the stable, yet the duke generally rode
the same horse and never mounted a friend on one of his horses.⁵
But for all that it was an ominous day for the elder Whitbread

* Vicary Gibbs, *The Complete Peerage* (1929–49). The Bedfordshire County
Archivist points out that this was a middle-aged man's comment on an *avant-garde*
fashion.

when the duke threw his fiery, partisan eye across the corporation of Bedford.

The tortuous story of Bedford local politics happily only concerns the reader so far as they affected father and son. When the father was first returned for Bedford the old duke — he was the grandfather of Francis — was becoming blind and enfeebled and was consequently relaxing his political grip on the town. Broadly speaking, the elder Whitbread represented the town, which was a two-member constituency, jointly with the nominee of the duke and the Corporation. This led him into strange company. For much of the time his fellow Member was a local baronet, but for two elections he fought in double harness with a racing man, familiarly known as 'Jubilee Dicky'. In 1769 there was an alarming moment when ardent supporters of Wilkes appeared at Bedford; one was a London alderman and another was a clergyman who had just announced that for such a splendid cause as that of Wilkes 'he would dye his black coat red'. These villains, who had some local interest, arrived as opponents of the Duke of Bedford and were successful in carrying the election of the mayor against the nominee of Woburn. But through all these alarms and excursions Whitbread's father remained in possession — the Member of Parliament for Bedford. As early as 1785, he told his son, who was still an undergraduate, that the way to come into Parliament respectably was 'by invitation, not by contention'. He meant presumably by this that the invitation of some borough monger, in the way that Sir James Lowther ordered the electors of Appleby to return Pitt to the House of Commons, was much more respectable than jostling for the approval of burgesses. Electoral respectability evidently varies from generation to generation. And it is strange to see that Whitbread at one time had ideas of buying the manor of Gatton. This was a property among the chalky hills between Caterham and Redhill, which carried with it a seat in the House of Commons. When a general election came round the servants' hall was transformed into the polling-booth; here the butler presided with all the importance of a returning officer : the solitary voter, after he had done his duty by voting for the lord of Gatton, was regaled by the returning officer with a glass of sherry. Perhaps it was fortunate for Sam Whitbread the radical that he was not embarrassed by this too safe seat, and was free to proclaim himself the spokesman of the free citizens of Bedford. His heart was clearly set on Bedford — even if his candidature involved a whisper of political patricide.

The first symptom of all this appears in a letter which Whitbread wrote to his father from Bordeaux, when he was abroad in the summer of 1787. The letter is dated 22 June :

. . . You know my opinion of Wendover. I still think that you would find that you paid your money for a seat as insecure to the full, and much more expensive than Bedford.* You must be a better judge than myself of such affairs and therefore will use your own discretion. My opinion of politics I gave pretty fully in my last.† I will only apprise you of one thing — that it would be highly necessary if you would decide soon what part you mean to act at the General Election. Whether you mean to continue in for the Borough or put up for the County or whether you mean to propose me for either — which indecision prevented your having the County twice. You will pardon this hint and I hope attend to it.[6]

In the eighteenth century sons did not address their fathers in quite this blunt fashion, and we may suppose that the father, reading this missive, would have received it with that severe comment 'undutiful'. But if bluntness of speech is a failing of strong characters Whitbread was richly endowed with it. All his life he seemed unable to calculate the effect of this bluntness on the recipient of it. There seems a possibility that his father was hoping to bring in John Howard with himself for either the town or the county. He had tried to persuade Whitbread, when the latter was abroad with Coxe, that if he (the father) died his executor should issue a statement that Whitbread had determined never to put himself forward for Bedford as long as John

---

* Wendover, in Buckinghamshire, was on the Icknield Way and therefore tolerably accessible from Bedwell. It was a so-called rotten borough and was one of the constituencies abolished by the Reform Bill of 1832.

† Unluckily this letter has not survived.

Howard lived.[7] Two years later he was writing to Howard who was examining prison conditions in Russia and (as was said at the time) was 'diving into dungeons' 'the Duke and Corporation are making freemen in plenty : but will neither affect you nor me — not worth either of our thoughts. . . .' What exactly happened it is not easy to say. One thing however is clear, when the general election came in the summer of 1790, the father was unable to carry the day in the town which he had represented since 1768, and had to hand on the torch to the son. Personal and family considerations in those days weighed quite as heavily as political ones : even the father would have seen that it was more important for a member of the family to be returned, for a Whitbread to sit for Bedford, than for the family influence to be shattered by a public combat between a Pittite Whitbread and a Foxite Whitbread. Here is his description of what happened in a letter to John Howard written from Portman Square on 1 July 1790 :

I have had a miserable time to a great degree and gave it up myself a day or two before election* and my son took it up with violence and has carried it. . . . I also lost by too much kindness however it is all over and nothing could be more wretched than I have been during the time — though I was not active in the scene.

A few days later he was writing from Teignmouth 'This place is beautiful for situation. Sam and his wife here. . . . I am pretty well, but not recovered the storm to my soul, and my son is not kind nor respectful.'[8]†

The election took place in the high summer of 1790, and at Bedford there were three candidates. Whitbread, Colhoun, who had sat with the elder Whitbread in the previous parliament and Peter Payne — a clever, wild son of a Bedfordshire baronet and thought by many to be a bastard. As soon as Colhoun was seen to be safe, the Corporation of the town which was respectfully watching for a sign from Woburn, supported Whitbread, and he

---

* This presumably means before the poll opened, which lasted for several days.

† The Elder Whitbread subsequently sat for Steyning in Sussex from 1791 till his death.

and Colhoun emerged victorious from this somewhat bloody field. On 13 December 1790 Payne petitioned against Whitbread's return charging him with corrupt practices. The petition was dismissed by a select committee of the House of Commons.[9] Thereafter the duke and Whitbread controlled the political destiny of the town of Bedford. There is in all these matters an important point to notice. Many people made great sacrifices of time and money to enter politics. Whitbread made both of those sacrifices. But in addition he made an even greater one. Had he not played the part of an inverted Isaac, prepared to make a political burnt-offering of his father among the red bricks of Bedford?

But that was by no means his only attempt to batter his way to Westminster, because he simultaneously made an attempt on the county of Bedfordshire. The county was represented by Lord Ossory, an Irish peer who is agreeably familiar to readers of Horace Walpole's letters, and St. Andrew St. John, who was brother to Lord St. John of Bletso who had married Whitbread's sister. Mr. St. John was a staunch Foxite Whig, though his electoral hold over the county could best be described as shaky. He was elected by a majority of one in 1784, unseated and then reinstated by order of the House of Commons. Like many a sound Whig, including the great leader himself, St. John was not exactly scrupulous in money matters. Whitbread knew of this, and he evidently implied that it might be unwise for St. John to continue as member. Lord St. John then weighed in with one of those formal, alarming letters, winding up with a stilted assurance of being a faithful servant. He firmly stated that no one could possibly object to Whitbread wishing to represent the county of Bedford which 'is an honourable pursuit' but to try to deprive a near connection of 'an honour in possession is no strong mark of friendship or even judgment'.[10]

Whitbread's entry into politics was decidedly bellicose, and as has been seen the heavier blows were reserved for his own family. There was always hanging over his political career a marked ruthlessness explained possibly by a certain insensitiveness and coarseness of fibre but justified by his complete identification of himself with the cause for which he was fighting. He fought with fervour because he felt fervently. The methods by which he seized a place in Parliament are proof of the intensity of his political feelings. They also suggest that a career which began in storm would be pursued fearlessly and remorselessly. It was.

Whitbread's first Parliament assembled on 25 November 1790. His reputation was established within eighteen months. At the end of February 1792 he opened a debate, in a powerful speech, respecting the armament against Russia. Six years earlier Catherine the Great had fought the Ottoman Empire and made deep gashes in that now brittle structure round the Black Sea. After a long siege the Russians captured Ochakov, east of Odessa, on the Black Sea. By 1791, Prussia and Britain were threatening Russia with war unless she handed back this blood-stained fortress to Turkey. On this issue Whitbread made his first considerable speech, and the debate is not completely engulfed in oblivion because he was answered in a maiden speech of force by the future Prime Minister — Liverpool. Whitbread's argument was inevitable — the argument of the pacific against the adventurous. What had Ochakov to do with us? The possession of Ochakov, either by Empress or Grand Vizier, was 'a consideration wholly foreign to the political or commercial interests of Great Britain'. In all his speeches he was prone to appeal beyond the House of Commons to the people of England and he spoke of his satisfaction in feeling that, though he was one of the humblest of the Foxite Whigs, 'their voice was in unison with the voice of the people'. He enjoyed the thrust of debating, generally driving home what he had to say with sarcasm. On this occasion he remarked that he hoped Ministers were careful to find Ochakov on maps of only the smallest scale, because casting their eye round the globe they might be reminded that what was aggrandisement, when practised by the Empress in Europe, was only sound policy when practised by the British in Asia. With the argument that Pitt had to be supported because he was a financial genius — an argument which has crept into some of our history books — he said that it was merely an attempt to throw the gaudy veil of national wealth over 'political imbecility'. 'Three per cents at 96 is a complete refutation of every argument you can bring against his political conduct.' In his speeches his arguments were invariably more copious than select: his was a mannered style of speaking, but it was effective. Fox expressed great admiration for this speech, supported Whitbread with a speech of his own, but the motion was rejected — 116 voting for the Foxites and 244 against them.

Another characteristic of Whitbread as a debater was quickly noticed. He was completely reckless in the topics he discussed. How well we know the words of caution which freeze the courage of even the most ardent spirit. 'Perhaps not quite the time . . . wait — and we shall see more clearly how things are going to turn out . . . you may antagonise a lot of moderate opinion . . . nothing will be lost by giving time.' So the words drone on. But to Whitbread such cautionary advice was never a bridle, always a spur. In May 1797, when the Fleet was in mutiny at Spithead and had elected a parliament of delegates from each ship, Whitbread rose in his place to move a motion of censure on Mr. Pitt for his conduct with respect to the seamen. Before he could speak the member for Cambridgeshire, Mr. Charles Philip Yorke, a Whig — but a Whig who was invariably behind authority and who was to clash with Whitbread many times in the House of Commons in the future — rose 'to conjure Mr. Whitbread' to postpone what he had to say. 'The country was in danger and he called upon the House to endeavour to save it.' Whitbread was undeterred and explained that it was just because the crisis was 'awful beyond example' that he intended to proceed. He thought that the mischief had arisen through a failure by Pitt to let the men know, in time, that their demands would be met. And as was so often to be true of his career hereafter, the appeals for moderation only made him lay about with greater vigour. Pitt was guilty of 'culpable negligence' . . .

'if the House do not pass a vote of censure upon the author of that delay, we shall as grossly neglect our duty, as he has neglected his'. He contrasted the celerity with which Pitt moved when there was a question of infringing the liberties of the people by suspending Habeas Corpus. He ended by saying that 'to all the other instances of incapacity they have added this new calamity — of magnitude unascertained and of consequences incalculable'. In spite of the advocacy of Fox, who seconded the motion, only 63 Members voted with Whitbread.

Whitbread also showed in these early years his concern with the unfortunate and the oppressed of whom, as a Bedfordshire magistrate since he was 24, he had direct knowledge. In the winter of 1795 he introduced a Bill in the House of Commons to enable magistrates to fix a wage below which a labourer might not be paid; the Bill also provided that an employer, paying less than the fixed minimum should be liable to imprisonment. In those days the magistrates had the power to fix the maximum but not the minimum wage. One year before this the Berkshire magistrates, dealing with particular cases of distress at Speenhamland outside Newbury, had agreed to supplement the lowest wages from the poor-rates. There were degradations about this which were to make the Speenhamland system, over the years, execrated by working men. The Bill introduced by Whitbread was an altogether fairer method and he proclaimed that it was his hope by his Bill to redress the position of the labouring classes which was such as 'no liberal or feeling mind' would tolerate and thereby to stop the drift from the country-side to the towns and to the armed forces. This was supported by Fox, and opposed by Pitt; it was negatived on second reading.

E

CHAPTER FIVE

Friend of the People

THROUGHOUT the 1790's, as an informed debater of fearless-
ness and force, Whitbread moved to the front of the Whig Party—
a position in which he was quickly recognised by the House of
Commons itself. And the 1790's were years when Whigs had to
rely less on the strength of party than on the strength of
persons. For amidst those thunderous events in France — their
sound rolling across the Channel — many a once faithful Whig
began to turn away from party and Fox and to think of country
and Pitt. 'The days of the age of conversation were already
numbered : the age of events was at hand'.[1] Fox's salutation of
the event of 14 July, when the Bastille fell, is well known and as
his opinion was not materially different from what we may have
assumed Whitbread to have felt — all Whitbread's speeches
about the relations of France with this country during his
twenty-five years in the House of Commons reflect Fox's point
of view — it may be helpful to recall exactly what Fox did say.
His views on the events in France of the summer of 1789 are to
be found in a letter to Richard Fitzpatrick and perhaps of all the
Whigs the one who was closest to Fox. Fitzpatrick was a gouty,
gambling general. Wit, botanist and balloonist — he ballooned
on his own from Oxford to Kingston Lisle in Berkshire — he was
to cross Whitbread's path many times in the years ahead. And,
as is perhaps too often the case with men of his type, politicians
were apt to dismiss him because his life was unorthodox and, for
a serious politician, unexpected. Yet man's mind is not made
less receptive to large ideas or to new ones by sitting round the
green baize, studying the anatomy of pistils or sweeping
through the cerulean blue. So Fox found. The adventurous

general was not only his familiar but the counsellor from whom he accepted advice and on whom he tried his own thoughts on matters of public moment.

July 30 1789

DEAR DICK

I was not surprised to hear you meaned to go off to Paris, but am very much so at your having put it off. If you go you had better come this way, as I should be glad to talk it over with you a little, and it is not quite impossible but I may go too. How much the greatest event it is that ever happened in the world! and how much the best!* If you go without my seeing you, pray say something civil for me to the Duke of Orleans, whose conduct seems to have been perfect: and tell him and Lauzun,† that all my prepossessions against French connections for this country will be at an end, and indeed most part of my European system of politics will be altered, if this Revolution has the consequence that I suppose.

Yours ever
C. J. FOX

Generally speaking many people of all parties would have shared Fox's view that the changes in France marked the end of the expansionist, imperial policy of the Bourbons, and that a constitutional revolution would discipline the ambitions of France and end the ancient rivalry between her people and the British. Governments, however, seldom alter national temperaments — as the world was painfully to discover again after 1918. When it became clear that the Revolution in France, like a child's jack-in-the-box, had produced a startling apparition instead of the sober constitutionalist expected, then indeed terror reigned on both sides of the Channel. Far from being weakened France was seen to be bursting for a quarrel and only too ready to push forward her ideas (newfangled and horrible) in a form of warfare which was political and new. Opinion

* Lord John Russell, who edited this correspondence, here adds a footnote: 'The taking of the Bastille, I suppose.' Yet Fox possibly meant (especially from the reference to the Duke of Orleans which follows) the whole French constitutional and revolutionary developments of that summer — especially the meeting of the States-General (C. J. Fox, Memorials and Correspondence (1853), i, 221).

† A progressive representative of the nobility in the States-General.

rapidly hardened after three years of the Revolution and the
majority of Englishmen felt that the experiment in Paris was a
monster which must, at all costs, be destroyed. One symptom of
this prevailing alarm was that, in 1792, the great Whig Party
cracked in half. Led by Portland — not perhaps a great
politician but one of our few musical dukes — dozens of Whigs
began to join Pitt: they included the powerful brethren from
Stowe — George, Marquis of Buckingham, William, Lord
Grenville and Thomas Grenville. These brothers have been the
target for some delightful shafts from Lord Rosebery, but they
were to figure with dignity in Whitbread's life and, unlike many
political renegades, they were at least to return to the citadel of
truth. Among other dissident Whigs were Burke and perhaps
the most graceful and accomplished of them all — William
Windham. The last was, in office and as an orator, the most
considerable of all these recruits to Pitt. Fox said of Windham
(perhaps a shade cruelly) — he owed his fame to having been
much frightened.[2] But if the truth must be told the fright was
general. Indeed there were only here and there a handful of
faithful Foxites who (like Og, King of Basan in an earlier age)
carried into the nineteenth century that remnant of giants who
once bestrode the party of Whigs. Whitbread was among these
survivors.

   In politics fright tends to put opinion on the defensive — but
also on the most savage and unreasoning offensive against those
who seem in any sense in sympathy with what has caused the
alarm. So it was that the Whigs found themselves not only
excluded from office, not only deserted by old friends but
branded as friends of those who were enemies of the state in its
hour of danger. An additional and possibly the principal
reason for this was the question of reform. Throughout the later
decades of the eighteenth century there was mounting criticism
of Parliament — and particularly the criticism that the King had
too much power over the House of Commons or that men were
kept out who should have been Members of Parliament. There
were contributory streams of thought which combined to make

reform a formidable issue. There was a quiet current of opinion, carrying with it dissenters who objected to their exclusion from the House of Commons under the Test Act and constitutional antiquarians who looked back to a golden age when they thought the franchise was widely based. A typical representative of these genteel agitators was the Reverend Christopher Wyvill — an absentee Essex rector who lived in a magnificent home — Constable Burton in the North Riding of Yorkshire. Of all political questions constitutional reforms attract the bore as surely as a drop of ale attracts the wasp. Wyvill does not escape this harsh judgment; of one of his pamphlets Horace Walpole wrote : 'I never saw such a composition of obscurity, bombast and futility.' Yet although the human frame shudders at the sight of his interminable letters and crabbed handwriting to Whitbread, the shudder is stiffened by respect for the learning, the assiduity and the shameless waste of other men's time which distinguished the rector of Black Notley. We feel that right was on his side. Through the later decades of the eighteenth century these quiet, library-inspired quests for reform were disturbed by spasmodic, violent agitations of the stream. Wilkes and, even in his weird way, Lord George Gordon were symptoms of the more turbulent forces in the country behind reform. Such popular explosions of feeling had the inevitable consequence of making the task of the moderate and respectable reformer more difficult. But two things in the 1780's strengthened the respectable forces struggling for reform. One was fortuitous — 1788 was the centenary of the Glorious Revolution. Centenaries in those strenuous times, when men looked to the present and thought of the future, were seldom observed. This heaven-sent occasion was therefore seized not so much to celebrate the past as to instruct the present.

In November 1788, on the anniversary of King William III's birthday, an immense concourse of reformers met for a banquet in the London Tavern. Those who picture a tavern as dark and murky, with sawdust on the floor, here a settle and there an ingle-nook, with a wide chimney and a crackling fire all set for toddy and negus, the whole redolent of hops and villainy must revise their opinion of the London Tavern. This had been built twenty years earlier in Bishopsgate. Inside was the Great Dining Room adorned by Corinthian columns — forty feet long and nearly as many feet in width. Above it was the ballroom, which could be used for banquets, and had galleries and a fine-toned organ. In the cellars were bottles of wine innumerable, and a great vat in which might be seen two tons of turtle sporting and floundering before the last agonising journey to kitchen and soup-tureen. The London Tavern had the merriment of the Savoy Hotel combined with the high purpose of the National Liberal Club. It afforded a cheerful but solemn setting for the celebration of the birth of that rather dull King — William III. On the evening in question the chairman was Lord Stanhope who was tersely — though not altogether inaccurately — described by Horace Walpole as 'a savage'. Several of the London clubs likewise celebrated the event with illumination and gaieties. In Derby-shire — at the extremity of the Dukeries — an immense conglomeration of Cavendishes, Osbornes and local baronets foregathered, attended by their tenants and stimulated by revolutionary banners, for feasting, laudation of one another and largesse. But one person, King George III, for whom these lessons were principally intended was lost to their message. He was hopelessly mad.

The other force, which strengthened reform, was its adoption in earnest by the Whig Party. The Whigs had of course tactically agitated for it inside Parliament for many years but their enthusiasm for the cause was first shown emphatically to the world by the formation of the Whig Club in 1784 — at the time of the emergence of Pitt when their parliamentary fortunes were low. As Whitbread was always a prominent member of this concern it is important in his biography. Like the multipli-city of clubs formed at this time from The Club downwards, it met regularly for a tolerably convivial evening. Dinner was 5s. a head and was served at 4.30 in the afternoon. There were these standing toasts :

1. The glorious and immortal memory of King William III
2. The constitution according to the principles asserted at the Revolution
3. The Rights of the People
4. The Friends of Freedom
5. The cause for which Hampden bled in the field and Sidney on the scaffold
6. May the names of Russell and Cavendish be ever united in defence of the liberties of their country
7. May it be the character of the Whig Club never to slacken their efforts in adversity, nor to forget their principles in prosperity
8. The House of Brunswick and may they never forget the principles which seated their family on the throne of Great Britain
9. May the triumph of our revolution prevent the necessity of another

The importance of the Whig Club is that it linked the Whig hierarchy, the Whig Members of Parliament, with the agitation for reform outside Parliament. The club was popular rather than privileged; it was an attempt to sound the battle-cry of reform beyond the House of Commons, beyond the constituencies, with their limited franchise, to the public itself. Certainly the club was formidably aristocratic with Fox, Windham, Fitzpatrick as members, together with a pleasant enrichment of strawberry leaves and coronets. But — and this has possibly been insufficiently noticed — there was among the lordly ones a sprinkling of middle-class support. Members included a silk mercer, a woollen-draper, a glass manufacturer, and Mr. Harry House, the wine-merchant and oil-man, with Amos Chaplin the bootmaker and Thomas Lonsdale the laceman.[3] A dinner at the Whig Club must have been an exercise in manners both for dukes and drapers.

Further evidence of a fairly broad-based membership is suggested in the list of candidates for 1804. These included Mr. Edward Griffiths of Caernarvon and Mr. Jeremiah Crook of Bolton. The latter was proposed by Fox.[4]

To all these theorists in England the Revolution in France seemed like a fairy tale which had sprung to life. They applauded what was happening : they went on visits to that troubled country : they redoubled their activities at home : they corresponded with French reformers. When Lafayette was in dire straits after the Terror it was Whitbread who organised a purse for him, heading the dukes and lords of the Whig Party with a gift of £500. General Fitzpatrick, who was trembling on the edge of bankruptcy, contributed half that sum and endears himself to us by qualifying his generosity in a letter to Whitbread 'if it is not giving too much colour to the *groundless rumours* of my opulence'. Lafayette sent Whitbread a charming letter of thanks — 'a tribute of the gratitude which your generous exertions on my behalf could not fail to excite'.[5]

Yet for all this the contacts of the Whigs with the French Revolution were to be the kiss of death. This first became clear in the summer of 1791 when the Birmingham mob which, according to all the theories of the Whig Club ought to have been prattling about reform, rioted and burned the house and library of a moderate partisan of reform — Joseph Priestley the distinguished scientist and theologian. All that could be said against Priestley's constitutional opinions was that, himself a dissenter, he had advocated the repeal of the laws excluding dissenters from the House of Commons and that he had attended a 1688 centenary banquet in Birmingham. He had also used the imaginative phrase 'grains of gunpowder' to describe his theological writings. The consequences of these too flowery words might remind publicists that prosaic language is often safest. Whitbread took up the outrage against Priestley in the House of Commons with the greatest fury — he started his speech by brandishing thirty-six affidavits to show that the Birmingham magistrates had been guilty of negligence. He described how two of the magistrates, when the crowd cried 'Church and King', had taken off their hats and waved them round their heads, and how one of the crowd had then asked whether he might have leave to shake a little of the powder out of Dr. Priestley's wig. At this a Member of the House of Commons laughed. Whitbread turned this to his own advantage by saying that the Member was only doing precisely what the magistrates had done. His speech was extraordinarily powerful, resting on the contention that the tumults in Birmingham had arisen purely from religious differences 'which cannot be the object of political control, as they respect not man but God'. But the hearts of Pitt and his cohorts were hardened.

This association with the reformers outside Parliament was courageous but extremely dangerous. There may have been no danger that Grey's house in Hertford Street or Whitbread's house in Wimpole Street would be razed to the ground by a London mob, but they were making themselves targets for the war fervour and hatred which in time of war, always burns most fiercely among non-combatants. The Crimean War was to teach John Bright and the Great War was to teach Lord Lansdowne that the holder of the olive branch through the passions of war fills one of the least enviable positions in English political history.

The first important step along this well-mined road was taken some months before the war with revolutionary France began. Stung no doubt by the treatment of Priestley and other respectable partisans of reform and led on no doubt by their youthful generosity of heart, the three young members were largely instrumental in forming the Friends of the People. The most active spirit in this adventure was probably Lambton though Whitbread was scarcely less keen: Grey warmly supported them, though he subsequently grew to think that the step had been unwise.

The Friends of the People was established on 11 April 1792 and the first general meeting was held nine days later in the Freemason's Tavern in Great Queen Street near Lincoln's Inn Fields. Lambton presided. The meeting approved unanimously an address to the people of Great Britain which had been drawn up by a small committee on which were the three friends, Sheridan, Philip Francis,* two other Members of Parliament

* He has received much attention from historians as the reputed author of the Junius Letters. He was, at this time, M.P. for Bletchingley, a very bad speaker but

and four others who were not in Parliament. The declaration
was pointed 'First — To restore the freedom of election, and
a more equal representation of the people in parliament. Second
— To secure to the people a more frequent exercise of their right
of electing their representatives'.* This was then followed by
125 signatories, a quarter of whom were Members of Parliament or peers. Whitbread signed as 'Sam Whitbread, jun. Esq.,
M.P.' Lord Edward Fitzgerald was among those signing: Fox
was not. The signatures were followed by an Address to the
People of Great Britain, which was effective, though unkind
critics might have said that it was a cross between a sermon and
a paper read to a society of antiquarians. France was alluded to
— 'The example and situation of another kingdom are held out
to deter us from innovations of any kind. We say that the
reforms we have in view are not innovations.' Blackstone was
quoted to the effect that the Executive of the Government had
been immensely increased, which was never the intention of our
'patriot ancestors'. At this point it is important to emphasise that
there were two other reforming societies in existence, each with
cumbersome titles. Both were decidedly suspect by the authorities. One was the Society for Constitutional Information, with
an expensive membership: the other was the Corresponding
Society for Constitutional Discussion, inexpensive and with a
partly artisan membership. The fear of the authorities was that
either or both of these societies might form a powerful force,
with delegates meeting in London, to exert pressure on Parliament and to draw into England poisons from France. The
intolerance, springing from fright, which afflicted even reasonable
men and women at this time was horrifying. Sir Joseph Banks,
the enlightened traveller, refused permission to a friend of the
poet Coleridge, who wished to consult his library for some
information about tanning, because this man was suspected of

extremely active in all these advanced politics. He had the temerity to tell Burke
that his passage about Queen Marie Antoinette in *Reflections on the French Revolution* was 'sentimental'.

* General elections were governed by the Septennial Act.

contact with the Friends of the People and with advanced politics.[6] The plight of these enlightened advocates of change has perhaps never been better expressed than in some words of William Hazlitt 'they were assailed with all the engines of power, . . without the possibility of their defending themselves "from the pelting of the pitiless storm" that poured down upon them from the strongholds of corruption and authority.'[7] As was almost inevitable, one of the Constitutional Information Societies — the Sheffield Society, with a membership of over 2,000 — was quickly in touch with the Friends of the People. With a sprinkling of flattering phrases about 'great deference', 'your honourable society' and 'your superior judgment' they urged that a convention of reformers should be summoned to meet in London from each county or district. Grey, writing as a chairman of the committee,* urged 'wariness' otherwise they would find themselves accused of 'measures of desperate tendency and undefined extent'. He warned the Sheffield men against 'ardent indiscretions' but rather unexpectedly, on the particular point of the Convention, confessed 'we do not feel ourselves able to decide'. These were the events which set off the explosion which shattered the Whig Party. This was the occasion, seized by the Duke of Portland and his followers, to break away from Fox — though it was naturally an occasion which has to be viewed against the wider background of events in France. Five Members of Parliament, who were members of the Friends of the People protested against the correspondence with Sheffield, and their names were expunged from the books of the Society. At the same time Lord Lauderdale,† through his brother Tom Maitland, wrote to Whitbread urging that he and Lambton and 'our steady friends' should show the utmost caution.[8] Whitbread was later to describe the attitude of the Friends of

* This was a position which varied, probably according to ability to attend the meeting. Sometimes Grey signed as chairman : sometimes Lambton and sometimes Whitbread.

† He was one of the moving spirits in the Friends of the People. Never very elegant, he proclaimed himself a Jacobin and was familiarly known as Citizen Maitland.

the People as one of 'intrepid moderation'. After a pause of six months a further meeting was held in the Freemason's Tavern, with Whitbread presiding, and the Friends attempted to define their position less ambiguously. They remained unshaken on the subject of reform to the accomplishment of which they were bound 'by every tie of honour and duty'; but they reiterated that it could only be accomplished by lawful and constitutional means. 'Mistaken zeal is always at the mercy, and too often under the guidance of real treachery.'[9]

Naturally it is easy enough to smile at the Friends of the People. 'Largely aristocratic', 'exclusive'[10] 'rather innocuous would-be Mirabeaus'[11] are charges easily levelled at Whitbread and his friends. They will be readily accepted by all who think that political feeling is driven forward in the bearing-rein of class. The letter from Grey to the Sheffield men is perfectly sincere. Professor G. M. Trevelyan is far closer to the truth when he devotes many pages to the Friends of the People in his biography of Grey and tells us that too little heed has been paid to their origins considering their 'importance in our political history'.

The writer of the article on Grey in Earlier Editions of the *Encyclopaedia Britannica*, an ardent admirer of Burke, depicts the 'Friends' as they must surely have seemed to many of their contemporaries — 'A portentous association' existing to present in Parliament 'its menacing petitions. Such petitions were in fact violent impeachments of Parliament' . . . 'Grey was overborne by the fierce Jacobinism of Lauderdale, and found himself the parliamentary mouthpiece of this dangerous agitation'.[12] The Friends of the People was no society of 'play-boys': it was formed to support those who were being victimised for their opinions and were about to be punished for them. It was not formed for patronage but for succour.

The Government retaliated by starting proceedings against a number of reformers, and at the end of 1795, after George III was insulted on his way to open Parliament, introduced the Seditious Meetings Bill. Whitbread kept a copy of the Bill, and in the margin he wrote that there was nothing in the measure to prevent the circulation of scurrilous pamphlets, and that it was aimed at the London Corresponding Society who were said to be the disturbers of the tranquillity of the Kingdom for which accusation 'there was not one tittle of proof'.[13] In the Commons he described the Bill as no less detestable than 'any of the most despotic measures of the most accursed tyrants upon earth'. He foresaw the people sinking 'under a government of tyranny, of persecution, and of blood; aye of blood!'

Unlike many another loud voiced champion of the victims of oppression the Whig leaders gave sympathy which was not only theoretical and argumentative but personal and practical. When Arthur O'Connor, one of the leaders of the United Irishmen, was arrested in Margate on a somewhat flagrant attempt to charter a fishing-smack to take him and some of his associates to France, Whitbread with Fox, Grey and other Whig leaders went down to Maidstone and gave evidence on behalf of the Irishman. Their evidence helped to secure his acquittal. Writing to his wife, Whitbread said: 'If you had witnessed the anxiety with which poor O'Connor looked round for his friends, and the pleasure it appeared to give him to see me, I am sure you would have rejoiced.'[14]

Then there was the far more painful case of Thomas Fysshe Palmer. Palmer, educated at Eton and at Cambridge, was a convert to the Unitarians from the Church of England. In the 1780's he settled at Dundee, greatly admired by what was called in the language of the day a 'congregation of humble worshippers'. He was something of a theologian and wrote a paper to prove that the crowing of the cock heard by St. Peter was really the sound of a trumpet. Among his humble worshippers were undeniably some supporters of Parliamentary reform, Dundee being one of the strongest centres for reform in Scotland. In 1793 Palmer's friend Thomas Muir was sentenced in Edinburgh to fourteen years at Botany Bay for sedition: the following year William Skirving, the secretary of the Scottish convention for reform, and Margarot and Gerrald, two delegates from England, received the same brutal sentence from the same Scottish judge. In 1793 Palmer was tried for 'leasing making' — a term in Scottish law meaning the use of words which tend to excite discord between the sovereign and his people. 'Oh ye sons of men, how long will you seek after leasing?' cried the psalmist. The Scottish justices showed that they thought, with the psalmist, that men who sought after leasing should not be lightly treated. 'No man has a right to speak about the constitution, who is not a landed proprietor', said one. Another observed that the only adequate punishment for what Palmer had done was torture. From such barbarians the old Etonian was possibly fortunate to escape with seven years in Botany Bay. Fox dryly wrote to his nephew : 'At home we imitate the French as well as we can, and in the trials and sentences of Muir and Palmer in particular, I do not think we fall very far short of our original.' And then with a splendidly aristocratic contempt for mere life he adds 'transportation to Botany Bay is less severe (and to a gentleman that is not much) than death'.[15]

The indignation of the little band of Foxite Whigs in the House of Commons was unbounded. Of Palmer, Whitbread said 'I have seen him, known him and had the honour of corresponding with him; he is a man of the most engaging manners and of the most enlightened mind. The greatest proof, if any proof were necessary, of his firmness and fortitude, was the undaunted and philosophic mind, with which he bore up against this unheard of oppression. He was a man on whom "The Gods themselves may look with envy".'[16] When all the efforts of the Whigs had proved unavailing and these dangerous men were securely in Botany Bay, Palmer wrote to Whitbread and, long years after it was written, the faded letter can only be read with a shudder of horror for the White Terror which the Whigs could condemn but not dispel.

DEAR SIR,
  On the arrival of Governer Hunter, Messrs. Muir, Skirving and myself delivered to him the enclosed memorial, which he transmitted

to the Secretary of State by the first opportunity. He has had an answer to it by the last ships which came from the Cape, and yesterday he favoured me with the contents.

He tells me that he has instructions from the Secretary of State to detain us in this place until the expiration of our sentences, which are accompanied with the opinion of the Crown Lawyers that it is perfectly legal for him to do so. He tells me also that the opinion of the Lord Justice Clerk and Lord Advocate and of the Scots Judges could not be sent by the same conveyance as at the time of sailing they were all in the country.

You will doubtless observe the duplicity of Ministry. To obviate the odium occasioned by the illegality of our sentences, and to soften the public mind their creatures at Edinburgh declare that our sentences are completed on our arrival, and that we are at liberty to go to any part of the world except G. Britain, at the same time they give their servants here the most peremptory orders to keep us in custody at N.S. Wales.

I think that I am warranted in saying that this custody has already been the death of two of us. Mr. Skirving* on his deathbed declared to me that he never recovered the starvation of the short allowance in the year '95, and Mr. Gerrald's death was hastened if not occasioned by the quick vicissitudes and strong heat of this climate insupportable by his feeble constitution. Mine is greatly impaired. I hear the same of Mr. Margarot. Now if the Scots lawyers . . . be rightly founded in their assertion that we are at liberty to depart when we please, the detention of us appears to me to be little else than a cold blooded process of murder. And this by the express orders of Ministry.

If you find a proper opportunity you may possibly think it right to bring this before Parliament, but this must be left to your own judgement on which I have the highest confidence. Accept Sir my sincerest thanks for your zealous and able endeavours to serve me. I believe the whole Kingdom joins me in gratitude for your great exertions to stem the torrent of despotism, and restore the violated rights of Britons. With warm wishes for your happiness, I have the honour to be Sir with great gratitude.

Your obliged humble servant
T. F. PALMER.

N.S. Wales, Sydney, August 14, 1797.[17]

That the dangers linked with Reform, particularly the risk of repression against individuals, had sunk deeply into the

---

* Skirving died within a year of reaching New South Wales.

consciousness of the Whigs is implied from an opinion expressed by Whitbread many years later. In 1808 Whitbread was asked to sign a requisition to the sheriffs of Middlesex in favour of parliamentary reform. He declined to do this and explained that unless there was a general feeling in the country, favourable to reform, the agitation of the question 'may afford opportunities, as it has heretofore done' of a curtailment of British liberties.[18]

On 16 November 1795 Fox organised a protest against the Sedition Bill in his own constituency of Westminster, and the leading Whigs (Whitbread among them) appeared on the hustings in Palace Yard. Joseph Farington, R.A., has described the scene after the meeting when Fox, supported by the Duke of Bedford, Grey and other Whig chieftains, rolled through the streets 'among a crowd of low people and black-guards who huzza'd manfully'.[19] To the advocates of the world of privilege the supporters of change are often rapscallions, and the conservative Farington was no doubt comforted by the knowledge that Fox's spirited protest did not deflect the progress of the Bill.

In a less spectacular way Whitbread, from the beginning of the repression, had attempted to rally opinion against it in his own part of the country. Moreover throughout the 1790's he was active, with the Duke of Bedford, in addressing large meetings in the county with the object of petitioning the King in favour of peace and of dismissing the Ministers. In May 1792 the Government had issued a royal proclamation with the idea of stiffening magistrates in the control of riotous meetings and of seditious publications. After this proclamation a public meeting was held at Hertford when Lord Grimston, the builder of Gorhambury, opened the business by moving an address to the King to thank him for the proclamation. Whitbread sprang up to oppose this — making the good point that the proclamation tended to turn the magistracy into police spies.[20] In collaboration with Mr. Brand, 'a very elegant and expensive commoner' who lived at The Hoo near Welwyn, he prepared a draft letter announcing the formation of a local society on the principles of the Friends of the People.[21] At the same time Whitbread was writing optimistically to his father-in-law 'The Friends of the People are rising to their true level, and becoming every day more popular'[22].

The rector of Hertingfordbury (close to Bedwell) wrote to Whitbread to ask for his signature to a document of a 'patriotic' character about sedition.* Replying on 28 December 1792 Whitbread said 'I own that I can not see the necessity for so novel a proceeding in this parish, where I am not conscious that the seditious doctrines alluded to have at all penetrated, and which — from its situation and other circumstances — can not be expected to have any great effect by way of example'.[23]

How different, how painfully different was the meeting of parishioners at St. Luke's — the church close to Chiswell Street and the Brewery. Here the father was in the chair, supported by the Reverend Henry Waring, the rector, and with his most faithful henchman from the Brewery, Jacob Yallowley. The meeting passed a resolution that 'we should be ungrateful to God, rebellious to our King, and forgetful of every domestic claim if we did not stand forth upon the present occasion', in support of Pitt and the Government. Finally Whitbread was thanked for his 'truly patriotic conduct' in the chair.[24] Plaintively the father wrote 'My son is *very very very* much with Fox and Co.'.[25]

* The vicar was not calculated to win Whitbread's support. He had fought with gallantry at Dettingen and had then changed the red coat for a black one. He married Peg Woffington's sister, who had been on the stage; he was rewarded by the King with three rectories in Hertford in addition to Hertingfordbury.

CHAPTER SIX

Country Life and Neighbours

WILLIAM HAZLITT, though ten years younger than Whitbread and blessed like him with vigour of mind and intensity of feeling, once remarked 'When I am in the country I wish to vegetate like the country'. Whitbread was the precise opposite. He brought to country-life the zeal and insatiable energy with which he pursued his political career at Westminster. Improving his country house, laying out his garden, preserving his pheasants, hunting the fox, governing the county and maintaining law and order — all showed the mark of his active individuality. He never viewed the country as a refuge from the town but only as a different setting for the display of the same eager benevolence. The twentieth century, with its nose for social difference well developed, may easily imagine that those who lived in his neighbourhood might have looked somewhat critically at his riches — made disagreeably repugnant by the addition of Foxite opinions. A rich radical in the country is always a target for comment — and sometimes for ladies' whispers and a general pouting of lips. In the eighteenth century, country life was more tolerant than it became in the nineteenth century and, as has already been said, there was a tradition of the Left in Bedfordshire, as there was also in the other counties immediately to the north and east of London. Here and there a few sad squires and a few corpulent, clerical pluralists may have grumbled at the new man who had come to take possession of the land. Probably such people existed and whined, but no evidence of their whimpers has come down to us. On the contrary Whitbread seems to have enjoyed the innocent pleasures of country society, and he would have sharply disagreed with Horace Walpole who tells us that one of the chief disadvantages of country life was 'that unpleasant Christian commodity, neighbours'. From the Duke of Bedford to John Thompson, who lived in Cardington village with his mare and chaise cart,* he loved them as himself.

Perhaps in the very early days of his marriage he was too much of an appendage to the old gentleman in the country to be wholly at his ease. He had mentioned to his wife before marriage that they could have Woolmers, which lay within the toss of a biscuit from Bedwell. It seemed to be mentioned as something quite out of the question but the negotiations for the house he wanted in Bedfordshire fell through, and to Woolmers the bride and bridegroom went. With Hatfield to the west, Bedwell to the south, Balls to the east and Panshanger to the north, Woolmers stood in a five-mile enclave of genteel and aristocratic park and palings. The estate was of moderate size — 186 acres in a ring fence. The River Lea, fortified in its earlier course by some languid little streams — the Maran, the Beane, the Rib and the Stort — flowed through the property. The Lea was helped on its progress to London by a spring which rose in Woolmers and discharged its waters through a pleasure garden of some renown. Whitbread's wife was a great gardener and when, after twelve years, they parted with Woolmers, the garden was described in the sale catalogue as being in 'the highest perfection'. The house was characteristic of the classical tradition with a fine bow-windowed drawing-room; all had been greatly improved by Whitbread. A modern embellishment to the house was a water-closet on the ground floor. The property was valued by Henry Holland the architect at £400 a year rental. It was finally sold in 1801 for £15,150 to Robert Dent.† As will be seen Whitbread had by that time been settled at Southill, and Woolmers would have been sold long since if it had not been

---

* 'It is my direction that John Thompson of Cardington shall have the use of the house and garden, which he now occupies and that my executors shall provide funds for keeping the mare he drives and his chaise cart, and if the mare shall survive her master I desire that she may upon his death be shot.' Extract from Whitbread's will.

† Brother to 'Dog' Dent, Member for Lancaster, who introduced a tax on dogs.

for Whitbread's affection for an old friend, renting the house, whom he did not wish to inconvenience. This was Thomas Tyrwhitt — a strange, laughable, little gentleman who was to become Usher of the Black Rod and the target for some affectionate but unseemly jokes between the Prince Regent and Queen Charlotte. Like many a courtier Tyrwhitt made up for reticence in public by violence of expression in private; Whitbread gave him great indulgence in this respect. During the negotiations over Woolmers Tyrwhitt wrote in the summer of 1801 'if one may judge of London atmosphere by the heat of our damned, corrupt, stinking House of Commons, your weather is as hot as that in Devonshire — before the Sessions are over I am sure that somebody will have a ball in the Thorax'.* Though viewed against the background of his day-to-day career in Parliament Whitbread may appear a too serious-minded individual he was able, in congenial masculine society — and unlike many an ardent 'leftist' — to enjoy the pleasantries and impertinences of a wider social life.

His life at Woolmers was still coloured by his father's persisting disapproval of the Greys. He was warmly attached to his half-sister Mary, and was responsible for her engagement to his brother-in-law George Grey, who was a naval officer of distinction, afterwards resident commissioner of Portsmouth Dockyard. In 1789 Whitbread's father wrote to his old confidant Howard 'my son is to me as when you left us and this about Mary is his doing and not proper'.[1] When Whitbread's first child was born he proposed to name him Henry Charles — both Grey names — but in this particular the old gentleman had his way and William was substituted for Henry.† This child, born in April 1789, died in infancy. He was succeeded by four more children : Elizabeth, born in 1791; William Henry, born in 1795; Samuel Charles, born in 1796; and Emma Laura, born in 1798.‡

---

* It was only three years since Tierney and Pitt had fought a duel, though happily the balls flew wide of the thorax or any vulnerable part.

† William after Whitbread's maternal grandfather.

‡ William Henry succeeded his father at Southill and was Member for Bedford. He lacked seemingly both the ability and sensibility of the Whitbread family. He

One of the chief domestic events in Whitbread's life was the move to Southill at the end of the 1790's. This was a well-wooded estate sandwiched between the two monastic foundations of Old Warden and Chicksands Priory. Alive to the importance of shelter, and not indifferent to the lure of productivity, a buyer of property is generally wise to follow close to those pioneers of real estate development — the abbots and priors of the ancient faith. Southill had belonged since the end of the seventeenth century to the Byngs — a naval family of distinction and misfortune. (Admiral Byng after being court-martialled, and shot on the quarterdeck of the *Monarque*, lies in the family vault at Southill.) The first Byng to own Southill was created Lord Torrington : his grandson the fourth lord — an active Whig and for many years Minister Plenipotentiary at Brussels — got into financial difficulties and the house was let to Dilly, brother of the renowned London bookseller, familiar to readers of Boswell.* The bookseller described it as a calm retreat from the noise and bustle of London. Whitbread would have entirely agreed with this, as did Dr. Johnson, who stayed there with Boswell.

Whitbread's father decided to buy Southill because as he explained to John Howard he thought that his son would never apply himself to 'the trade' and that therefore it was sensible to increase his ownership of land. The purchase was not straightforward and the old gentleman complained 'I have bankrupts, lawyers and auctioneers to deal with'.[2] However all went through satisfactorily in 1795. Whitbread's father died in the following year and, after a decent interval, Whitbread evidently decided to move across from Woolmers. There was already a fine eighteenth-century house at Southill, enlarged from a seventeenth-century house by Isaac Ware some forty years

them, and so on and so forth for the present family

was twice married but had no children.

Samuel Charles appears to have been the favourite of his parents — certainly of his mother. He is the ancestor of the present family through his marriage to the daughter of the twenty-first Lord Dacre. He succeeded his brother at Southill.

Elizabeth married in 1812 the eighth Lord Waldegrave.

Emma married in 1817 Charles Shaw-Lefevre, the Speaker of the House of Commons, a partner in the Brewery and afterwards Lord Eversley of Heckfield.

* Lord Torrington's brother, the fifth lord, was the author of the diaries.

earlier. No doubt it seemed out of date to Whitbread and he decided, with the help of the fashionable Whig architect Henry Holland, to modernise and embellish it. The result is a house often loosely called 'Regency' but more correctly described as a late-eighteenth-century masterpiece : it is unchanged since that time and with the decoration and furniture of the day virtually as it was. The house and its contents have been the subject of an admirable study published in 1951[3] and it is perhaps only necessary to recall the earlier verdict of Mr. Christopher Hussey — an authoritative view which would be generally endorsed by experts in the arts — 'Southill must be acknowledged the classic example of the most civilised decade in the whole range of English domestic architecture'.[4] A trivial point emerges. Holland made his name in architecture as the adviser to the Prince of Wales over the rebuilding of Carlton House and, a little later, over the original design for the Pavilion at Brighton, and it is curious to reflect that Whitbread in later life was to compose in Holland's calm retreat at Southill his celebrated invectives against the occupier of Holland's Carlton House. How far Whitbread was himself responsible for the taste of Southill and its furnishings is of course difficult to say. But it would be quite wrong to deny all credit for these to the rich man who employed the leading architect. In no side of his life did Whitbread attempt to impose himself by the pressure of his riches : there was nothing about him to suggest his being the type of affluent gentleman who would utter those terrible words (which have led to the defilement of acres of England) 'I want the best, and I am able to pay for it'. A surviving letter from Holland shows that Whitbread was an appreciative and understanding patron, who suggested ideas rather than imposed them, and was content to be guided by the man he chose and trusted. He asked Holland to send him the plan of the building as it stood before the alterations — in itself a sign that he was interested in what had been achieved. Sending this, Holland added 'And now my dear Sir let me thank you again and again for the very handsome manner in which you have treated me through the whole business, and to assure you that I never transacted any that afforded me so much pleasure and satisfaction.'[5] Although Whitbread's poetic powers were not his most conspicuous gift, the sentiments which he wrote below the marble bust of Holland at Southill, and evidently composed in 1806 a few weeks after the architect's death, show affectionate realisation of Holland's genius :

> Business is often Friendship's end
> From business once there rose a Friend.
> Holland! That friend I found in thee
> Thy loss I feel when e'er I see
> The labours of that polished mind;
> Thy loss I feel when e'er I find
> The comforts of this happy place;
> Thy loss I feel when e'er I trace
> In house, in garden, or in ground
> The scene of every social round.
> Farewell! In life I honoured thee;
> In death thy name respected be.

Whitbread and his wife and family began their life at Southill in mid-October 1800 — a few months after Napoleon had routed the Austrians at Marengo and a few weeks before the even greater victory of Hohenlinden. Napoleon was master of civilised Europe and amid the panic which that engendered, Whitbread was one of the very few Englishmen to view the French leader rationally and without alarmist apprehension. So much was this the case that some of his less subtle opponents viewed the Lord of Southill as Napoleon's best friend in England. The French influence in taste and especially furniture, of which Holland was the leading exponent, was a conspicuous characteristic of the decoration at Southill* and critics of Whitbread were heard to whisper that the eagles in the drawing-room were a reminder to friends and neighbours of the eagles soaring to victory across the Channel. This was too ingenious : it was weaving a political motive into a contemporary and perfectly innocuous fashion.

* See particularly the chapter by Mr. F. J. B. Watson in *Southill, A Regency House.*

Life at Southill was marked by comfort and by some splendour, but not by extravagance or ostentation. Fox, who stayed there several times, describes his visit with the adjective, uniformly used, 'pleasant'. Certainly it was not luxurious, and once Fox had to approach the front door for the last half mile on foot, while men servants had to 'hump' the baggage, the drive being unfinished. In these early days the Whitbreads quickly fitted in with the neighbourhood and there were plenty of signs of those little civilities which show that newcomers are acceptable. Lord Ongley, a rough Bedfordshire peer who lived close by at Old Warden ended a letter to Whitbread with bucolic familiarity, 'Spouse desires to be remembered'.[6] Another neighbour sent an offering to Mrs. Whitbread of 'a well-hunted hare' — as though they thought in Bedfordshire that the circumstances of the kill enriched the jugging. And on the rather rare occasions when they were alone Whitbread would read aloud to his wife, tackling on one occasion the life of Catherine the Great which he was doubtless able to embellish from personal recollections.*

In the year of his father's death Whitbread moved to a more considerable house in London — 35 Dover Street. This he rented at £500 a year from the widow of the fashionable doctor, Richard Warren, who was reputed to have made £150,000 from his practice. Dover Street was then a magnificently aristocratic place to live, with just a surgeon or two at the Piccadilly end to lower the tone of the street. Next door but one was the London palace of the Bishops of Ely — a splendid house built twenty years earlier. From Dover Street, Whitbread could stroll to Brooks's in five minutes, and to the House of Commons in fifteen.

Whitbread kept careful accounts of his expenditure and these have fortunately survived. Although it is not possible to apportion the respective amounts spent in Dover Street and Southill, the figures throw an interesting light on the personal

---

* This was almost certainly the life of Catherine by William Tooke, chaplain to the Russian Company in St. Petersburg. Whitbread would have known him.

expenditure of a wealthy man when the nation (though at war) was moving towards the peaks of prosperity. The figures for each year from 1796 to 1812 will be found in Appendix 1 on pages 309 and 310.

The radical at Westminster shed some of his fire and fury when he stepped from his carriage at the entrance to Southill. With that fancy for exact information, which was a characteristic both of him and his father, he had had sunk by the front door some panels with the mileage to Hyde Park Corner and the mileage to Bedford. As he set out on the longer journey to Dover Street we may picture his mind filled with dark imaginings of the iniquities of Pitt and his government and with vaulting ideas of great changes and improvements in the lot of mankind. On the shorter journey to Bedford he would be engrossed by the topics of a narrower, more practical range — improvements at Bedford, poachers, the tribulations of the paupers, prices of grain and all those multifarious trifles which, in small communities grow — like stinging-nettles after rain — into problems. At Westminster he was belligerent; in Bedford-shire benevolent. Such a combination, though not unknown, is unusual. Those who adopt with ardour advanced political theories generally use the country as a retreat — not as a field for experiments in government. Whitbread's friend Horne Tooke was a case in point: he was an extremist and imprisoned for his opinions, and his idea of rural bliss was to keep a cow in Wimbledon.

Whitbread was an enlightened though conventional land-owner of his day. His first action on purchasing Southill was to enclose it. In 1812 Cardington was enclosed by Act of Parliament.* Enclosure, as readers of Cobbett know, marked the death of medieval England and was part of a long process

---

* The enclosure at Cardington is recorded in the fullest detail in the Whitbread papers at Bedford. Mr. Quentin Skinner has allowed me to see the essay which he based on the information in these papers. The evidence in this case hardly seems to bear out the possibly too simple verdict of the Hammonds that enclosure meant 'the removal of the sheet anchor of the poor'. So far as Cardington was concerned the costs of enclosing were very fairly met, and in no case do legal rights seem to have been overruled.

which meant the virtual elimination of peasant ownership, either of beast or acre, sole or in common, from the English countryside. But it is important to notice that it marked — but did not cause — the end of these time-honoured perquisites for the peasant cultivator. Enclosures were the symptoms of progress — an essential prelude to efficiency. Whitbread, who with his contemporaries was a landlord who improved his property, may have mourned old times and old ways but it would not have crossed his mind that enclosing land was materially different from cultivating it. The odium attached to enclosures was sentimental, largely posthumous — not contemporary.

If it could be argued that he took something away from the people of Bedfordshire he returned it a hundredfold by his zeal and attention to their concerns. Almost from boyhood he had been a Bedfordshire magistrate and the justice room at Southill, with easy access from the back-door, was where he was available for judgment or advice. He used to sit in the justice-room in his dressing-gown at half past eight in the morning, and he only left for his breakfast when the last person was satisfied. He kept a record of each case at petty sessions and of what was decided, not entrusting this to a clerk. But the vastly more important side to the work of a magistrate in those days was local government. The administrative side of Quarter Sessions — and Whitbread attended them regularly for a quarter of a century — was quite as important as the judicial side so that the J.P. was parish, rural district and county councillor rolled into one.

Whitbread's experiences in Bedfordshire were not without their influence on the higher councils of the Whig Party. There was, when he first went to Southill, an exceptional amount of distress as a result of the war; and the parishes, finding the expense of relieving this by corn or cash extremely costly, were prone to try to satisfy people by distributing cheaper foods like rice. This caused much discontent. Whitbread told Fox that in his area he relieved distress by a parish allowance of money, leaving the recipient to economise by buying rice if he so wished.

Fox thought that leaving the choice to the recipient was a thousand times more effectual than substituting rice for corn 'which I own I thought abominable'.[7] Equally Whitbread's knowledge of government at the top was of service in Bedfordshire.

He sent his estate-agent to draw up a report on the poorhouses, and among others the one dealing with the neighbouring parish of Haynes has survived. In one part of this poor-house there was a living-room 17 feet by 11 feet and 6 feet high. There was a sleeping-room attached, with a dirt floor and one side of the rafters and thatch unplastered. Another sleeping-room was over the living-room. In these three rooms lived a mother with her five children, and a father and mother with their four children. There were dreadful rags for bedding, two or three flock beds, and the children slept on the floor covered with rags and an old sack. The same conditions were found in the other part of the house. There was a cottage near the poor-house, which was used for the same purpose and where conditions were not materially different. On this and similar cases Whitbread consulted the Attorney-General whether a visiting justice had the right to punish the overseers where they found extremely bad conditions.[8] He also had reports made by his land agent on the schools in the area. At the school at Cardington eighteen boys were taught to read and write, and twelve of them were clothed. The total cost a year was just in excess of £40. The same number of girls were taught and clothed, though in their case knitting and needlework were substituted for writing. In the case of the girls this was done for £30. At both Elstow and Warden the children were largely taught in the Sunday Schools which, where there were no day schools, came into their own.

Though he could not do much for education, except out of his own pocket, he ordered the overseers to see to their poorhouses, repair the structure, pave the floors and provide a minimum of furniture and proper bedding for the inmates; all to be paid from the poor-rate. He was ruthless in pursuit of a particular overseer who escorted a sick man from the workhouse and then left him lying in a field which was just within the boundary of a neighbouring parish.

In 1798 the magistrates decided to build a modern gaol at Bedford, and here there is no doubt that the influence of John Howard through Whitbread was the driving force. Whitbread sent the plans to Henry Holland, and asked him to appoint someone to examine them and report on them, and the expense of this was borne by Whitbread.

Always interested in health, he had reports from the local doctors on the causes of death — especially among children. He closely examined the distressing case of poor Anna Fooks. For twenty-six weeks she passed no water : this mysterious drought was supposed to have ended by an upward discharge from the mouth. Though the Englishman at the turn of the century was remarkably robust he had some strange and naïve fancies where nature and the human form were concerned. Such things were however only incidental to his larger interest in the welfare of the residents of Bedfordshire. His father had bequeathed £8,000 to start an infirmary in Bedford and Whitbread was responsible for the building, and the development of the scheme. Either he or the Duke of Bedford was always in the chair at the meetings of management.

At this time a not very good joke came into use, namely that Bedfordshire ought to be renamed Whitbreadshire.* The jest was not good because it was not really true : if the county was searching for another name it was not necessary to go further afield than the great ducal abbey. Bedfordshire — at any rate in Whitbread's lifetime — was always Woburnshire. Disraeli in his novel, *Sybil*, said of the English aristocracy : 'Your order stands before Europe — the most glorious of existing spectacles.' Of the House of Russell this could never be said. For although Woburn was vast and magnificent, its occupants were always the reverse of gorgeous. Shy, tinged with oddity and

* Lord Upper Ossory, the elder brother of General Fitzpatrick, who lived at Ampthill and with certain aristocratic reservations greatly admired Whitbread said : 'Bedfordshire used to be called Whitbreadshire, but I deny that he ever ruled or governed me.' Lord Holland, *Further Memoirs*, (1905), 214.

avoiding attention if they could the Russell Dukes of Bedford might well have given Trollope the inspiration for his greatest character the Duke of Omnium. The greatness of that duke is felt because his sway dominates each page of the story but yet he scarcely appears. That duke used to entertain his neighbours occasionally to a gigantic dinner but the host always quietly slipped away with the coffee. The Dukes of Bedford were more attentive to their neighbours than that, but they spent much time in London and in Devonshire so that their immense influence in Bedfordshire could be described as one of acres — rather than personality. Yet a nod from the Abbey or a frown travelled through the county as silently but forcefully as the waters of the Ouse. Whitbread was possibly fortunate in that politics bound him to Woburn but, in addition to that, his was the type of character — original, clear-cut and owing little to tradition—which instinctively attracted the shy but questing mind of the Russells. When Whitbread came to Southill, Francis — the fifth duke — was living at Woburn in uneasy bachelordom : he was in his middle thirties, the same staunch, unrelenting Whig who had stamped out of the Duke of Portland's house when he found himself in company with conspirators against Fox. The duke, entertaining a party of friends at Woburn, began the fashion for short hair and the abandonment of powder. Because of his reputation for advanced political opinions a crop was regarded as democratic. The duke certainly possessed an aristocratic confidence in his own judgment : he once met the agitator Thelwall, who had just been released from the Tower. Thelwall was described by Coleridge as intrepid, eloquent and honest and totally different from the 'ragged cattle' who formed the majority of radical reformers. The duke's only comment was 'I thought him a dull man'.[9] Fox once complained that the Duke of Bedford lacked 'popular manners', and Whitbread said to Farington that 'he can not be familiar and general with strangers' explaining that this was due to shyness not to pride. *Burke's Peerage*, which is generally parsimonious with its eulogies, called him in its early editions 'patriotic and deeply lamented'. In the later editions the first adjective alone survives though what it conveys to the casual enquirer is difficult to determine. But if the Duke of Bedford was a shy man his immediate circle of friends, of whom Whitbread was one, never had the least difficulty in penetrating to the charm behind the reserve. To their consternation he died rather suddenly from a neglected rupture in March 1802. In the House of Commons Fox said that in his character there was something so great, so benign, so marked that it seemed as if he had been endowed with wealth and rank merely to set off his virtues. A hunting friend of Whitbread's, who was staying at Woburn at the time, wrote 'with the most poignant anguish' to announce that the duke was dying, expressing the simple, if touching, hope 'May the Almighty God, thro' whose permission he did so much good in this World bless him eternally in the one into which he is going'.[10]

The succeeding duke, John, was less ardent than his brother, quieter and less partisan, but with an understanding of the arts, agriculture and science and perfectly prepared to take his place in public life if the country had shown any inclination to turn towards the Whigs. From a letter to Whitbread, which was written in 1808, we can sense something of the duke's political opinions and something of the tenacity of whiggery:

I am but a fireside politician, and know little of passing events but what I learn from the newspapers . . . nothing but peace with Europe, and a reform of the public expenditure and of the various abuses which have crept into the constitution, can save us. We are a 'sinking country' however some may cavil at the expression, and a total change of system can alone sustain us and prevent our entire fall. . . . I am old-fashioned in my politics, and am for *old* principles, as well as 'old morality' . . . forgive my prosing.

There is a certain ducal charm in the reasons he gave Whitbread for being reluctant to speak in the House of Lords on the Catholic question 'You say that you *know* I *can* speak — as old Vinegar says in the Farce "I won't contradict you because it isn't good manners" but I *know* I *can not* speak. I feel however that I ought to say something, and if I can muster up sufficient courage (and it requires a great deal) to risk the almost certainty of exposing myself, I will. . . .'[11]

The diarist Charles Greville, who always employed plenty of vinegar with what he wrote, described the duke as 'an uninteresting, weak-minded, selfish character'. Although in Whitbread's life, the duke was always a force in the background rather than an influence through constant personal contact, there is nothing to bear out Greville's attack. He married the daughter of the Lord Torrington who sold Southill to the Whitbreads: Lord John Russell was their son. When he became duke he was a widower, and in his effort to remedy this lonely plight he did perhaps show some weakness. At the time there was a celebrated Duchess of Gordon, married to a half-mad husband: the duchess was a lady of the greatest vivacity and energy and of some vulgarity. Anxious for her daughters to marry prosperously she assured intending suitors that there need be no fear of insanity since there was no drop of Gordon blood in their veins. When Francis, Duke of Bedford died she plunged her daughter Georgiana into mourning on the grounds that she was engaged to him. Certainly the duke from his death-bed sent Lady Georgiana 'a very kind message' and, it was whispered, a lock of that hair which twenty years earlier had been viewed with disfavour by Horace Walpole. All these particulars were faithfully reported to Grey at Howick by Whitbread. In the following year the sixth duke married Lady Georgiana, who thus became the third daughter of the Duchess of Gordon to follow the mother's example and find nuptial bliss among the strawberry-leaves. Whitbread was staying at Woburn a few months after this marriage and he wrote off to Grey:

I continue to like the Duchess; allowances must be made for what you may have heard of her carriage in her new situation; and she would be more than human if she was not a good deal elated by her situation at first. Added to all this, the freedom of a Scotch Manner and the Recollection of her mother may have produced sensations in some quarters. But I like her, she is cheerful, desirous to please, uncommonly kind and attentive to Bess,* and is improving every day. In short I like her.[12]

But whatever weakness there may have been in the duke's private character, politically he was one to whom Whitbread ever turned in difficulty and from whom he ever received advice which was uninfluenced by the excitements and frictions of conventional political association. To the end of his days Whitbread found Woburn at once a refuge and an inspiration. Edward FitzGerald, visiting the great house long after this time, thought that there was 'not much character in it', and he added that an old squire's gable-ended house was 'much more aristocratic'. So perhaps the Victorians were to feel. So perhaps an earlier generation felt, instanced by Horace Walpole saying that he admired Woburn rather than liked it, though he gave his highest praise to the setting and surroundings. The house was heavily altered in the middle of the eighteenth century by Henry Flitcroft — his changes being sufficiently indicated by his nickname of Burlington Harry. But the formality of the Augustans never quite destroyed the Gothic in the background, and as the Whig leaders planned and feasted they were reminded by the portraits on the walls of faithful adherents of the popular cause, of great names in Tudor history and of more shadowy ancestors of earlier days from the west country.

At one of the informal Woburn gatherings of the Whigs — it might consist of Fox and perhaps half a dozen friends — the headquarters would be the library where they would, according to Charles Grey, talk or 'lounge over' books. Rather unexpectedly Fox would play a game of real tennis : there would be dinner at four followed by a saunter outside, a hand of whist and supper. 'We sit up rather too late, and dine rather too early for the hours we keep.'[13] It was staying here in 1803 and after a long talk with Fox on politics that Whitbread admired the bust of the statesman which stood in a classical temple recently designed by Henry Holland. William Lamb had written some lines which unfortunately tempted Whitbread to try something

* Whitbread's name for his wife.

JOHN, SIXTH DUKE OF BEDFORD, 1766–1839

By Sir Thomas Lawrence

CHARLES, SECOND EARL GREY, 1764–1845

By Sir Thomas Lawrence

better — the lines which are below the bust of Fox in the Southill Library.* And just occasionally the party at Woburn became a shade less civilised. There was the occasion, described by Creevey, when Sheridan made some vitriolic remarks about Fox in his absence. Adair, Fox's friend, challenged him to a duel. The challenge was accepted. Whitbread, who was also in the party, was successful in making it up between them.

CHAPTER SEVEN

With the Oakley Hunt

WHITBREAD'S position in Bedfordshire, strong on his own account and strengthened through association with Woburn, became unimpeachable through his prowess in the hunting-field.* Extravagancies or unorthodoxies of opinion were all forgiven and forgotten amid the excitements of a day with the 'tally-ho's' in the Oakley country. The Oakley Hunt took its name from Oakley House — a property of the Dukes of Bedford then generally the home of the eldest son, Lord Tavistock, and the country ran some twenty miles north-west of Bedford and roughly the same distance in depth, though widening out at the Buckinghamshire border into something the shape of a pear. In the nineteenth century the hunt achieved some notoriety owing to Grantley Berkeley — a quarrelsome aristocrat of dubious lineage — who was for a time its master. But at the beginning of the century it was financed by Whitbread, the duke and Mr. Lee Antonie, the hunt having been formerly financed and managed by the duke. Lee Antonie was the grandson of a celebrated Lord Chief Justice, Sir William Lee, and he took the name of Antonie on inheriting Colworth, a property in the north of the Oakley country. He was master of the Oakley Hunt from 1798 to 1809. 'My dear squire', as Whitbread invariably addressed him, was a man of character and force in Bedfordshire. He sat for Bedford, with Whitbread, for ten years from 1802. The force of private friendship in politics at this time is some-times overlooked. Lee Antonie wrote to Whitbread that

* Whitbread's younger son, writing in his 80th year, said: 'my father was a perfect horseman.' Miss Godber's article on Bedfordshire foxhunting in the *Journal of the Bedfordshire Historical Record Society* (vol. xliv) has been of great service to me.

although he gloried in the Whig cause which I have ever espoused 'nothing but having the honour of being your colleague would have induced me to come forward'.[1] But he passed through Bedfordshire like the post, in the Wisdom of Solomon, which hasted by leaving no mark for the future. Antonie has gone and even Lee has vanished to the unremembered pages of Burke's *Extinct Baronetcies*. But the squire played his part in the life of Whitbread, and brought out in Whitbread certain unexpected depths not only of delight in life but of true attachment to others. The duke and Whitbread found the money for the Hunt: Antonie was responsible for the management: 'that there can be no Pack of Hounds unless you will manage them is quite certain, and it would be utter destruction to me if there were none'. 'That you are the very mirror of squires in punctuality and strict observance of your word, all the World allows: and none with more experience of the truth than I . . . Adieu may we be at peace. May we have a good crop of hay and corn, and may we meet again in Good Health for the beginning of another Good Hunting Season.'[2]

No doubt one of the reasons which encouraged Whitbread to move to Southill was sport. At Bedwell fox-hunting was little appreciated. Whitbread's father wrote in 1789 to his friend Howard, and the implied disapproval is not effaced by the decades which have passed. 'My son is near me at present but moving soon to Cardington and other places for Hunting.' And replying a few years later to a request that he would arrange walks for hound-puppies at Bedwell Whitbread replied 'I will see what I can do for you, but our tenantry are so unused to fox-hunting that they may perhaps not be so courteous on that head as others more *apprivoisés* might be'.

But the glory of the Oakley Hunt — so far as Whitbread was concerned — was transitory. The hounds and horses, the men to look after them, the mill for the meal were all happily at work in 1798 but the cost grew alarmingly. Two years later he was sadly writing to Lee Antonie 'a reduction in the establishment at Oakley must take place'. When they had started he had thought that the expense could not exceed £2,000 a year, but within two years the price of oats had shot up so that he had had to send to Hertford and London for them. But his third and last reason was perhaps the most significant 'in the present state of the country I do not think [it] quite decorous to go on with the same consumption of corn as would be justifiable and proper in more abundant times'.[3]

Four years later, writing confidentially to Lee Antonie, he explained that he did not feel justified in continuing even the more limited arrangement of 1800 'But in giving up my most favourite object of Amusement I do find a very great difficulty in expressing to you in terms adequate to my feelings how much I am impressed with your kindness to me in executing a task which none but yourself would probably have undertaken for any man, and you probably for none but myself.'[4] And the following year he had decided to put up his horses for sale at Tattersall's. It is not easy to say exactly why Whitbread gave up hunting. His wife very much disliked it, and any feelings from that quarter always weighed strongly with him. No doubt it was difficult, except during the parliamentary recess, to combine hunting and the House of Commons. There is an undated letter from Whitbread to Lee Antonie begging him to put off going to the country for an important division 'Pray, pray make this one more sacrifice. Don't damn me black and blue. Where is Ralph? That I may try and stop him.'[5] (Ralph Lambton was the uncle of Whitbread's friend and Member of Parliament for Durham; for the closing years of his long life he was 'confined to his couch' through a fall in the hunting-field.)

Whatever caused Whitbread's decision to give up the hunting field, it was unfortunate. Of a too robust physical system, he found that exercise in the hunting-field was the best means of keeping his weight from excess. We picture him on Buffalo at Roxton Spinnies, learning from experienced Bedfordshire hunting-men that a stump-bred fox always gives better sport than an earth-bred one. Of a tendency to despondency, he found the thrills of a good hunt and the brisk companionship of his own sex an alleviation to that lowness of spirit to which he was prone. Remembering that, we can enter into the feeling which inspired him to write to Lee Antonie when he finally parted with the Oakley establishment (though he very occasionally still hunted on odd days) 'I look back upon our joyous morning meetings with great regret. I miss them in a sensible diminution of health and spirits, and I have nothing to supply their place to my Body or my Mind.'[6]

Unfortunately the death of his father had also for some years past thrown into his busy life great additional responsibilities and anxieties.

No doubt too much should not be made of the conflicts between father and son. They were inevitable in two strong characters totally different in their tastes and outlook and sundered by firm attachments to different sides in politics. To Howard, who belonged to his own generation and shared a certain glumness where youthful gaieties were concerned, the elder Whitbread grumbled in that self-pitying fashion which could be expected from a lonely widower. But there were plenty of things on which Whitbread and his father saw eye to eye. For example both father and son shared an admiration and affection for Howard which was constant and unfeigned. When Howard died in Russia in 1790 the dignitaries of St. Paul's did him the signal honour of placing his statue in the Cathedral — the first statue admitted inside that building. Shortly before his father's death, Whitbread wrote to the committee responsible for making the arrangements for the statue (which was the work of John Bacon who also executed Dr. Johnson's statue now in St. Paul's) explaining that his father was not well enough to see them. The same letter makes it clear that Whitbread composed the inscription for the statue — 'I must trouble you with one, and that an *earnest request*, that my name may not appear as author of the inscription.'[7]

Shortly after this Samuel Whitbread the first died; his death took place at Bedwell on 11 June 1796. But although the old gentleman's body lay in Cardington Church his spirit of

benevolence went marching on. Whitbread was in possession of
the estates — of Bedwell, Cardington, Southill and land at
Purfleet and in London — and of the great Brewery, but his
enjoyment of them was controlled by the vast web of charity
by which they were bound. At the time it was said that Samuel
Whitbread died worth a million at least.[8] That was probably
correct. It was likewise stated that he had given away in
benevolence £3,000 a year. Both were prodigious sums —
judged by the standards of the day. The historian Lecky has
pointed out that as there are fashions in thought so there are
fashions in feeling, and that at the end of the eighteenth century
benevolence and philanthropy 'acquired a higher place in the
category of virtues'. Hannah More, whose religious tracts sold
in quantities comparable with a modern thriller, rather regretted
this spread of goodwill because it is 'a reigning error among the
better sort to reduce all religion into benevolence'.[9] Possibly
that might be said of Samuel Whitbread I. Certainly he followed
the fashion of benevolence — and perhaps helped to form it.
When he died his will covered 126 sheets; it was a book rather
than a document, a testament rather than a deed. There were
many charitable bequests and, as the *Gentleman's Magazine*
wrote at the time 'the many legacies left to old acquaintances,
friends, rectors, curates and tenants and distant relations are
almost incredible'. These legacies were said to amount to
£124,000. Many years later, a royal duke learning that his
aunt had bequeathed him a substantial fortune, was heard to say
'that was a beautiful will'. No doubt Samuel Whitbread's will
was also beautiful. But its beauty depended on someone to carry
it out. Legacies are well and good: they merely require a
backing of funds and an honest executor for their discharge.
Annuities are totally different: they have to rest as a charge on
some fund or estate and they need someone to see, year after
year, that they are met. Often, when Whitbread was walking in
the gardens or woodlands at Southill, he must have felt
conscious of the sly shade of a rural dean, of some whining and
impecunious cousin, of some bibulous old butler dependent on

his property for the security of their annual gifts from his dead
father. They were indeed encumbrances on his estate. And,
infinitely worse, their affairs occupied much of his time : the
beneficiaries became like a great Friendly Society, in which he
was by compulsion the friend of all. Here are two characteristic
clauses. His father left 10 guineas a year, charged on the
Manor at Cardington, to provide clothes for the inmates of the
four almshouses situated in the churchyard. Then 'out of respect
to the memory of John Bunyan' he left £500, to be laid out in
Consols, and the income to be applied to giving bread to the
poor in quartern loaves every Sabbath morning from October
to May. But it was, of course, the stream of gifts to persons
which caused the trouble. There was £500 due to Jane Akers
of Norwich for which Whitbread was trustee. A considerable
correspondence followed because Whitbread wanted it laid out
for Mrs. Akers and her daughter, while she wanted to buy a
baking business for her husband. Then there was Mrs. Nesbitt
to whom the elder Whitbread left an annuity of £100 'to assist
her in the support of her late brother's children which she has
very kindly taken upon her and I recommend to my son to be
her friend as long as she lives'. Begging letters from the
Nesbitts poured in to poor Whitbread all his life and a friend
wrote to him 'they have been a painful and expensive legacy to
you'. Then there was the elder Whitbread's butler's sister who
was given a promissory note for £280 on Whitbread. She lived
in Brecon, took up the matter with her Member of Parliament
and all had to be unravelled by Whitbread. And finally there
was the case of little Sophy Tyrrell whom we have no difficulty
in detesting. She and her mother lived in the south of France,
and all through the Napoleonic wars letters came to Whitbread
begging for little additions to the sum due under the will and
filled with scraps of information about 'dear little Sophy'. 'I can
assure you I spare neither trouble nor expense to make her an
accomplished woman . . . she is praised by all her masters and
mistresses. . . . Sophy made her first entrance in society, and it
has always been my endeavour to make her appear genteel . . .

Sophy likes to be well-dressed.'[10] If it is true as an Elizabethan writer tells us that the beggar's virtue is patience, it is surely equally true that those enduring the patient supplications of the beggar stand in dire need of the same virtue. The sensitive reader, picturing Whitbread at the height of an active parliamentary career, will grieve over these inroads on his time and kind-heartedness. Yet his patience never flags, and at the end of these appeals is often to be seen his minute to his secretary 'Pray tell me how this matter stands and send me the papers'.

In the beautiful will there was a technical fault, one of those little misfortunes which make even the sternest lawyer whimper. The will was dated 24 June 1795, and the testator did not survive for a year afterwards. Under the Statute of Mortmain, which dated back to the wild days of Edward I, charitable bequests had to be made more than a year before the death of a testator. Whitbread could have pleaded the statute which would have invalidated any or all of the charitable bequests. This course was suggested to him, but he preferred to carry out what he knew were his father's intentions.[11] Always generous-minded he wrote to a member of the family 'My father has distributed his fortune according to the nobleness of his nature'. And then he added 'to me he has been particularly generous'.[12] Of what was devised and bequeathed that might have been true, but that remark was certainly not true if we consider the burdens of correspondence thrown on to the shoulders of a busy man.

One particular ambiguity in the will gave rise to many a headache : it provided that if the trustees wished to sell land they might invest the proceeds only in freehold land of an equal value. A learned gentleman in Lincoln's Inn was consulted and, as was not uncommon among his brother conveyancers, he treated the problem, rather as a fascinating gambit on the chess-board than as something affecting human beings, and gave his opinion that if land was sold the proceeds must instantly be placed in a similar purchase of land and must not even temporarily lie at the Bank.

And, perhaps more serious than everything, were the trustees

— men of rectitude but uncongenial to Whitbread the beneficiary. One unfortunately went mad — 'his intellects are quite gone'. Whitbread's brother-in-law, James Gordon, then renounced the trust, leaving a cousin Jacob Whitbread of Suffolk as sole trustee. Whitbread proposed to appoint his political friend and neighbour Thomas Brand, but Jacob Whitbread sent him a highly offensive letter suggesting that Whitbread and Brand were aiming to get control of the trust. Whitbread wrote to him 'You deceive yourself in supposing that I would condescend to suggest, or Mr. Brand to be a party, to such a deceit as it is your object to guard against'. His younger sister Lady St. John added to his embarrassment by writing 'With the mental gifts bestowed on you I should have hoped for a better choice of trustees'. She had evidently inherited some of her father's censoriousness and then softened the blow by writing 'If you think I am wrong do not be displeased : for to differ in opinion is pain — both, as to thinking you in error as well as to expressing it'.[13] To Charles Grey apropos his original trustees he wrote — and it was a cry from the heart — 'Pray take care whom you name as Trustees for your children : I am cursed with such as no Man ever had. To stir at all, and to do the most beneficial acts for my children requires the Riches of Croesus and the patience of Job.' And the significance of the last sentence will not be overlooked 'You are very fortunate in having the control over your own property'.[14]

CHAPTER EIGHT

Cares of Chiswell Street

THE idea that wealth flows from a brewery with the same easy liquidity as the product which is made there is widely believed. It is a mistake. In the eighteenth century great fortunes were of course founded on beer : but they rested on nothing so stable as — for example — the skill and exploitation of the great English 'nabobs', or the northern mines which enabled the son of Whitbread's friend Lambton to jog along on £40,000 a year. Brewing was a highly technical trade, certainly capable of producing great profits, but demanding a constant refreshment of new capital which, in a difficult year, it was capable of devouring. When Mrs. Thrale sold her husband's brewery she wrote — and this was profoundly true — 'I have by this bargain purchased peace and a stable fortune.'[1] Whitbread was, of course, always a rich man, but the dependence on Chiswell Street wove into his wealth a thread of instability. For one of his particular temperament this was unfortunate. In addition it was, as will be shown later, a millstone to him politically. In a codicil to the famous will his father had said 'in case my son shall be desirous to sell and dispose of the trade and the property thereto belonging (which I recommend him to do)' he was to allow three clerks to purchase shares and lend them money to do so. Whitbread's decision to cling to the Brewery was a mistake of magnitude. Some have thought that Chiswell Street was no place for the husband of a Grey, for the associate of dukes, for the friend of Fox. That shows a misconception of English life. Social or snobbish reasons played no part in the decision. His interests lay in the wider fields of politics and public life. A Member of the House of Commons rising to fame in St.

Stephen's was out of place (and wasting his time) peering into a vat in Chiswell Street. And he made the common mistake of thinking that he could cling to the Brewery without really working there. He made this perfectly plain when he wrote to Charles Grey that the Brewery was 'a tolerably easy source of income without making too many demands on my time'.[2]

For some time after his father's death he carried on the trade alone — just as the old gentleman had — with a capital of a quarter of a million. On 9 July 1798 the capital was increased to £300,000 and Whitbread took in three partners. He followed his father's advice and one-ninth share each was taken by two of the clerks. The first of these was Jacob Yallowley. He was one of those devoted men — not ambitious of great wealth, not concerned to sway his fellows but perfectly content to serve the trade in Chiswell Street — his outlook only widened by a villa on Winchmore Hill — a comfortable, summer's walk from the Brewery. His portrait by Romney is at Southill. He died two years after the partnership was formed and Whitbread wrote, 'Poor Yallowley is a very great loss indeed.'* The other clerk was Robert Sangster whose portrait, also by Romney is at Southill. Like Yallowley he was a devoted friend and servant of the family and really acted as Whitbread's 'stand-in' at Chiswell Street. He was still active in 1812, and in 1790 Samuel Whitbread had noted with satisfaction that he had then served for twenty-six years. The third partner was very different from these two quiet gentlemen. Timothy Brown was noisy, opinionated and quarrelsome: he was rich and radical, and revealed to the world a combination which is happily rare — a banker with dangerous views. He was known as 'Equality' Brown and once in writing to Whitbread he alluded to the administration of the feeble Dr. Addington as 'the government

* In the eighteenth century part of the business of both brewers and distillers was in the nature of banking. Currie's bank emerged from this connexion, and also always had close links with Whitbread's. One of the partners in Currie's was another Jacob Yallowley, and another partner was the trustee for a Whitbread who went mad. The elder Whitbread himself had at one time a considerable account with Currie's. (Information provided by Glyn, Mills & Co. Ltd.)

of the Bastille'.³ In the terms of the partnership there was an
important clause which explains why Whitbread was always
free to pursue his own life irrespective of the Brewery. By the
terms of the partnership he was freed from personal attendance
at the business — only retaining for his own use 'two rooms
over the counting house, the strong room and the vaults used for
the storage of wine'.⁴ He was able to use the clerks and facilities
of the Brewery for his private and business affairs, and he was
in reality a sleeping-partner. But his origins and powerful
character meant that, in any moment of crisis, the sleeper could
always awake. If he left to others the day-to-day running of the
business : the actual finances of the Brewery and arrangements
with the partners were always his concern.

After a year Whitbread's share and Brown's share were
reduced by the inclusion of three additional partners — Sir
Benjamin Hobhouse (with west-country commercial interests),
Jacob Whitbread from Suffolk, and Joseph Godman. As will be
seen from the table opposite Whitbread's share of the partnership, in the following year, was in the region of £100,000.
Yallowley had died and his share reverted to Whitbread.
Part of this he pledged to two friends. He had a straightforward commercial transaction with a Hertfordshire neighbour — William Wilshere. Wilshere was a country attorney
and small landowner, and he acted in a general advisory
capacity to Whitbread over the estates. He invariably signed his
letters to Whitbread 'Your grateful and faithful servant'. The
reason for gratitude was obvious : his faithfulness was questioned (though unfairly) by those responsible for Whitbread's
affairs after his death. In 1801 Whitbread sold to Wilshere
one-tenth share of his share in the trade, and for this Wilshere
paid £16,000. There can be no doubt that out of this transaction
Wilshere did extremely well : as was true of all the partners he
was paid 5% on his capital, in addition to a share in the profits.
But if he made money rather too easily out of Whitbread he
appears to have given him constantly sound and disinterested
advice. He also borrowed £8,000 from Richard Holden Webb

in return for a three-twenty-fifths share of Whitbread's share (two-ninths) in the partnership. The financial background to Whitbread's share is explained in this table.

Year (1)	Partnership capital (2)	Amount owned by S.W. II (3)	Interest included in column (3) taken by —		Net interest of S.W. II (6)
			Wilshere (4)	Webb (5)	
	£	£	£	£	£
1796	250,000	250,000	..	..	250,000
1798	300,000	133,333	..	..	133,333
1800	300,000	66,667	..	..	66,667
1801	300,000	100,000	10,000	8,000	82,000
1802	333,333	116,667	26,667	8,000	82,000
1803	333,333	116,667	(a) 33,333	8,000	75,334
1812	400,000	112,500	33,333	8,000	71,167

(a) The additional share taken by Wilshere was advanced during 1803–1805.

Wilshere's share was of course considerable. Some critics have thought that he exercised a baneful influence over Whitbread's fortunes. Long, long after this Lord Brougham, who had been one of Whitbread's staunchest political allies, wrote to Whitbread's son to ask if he could find a particular paper which he needed for his autobiography. Replying, Whitbread's son said that the paper could not be found and that Wilshere 'of whom you will have no very favourable recollection' had, with Charles Grey, destroyed much of the correspondence. A possible explanation for this unfavourable recollection is that Wilshere, partly by reason of his enrichment through the Brewery, had acquired certain manorial properties. One of these entitled him to present the first cup to the Sovereign at the Coronation Banquet. He did this menial civility with some *éclat* at the coronation of George IV : this ceremony — especially if it were made possible by money derived through Whitbread — would have been particularly obnoxious to the Whitbread family and Brougham, who were all ardent partisans of Queen Caroline, who was denied any part in these medieval junketings.* Whitbread's financial position, at the end of his

* It is fair to notice that William Whitbread, Whitbread's eldest son, who was never among the wisest of mortals, put in a claim to act as almoner at the Coronation of George IV on the grounds that he was possessed of one third of the

life, made suspicions inevitable, but all that could be said against Wilshere was that he did well out of an honourable, commercial transaction and that if this was the consequence of Whitbread realising a part of the Brewery profits the most prudent course for Whitbread would have been to realise the whole.

His father seems to have summed up the position exactly when he wrote to Whitbread : 'As you are a perfect stranger to the whole, nobody can give you so good advice as them that understand it thoroughly, and these are your own clerks.'[5] Yet it was rather the financing of the Brewery than the running of it which was to prove Whitbread's greatest anxiety. He borrowed money from the Greys, from his Whig friends, from the purchaser of Bedwell and from even the impoverished General Fitzpatrick. On many of these loans a high rate of interest was paid, (though there may well have been some consideration of augmenting Fitzpatrick's slender income to explain the inclusion of his impecunious name among the creditors).

The truth was that Whitbread, at any time, would have had difficulty in selling the Brewery for his father had charged it with the satisfaction of the legacies and annuities in his will. No doubt to those who are not rich the cares and anxieties of a fortune seem easily borne; their presence at least removes others of a more grinding nature.

An entertaining contemporary of Whitbread's when he heard that a friend was sinking under the responsibility and anxiety of a large fortune remarked that such a burden was just what his health needed. But the point was this. Whitbread's career was elsewhere than in Chiswell Street : his interests were other than porter : he gave to the affairs of the Brewery the short time he could spare from his main preoccupations. Yet the knowledge that his own and his family's prosperity — not to speak of that of several of his relations and friends — depended on the partnership made the cares and anxieties not imaginary but real.

barony of Bedford. His claim was dismissed. He was one of the handful of Members of Parliament who attended the Thanksgiving Service in St. Paul's when the proceedings against Queen Caroline were dropped, and it is unlikely that his attendance on King George would have been particularly agreeable.

CHAPTER NINE

Entourage at Southill

ONE extravagance Whitbread indulged, and it was a princely
one. He liked a court of his own. Not a court of fair ladies and
still less of dazzling youths : it was not necessarily, like Queen
Victoria's court, 'pure'. His retinue was down-at-heel rather
than elegant, consisting of political secretaries, estate advisers,
and beggars. He moved through Bedfordshire life not unlike
some minor Florentine prince — the centre of a strange throng,
disparate but united in dependence and devotion to their prince.

As estate agents he employed a father and son — James and
Thomas Lilburne. James Lilburne had been a schoolmaster and
was perhaps more at home with a gradus than a ledger; he is
described as having 'extraordinary' notions of business. His son
was more practical, and together they made a useful team. They
were housed and paid £700 rising to £800 between them, and
could take on some private work. Though they were certainly
competent, they were a quarrelsome pair — advancing to battle
against gamekeepers and Whitbread's other personal servants
with every prickle sharpened for action. They were possibly
connected with that family in the seventeenth century which
produced those famous brothers — one a political agitator and
the other a regicide : and if that was the case they displayed in
the glades and fields of Southill all the fighting qualities of their
ancestors. In 1804 when Whitbread was in London the
Lilburnes sent him a letter of whining grumbles complaining of
things 'so distressing to all that is dear to us on this side of the
grave', and hinting at resignation because they did not think
they had the spirit to go through the business of collecting the
rents. The association of high spirit with rent collecting is

unexpected. To this effusion Whitbread wrote an indignant if somewhat oratorical reply. It began abruptly — 'Lilburne' and went on :

If I were to give way to the expressions your very extraordinary conduct excites I could write you a volume. But control is necessary to all our feelings even upon the most serious and trying occasions. . . . I can not believe that you will not upon reflection be sorry for hinting even at quitting your employment. You knew when you wrote how difficult it would be for me to supply your place, not so much from the ability with which you filled it, as from the unlimited confidence your integrity has induced me to place in you. . . . You are to decide for yourself. I have said all I can say about stopping these nonsensical squabbles. . . . You ask of me impossibilities if you ask me to prevent who pleases talking of you and your work as *they* please. You deceive yourself if you fancy *you* are wholly blameless in these trifles. Before you go further I advise you to consult Mr. Wilshere who has a real friendship for you. Whatever line you may pursue I shall never forget your former services and attachment; in the recollection of which I shall never cease to be your friend, S. Whitbread.[1]

That is of course a letter of authority, of master to man in an age when masters were few and men were plentiful, and we feel that his relations with his servants were those of the centurion— 'Do this, and he doeth it'. But even in a matter like this — tiresome, trifling and provoking as it was — the essential reasonableness of Whitbread's mind is revealed. In public as in private he could be hasty, he could be rough and he could exaggerate, but behind those characteristics was a mind whose mainspring was a sense of justice. The Lilburnes stayed : with their master, they both lie in the vaults of Cardington Church.

In all matters concerning the town of Bedford (apart from politics) his confidant was Mr. Theed Pearce, who was clerk of the peace for the county. A vast accumulation of letters from Pearce is among Whitbread's papers. He also turned to another Bedford man for political information and guidance. This was Thomas Belsham, who was the son of a dissenting minister at Bedford : those too prone to judge the lineage of dissenting ministers by the standards of the nineteenth century may be reassured to know that he was also the great-grandson of Lord

SOUTHILL PARK, BIGGLESWADE, BEDFORDSHIRE, IN 1965

SAMUEL WHITBREAD *c.* 1799

By John Opie

Anglesey, though it is proper to add that this peer was described
by Pepys as 'one of the greatest knaves in the world'. Many of
Whitbread's more orthodox political associates would not have
described the great-grandson in conspicuously different terms.
Explaining the reason for Whitbread's unpredictable politics
Lady Holland wrote that he was 'goaded by a scribbling
gazetteer of the name of Belsham'. After meeting Belsham she
wrote: 'His manner and appearance are positively offensive to
all the senses.'[2] In an account of him when he died in 1827 he is
described as having lived 'in great intimacy' with Whitbread,[3]
and the Whig hierarchy was decidedly nervous of this radical
provincial, and of his influence over Whitbread. He was,
perhaps, primarily an historian: his principal work was a history
of Great Britain from the accession of William III to 1802 in
twelve volumes, many of them devoted to the politics of the
reign of George III. Belsham understood English politics and
did not believe that public affairs are governed by the interests
and personalities of individuals but rather thought, as did the
Whig historians, that association in party was the motive
power of English political action. Again there is a considerable
correspondence on the issues of the day from Belsham to
Whitbread and he was constantly at Southill. His opinions were
advanced and his courage was high. In 1792 a 'patriotic' or
conservative meeting was arranged in Bedford by the mayor:
afterwards 'the populace', as Belsham calls them, burned Paine
and Priestly in effigy. The mob then moved to Belsham's house
and sang, over and over again 'God Save the King'. The brave
historian sat at his window all the time and, although it was late
December, he threw the sash open once or twice to show that he
had no fear of his fellows or of their provocative song.[4] Whitbread paid him an annuity of £200.[5]

Whitbread was a considerable collector. He had of course
inherited important pictures from his father,[6] and he added to
these Wilkie's 'The Cut Finger' and 'The Blind Fiddler'. He
was influenced in these matters by Humphry Repton — the
landscape gardener and architect, who sent Whitbread some

H

Universitas
BIBLIOTHECA
Ottaviensis

comments on 'The Blind Fiddler' to the effect that the composition, drawing, colouring and expression of the painting 'seem
to have reached the highest pitch of art — as a cabinet picture of
low life — without the vulgarity of Teniers — the deformity of
Ostade's figures or the filthy portraiture and costume of
Morland's'.[7] The famous picture of Gainsborough's daughters
came to Whitbread almost certainly through Sheridan. On Fox's
advice he bought Romney's unexpected picture of 'Milton —
Dictating to his Daughters' which Mr. Oliver Millar has
described as an attempt 'to escape to something less bound by
the conventions of the time'.[8] How difficult that was is shown
by a prosaic comment on this fine painting by Whitbread's
brother-in-law, Charles Grey 'I am sorry to tell you that I have
discovered your beautiful picture of Milton and his daughters
to be historically false. He had three daughters, none of whom
could write; and he always employed Elwood or some other
person to transcribe for him'.[9]

A rather surprising indication of Whitbread's interest in
the arts was his patronage of three minor English painters who
were largely dependent on him and his hospitality — George
Garrard, Sawrey Gilpin and S. W. Reynolds. George Garrard,
who originally attracted the attention of Sir Joshua with his
painting of 'Mr. Whitbread's Wharf,' when he was 24, did
several successful topographical paintings for Whitbread,
including one of the rebuilding of Southill. He achieved some
renown as a modeller of animals, and a collection of these are at
Southill. Mr. Oliver Millar suggests that the many examples
of Garrard's work at Southill imply that his patron had a more
understanding approach to the countryside than he could have
found in the more fashionable artists of the day such as Stubbs
and Ben Marshall.[10] To his hunting-friend Lee Antonie Whitbread wrote 'Garrard is a very ingenious little fellow who has
been patronised by me and my Father for more than twenty-five
years, and in some branches of Art, such as the modelling of
cattle, he is superexcellent, besides being a capital painter and
sculptor. I think his eagle and bull in the greenhouse at Woburn

Abbey may challenge competition with any work in any age.'
The Regency collectors knew what they liked, and were never
afraid to proclaim their likes from the house-tops.

The second artist whom he patronised was Sawrey Gilpin,
who belonged perhaps to a higher order of artists than did
Garrard; he was an academician, and has been described as one
of the best painters of horses which the country has produced.[11]
The delightful overdoors at Southill, filled with birds and
animals, were his work. He belonged to a very much earlier
generation than Garrard, who was his son-in-law. When he was
a man of nearly 70 he got into some kind of scrape, apparently
being involved in a matrimonial tangle. The letter which he
wrote to Whitbread on this occasion is worth quoting, partly as
a specimen of an immense, similar correspondence from other
hands and partly as an illustration that Whitbread was not
afflicted by the supposedly hard heart of the rich. 'April 2 1800.
I really do not know what to say to you, my dear sir : about
myself I can say nothing but what you know already — that I am
the greatest of all fools, and yet such has been yours and Mrs.
Whitbread's kindness that I think you will bear with my folly
better than any other person that I know.'[12] To an extent the
censorious might accuse Gilpin and Garrard of battening on
Whitbread : but at least they protected him from the impor-
tunities of other members of their family. One of Gilpin's sons
wrote from near Tadcaster to beg Whitbread to give him enough
money to cease 'languishing as a Yorkshire clergyman'.
Garrard, the brother-in-law of this importunate vicar indig-
nantly wrote to Whitbread that when last he had seen his sister
and her daughter they were 'as fat as moles', and when the
Yorkshire clergyman appeared 'the door was scarce wide
enough to admit his carcase'.[13] And the unexpected usefulness of
artists in domestic life was shown once when Whitbread and his
wife went to stay with Lord Robert Spencer at Woolbeding :
they were quite happy to leave their children at Southill in the
care of Sawrey Gilpin. In a letter to Mrs. Wilmot,* a relative

* See below, pages 287–8.

of the Greys, Gilpin wrote describing the delights of Southill for the studious — 'I am apt to be idle at Southill — in the superlative I mean — for I am everywhere comparatively so, but at Southill there is a stupendous mouse-trap in the form of a Library and when a poor, nibbling mouse happens to shut himself up in it, how is it possible for him to escape?'[14]

To the last of the triumvirate — S. W. Reynolds — Whitbread's generosity was most conspicuous and consistent. Reynolds was a younger man than the other two; he was still in his mid-twenties when Whitbread moved to Southill. He is today principally remembered for his engravings, but he was also drawing-master to the daughters of George III, and his landscapes, though rare in this country, are admired. His 'Old Woman in Bed', which is at Southill, is an interesting picture. In 1810 a society was formed for the encouragement of engraving, under the patronage of that proud and foolish Duke of Gloucester known as 'Silly Billy'. The subscription was 100 guineas; Whitbread was an original subscriber and wrote to his friend Lee Antonie asking that he should also be a subscriber. In this letter he said 'I am anxious to promote its success because I know the difficulties under which the artists, in that line, labour — and that even poor Reynolds with all his activity and genius can hardly put bread into the mouths of his children. Others below him must starve. *Mes amours à Madame.*'[15]

He was, in this particular, writing from knowledge. In 1801 Reynolds wrote the following letter to Tom Adkin, knowing perhaps that he was assured of a kindred feeling in the heart of that sympathetic bankrupt. 'You, my dear Mr. Adkin, know the cause of my present distress, but you can have no possible idea what I have suffered since I saw you. Oh! God what a wretched thoughtless fool I have been. His Majesty has signed the peace : war is over, but I have not a penny to buy a squib.' A few days later he catalogued his debts which came to £645 including £15 to the cheesemonger and £40 to the baker. In an effort to save himself he had mortgaged his future engravings to one of those rapscallions (half dealer and half usurer) who hang, like

vultures of vision, above the efforts of every promising artist.
This worthy, who bore a hint of the antique in the spelling of
his name, was called Jeffryes, and he wrote to Whitbread that he
had purchased Reynolds's portrait of Whitbread 'I propose to
wait upon you with the fifty proof impressions you agreed to
take of him'. This was presumably the Gainsborough portrait of
Whitbread which was painted when he married in 1788, and
Reynolds's sale of his work on this picture and others to Jeffryes
no doubt explains the allusions to his folly in the letter to Adkin.
Whitbread rescued Reynolds from his debts, but he could not
undo the transaction with Jeffryes. That personage wrote to
Whitbread at the beginning of 1802 — and the sentiments in
the letter must have been particularly unacceptable — 'Instead
of feasting and revelling at Southill he [Reynolds] ought to be
at his work-room in Poland Street for he may depend upon it
that unless he materially alters his conduct, he will ere long be
obliged to put up with apartments that are generally appropriated to the unworthy and undeserving.' Poor Reynolds! His
circumstances showed no signs of improvement: after 'a cold
and pinching drive' on the box of the Carlisle Mail he wrote to
thank Whitbread for the gift of a hare — 'in all probability we
shall have part of it on Christmas Day'. There can not have
been much feasting or revelling on that occasion off the
dismembered limbs of an animal which is at its most palatable
when entire. Just before this he had been reduced to sending to
Southill the tailor's bill for repair to his clothes marked, with
the nice commercial sense of his day, 'Lowest, ready-money
charge. No discount'. To his companion in tribulation, Tom
Adkin, he wrote, confessing that he was more deeply involved
with Jeffryes than he had first admitted 'I am the most
unhappy wretch living. Don't forget me.' Forwarding a true
statement of the case to Whitbread, with various letters of
Reynolds's, Sawrey Gilpin wrote in a style that showed true
understanding of human nature. He asked Whitbread to pay
attention to one point. 'Is it not obvious that the want of liberal
education, and connections introduces a kind of sneaking

timidity (it ought not to, I know) into the manners and
transactions of men who may have to do with superiors, and
may not this in the present instance, joined to an overwhelming
folly in calculating his resources, strike knavery out of the
charge against him? . . . Dear Sir, drop to his level if you can
when you read his letter.'

The appeal was not made in vain. Whitbread advanced the
£700 for the debts on condition that Reynolds would never
again put his name to a bill or promissory note, that he would
never sell any of his work before it was finished, that he would
use Sawrey Gilpin to sell off his pictures or plates and that he
would pay the interest regularly and try to discharge the
principal within two years. These proposals were drawn up by
Whitbread himself to be sent by Gilpin to Reynolds: the first
condition was perhaps the most important in Whitbread's
eyes 'You shall promise never to mention to your or his most
intimate friends from whom you have received the assistance'.
His generosity to Reynolds continued for the remainder of
Whitbread's life, and he employed Reynolds's eldest son as his
personal secretary, who was once grandiloquently alluded to by
Brougham as 'Secretary Reynolds'.[16]

This private circle, at once varied and talented was rounded
off by Julia Grant, who was Mrs. Whitbread's companion, and
Tom Adkin — grown a little fonder of the ruby since last we
met him, but endearing himself to every visitor to Southill — a
grateful friend who loved the feasting and festivity but ever
striving to pay something back by making himself pleasant and
useful.* One question remains. The following, which he had
attracted, looked to him with something of the fidelity of the
knights of old to King Arthur; but did Mrs. Whitbread, as could,
in a sense, be said of Queen Guinevere, control the destinies of
her husband and his retinue? Elizabeth Whitbread's character
was strong and forceful (this was true of all the Grey family)
and in addition her intellectual gifts were marked. Her collection

---

* There is a bust of Adkin at Southill done by Garrard in 1803.

of books has survived more or less intact,* and it includes a number in French and Italian, dating back to the 1780's. She had a complete set of the novels of Galt and — horrifying to her evangelical daughter, Lady Waldegrave — a prodigious collection of the romantic novels of G. P. R. James. But these were the solace of old age and widowhood. She had an Augustan rather than a Victorian mind. She was kind and somewhat unconventional. She showed this over Fox's marriage — though what was courageous in the 1790s may seem common-place enough in the 1960s. In 1795 Fox secretly married his mistress, Mrs. Armistead. The latter was living at Wyton near Huntingdon so as to qualify by residence to marry there. Fox went over to call on Whitbread and Elizabeth invited Mrs. Armistead to breakfast. To such civilities she was not accustomed, and she told Fox's niece long afterwards that she had never forgotten this kindness.[17] Old Mr. Whitbread would not have approved of that innocent breakfast-party, and it was, we may suppose, such acts of unconventional kind-heartedness which were to make her long afterwards the target for some severe shafts from her own evangelical daughter.[18]

Though it would be unjust to criticise Lady Elizabeth as harshly as did her own children, she was too exacting and too inconsiderate where Whitbread was concerned. The esplanation of this was that after the birth of her youngest child in 1798 she developed a tumour on the thigh : this was diagnosed as cancerous, and for months three doctors hinted that each day might be her last. When she very slowly improved, the doctors told Whitbread that her life henceforward depended on her being kept quiet and composed : he was assured that the slightest check might throw her back to her former state. As late as 1804 he was writing to an old family friend, 'The accounts you have heard of

---

* At Mr. Humphrey Whitbread's house in Cardington. Michael Sadleir, the distinguished authority on Victorian literature, attributed his interest in Gothic novels to a chance purchase in 1922 from Bumpus's bookshop of a little run of them, in three-quarters morocco, with Whitbread's bookplate. They included Mrs. Roche's *The Children of the Abbey*. It seems improbable that such things appealed to Whitbread and despite the book-plate it is likely that they were part of the reading of Lady Elizabeth.

Mrs. Whitbread's looks are true, for she never looked better in all her life than she does when she is able to mix in society, but alas! health is not her portion'.* So it came about that complying with her wishes became a habit. He never separated himself from her, even for a day, if he could possibly help it. In the House of Commons he would write to her two or three times during a debate, telling her how the day was going and sending a messenger with each note.

In order to make things easy for his wife he added to his other burdens by taking over the management of the children. When his mind was engrossed by politics his attention was distracted by nurses, governesses and tutors. In 1806 soon after Fox's death when he was absorbed by all the arrangements resulting there-from and particularly the wrangle in the Party over finding a successor for Fox in Westminster, he wrote to Grey that 'we received intelligence yesterday morning that the scarlet fever had broken out in Keate's house† which decided me to set out immediately to bring little William home'. He got home at half past three in the morning 'which is the great joy of his mother who, as you may suppose, had passed a most anxious day'.[19]

Almost every letter he wrote to Charles Grey contains some reference to Bess's health. No doubt these touching attentions had their compensations. Husband and wife were devotedly attached to one another : she entered fully into his public career : she was always a stimulating companion never a cushion : she was a graceful hostess much admired by his political cronies. But she increased instead of diminishing the load of life which was accumulating on his shoulders.

* A copy of this letter was found in Chiswell Street and sent to her after Whitbread's death (Chewton Papers).

† Then a housemaster and later headmaster of Eton famous for his savagery with the rod.

CHAPTER TEN

Joys of Opposition

F REEDOM — the poet tells us — has a thousand charms, and surely he must have included among them the satisfaction of fighting for it in a minority. All would admit that this was a charm which Whitbread was to savour all his life long. Moreover, association with a minority — such as Whitbread's devotion to Fox and the remnants of his party — fosters courage and constancy and possibly displays less agreeable characteristics, too much self-confidence and the joy of rousing antagonism for its own sake. These things could all be attributed to Whitbread in his political life. We can see that this is true from a small point of fashion.

At that period formality both in dress and deportment counted for much : comfort and convenience, so far as clothes went, were limited to what a man wore in his own home. Emergence over the door-step dictated a particular coat and hat, depending on the time of day. Perhaps the most ticklish occasions for the correct clothes were the dinners given by the Speaker for the Government and for the Opposition at the start of each session. At the Government dinner in February 1796 every guest was in full dress — that is, breeches and powdered hair. At the Opposition dinner it was noticed that even then three only were not in full dress — a general, Grey and Whitbread.

Now it will not be overlooked that trifles of this kind drew attention to Whitbread from the more conventionally minded. Moreover as he moved to the front rank of the Whigs he naturally became a target for his enemies on the other side. This is how a poet in the *Anti-Jacobin* viewed some leading

Whigs in the later 1790's (Francis, Duke of Bedford was
Leviathan) :

> And thou Leviathan! on ocean's brim
> Hugest of living things that sink and swim;
> Thou, in whose nose, by Burke's gigantic hand,
> The hook was fixed to drag thee to the land,
> With Erskine, Grey and Courtenay in thy train
> And Whitbread wallowing in the yeasty main.

The anonymous and scurrilous historian of the Whig Club,
already quoted, came near to the truth when he wrote about
Whitbread. He was described as 'following Mr. Grey as
close as his shadow'. The historian alluded to Samuel Whitbread's objection to his son's marriage, and he said that he
thought that he would never have consented to it if he had
foreseen how deeply his son was to suck in 'the poison' of Grey's
opinions. The writer goes on 'indifferent to the reproaches and
remonstrances of a father who has been but too indulgent to
him' he is only waiting to sacrifice the 'princely profits of the
brew house' to 'the character of being a patriot' and 'the honour
of belonging to the Whig Club'. Again that is more or less
correct because there is plenty of evidence that he was prepared
(though reluctantly) to abandon the trade in Chiswell Street if
that was essential to service in the Government. Then the
writer goes on to attack Whitbread as a speaker — 'his wild
and frantic ravings in all their native deformity'; if he tried to
make his fellow Member weep 'they are not infrequently
convulsed with laughter' : his attempt to make them smile
'excites a yawn'. Such charges were to be thrown at Whitbread
all his parliamentary life. He was too inclined to lapse into
rhetoric regardless whether the theme was strong enough to
support the flights of oratory : he was often — in the literary
sense — vulgar. 'He was the Demosthenes of bad taste and
vulgar vehemence', wrote Byron. He was a useful speaker —
never an elegant one. Someone once described an oratorical lord
as the Rupert of Debate : Whitbread's style of speaking was
also reminiscent of a charge — but rather of a charge by the

cart horses. Yet for all the hazards of his style, people listened
to what he said. And the explanation of this was that although
he often provoked his audience, he never failed to show that
his exaggeration of manner sprang from the intensity of his
feelings.

Looking back to issues long dead and gone, the observer
sometimes forgets how deeply they engaged the feelings of
those who lived with them at the time. Sydney Smith, gayest
and most courageous of mortals, was once obliged to confess
that the opening years of the nineteenth century were a time of
great tribulation for all professing advanced political opinions.
Though partial to overstating a case, he was not indulging
that partiality in this remark. As a Whig peeped at the harsh
world around him in the early 1800's he must have felt the same
kind of fears and the same sense of hopelessness which afflicted
a liberal in Bismarck's Germany or a legitimist in the France of
1830. The present was dark, and no glint of light could be seen
to promise something better in the future. The whole world was
reeling away from that reasonableness on which the strength of
the Whig party rested. Thomas Erskine, the distinguished
Whig lawyer and future Lord Chancellor, summed up this
feeling in a letter which he wrote to Whitbread in April 1805.
Explaining why he could not appear before King George III
during a period of court mourning he said 'I had no time to
dress, nor indeed anything to dress in as I have no weepers —
tho' there is so much to weep for.'[1]

In 1801, after nearly twenty years of office, Pitt fell from
power. Lawyers, divines and bigots within his own Government
compassed his defeat: they were outraged by his proposal to
give political tolerance to Roman Catholics, and would not have
disagreed with their ally, the King, when he described the
proposal as 'the most jacobinical thing I have ever heard of'.
Pitt's humiliation was complete: the King, who had made
him, parted from him without even the courtesy of farewell. But
in all this, there was no consolation for Fox and the Whigs,
except so far as it is agreeable to watch the discomfiture of an

enemy. There was no question of the Whigs with all their talent, all their ardour filling the gap left by Pitt and his colleagues; they were not even considered by the King or the House of Commons as an acceptable alternative. Instead, the nation had to accept one of the most laughable administrations which it has ever had to endure. At its head was Addington, the son of George III's doctor. He at once became a target for the wit and venom of the *beau monde* or the 'biu mond' as a not very elegant Tory peer described it. On one occasion he entered a crowded House of Commons and walked slowly to his place attired in all the sombre glory of the Windsor uniform, as though he were attending a household dinner at Windsor Castle. The Speaker happened at that moment to be reading out the Medicine Act: Members of the House, thus reminded of the origins of the pompous figure in their midst, were convulsed with laughter.[2] Addington neither saw the jest nor felt the ridicule. Yet Addington held his place, and carried the country into that strange interlude in our relations with Napoleon — the Treaty of Amiens. War broke out again in May 1803 and the country made it unmistakably plain that they wanted Pitt as Prime Minister — that they preferred a warder on the hill to a doctor in the House. The negotiations leading to Pitt's return to power were prolonged and elaborate: some thought that Pitt and the Whigs would come together: others that Pitt could only attempt a Government with the help of his old allies — the Grenvilles. But in May 1804 he came into office without allies. Fox and the Whigs were excluded: the Grenvilles, 'men of spirit' Fox approvingly called them, stood aloof. And under this Government it was not only men that were excluded: measures were forbidden as well. Soon after Pitt was installed in office, George III was driving down Bond Street and, to the alarm of passers-by, was heard to call out from the window of his carriage 'hot buns!'. This was interpreted by those who knew him as a cry of hostility to the Roman Catholics.[3] Some years earlier Pitt had given an undertaking not to bring the subject forward during the King's lifetime. The Bond Street cry strengthened that undertaking, and widened the cleavage between Pitt and the Whigs, who for many years had been committed to a relaxation of the political penalties on Roman Catholics. The Addington Government had not been altogether unpopular in the House of Commons — partly because the country gentlemen saw in it something for which they instinctively had a fellow-feeling. As one of them said, 'the Government was without those confounded men of genius in it'.[4]

Yet it was little use attempting to fight Napoleon without the men of genius. Reluctantly though sparingly the House of Commons agreed to a stiffening of the government with at least one man of genius — William Pitt.

Throughout all the difficult days of secession, of Addington's Government and of Pitt's return, Whitbread spoke over and over again, opposing infringements of liberty and prolongation of the war with France. On the eve of the war starting afresh occurred that terrible scene in the Tuileries when Napoleon shouted to the British ambassador in reference to the refusal of the British to relinquish Malta under the Treaty *'Malheur à ceux qui ne respectent pas les traités. Ils en seront responsibles à toute l'Europe'*. Probably Whitbread would have agreed with Napoleon, and we can sense the depth of his feeling from the letter he wrote to Grey when war started again 'As to spirits I can boast of none; for I am really and truly more depressed with the present situation of affairs than I ever felt at any Period of my Life. The war continues to be popular, or rather increases in popularity.'[5] Against this popularity the Whigs could only set the comfort of their own society. The Whigs under Fox in the 1790's were a close fraternity, suffering for the cause, but sustained by private friendship and by the applause of that towering personality who was at their head. 'The fewer men, the greater share of honour.' To be among that happy band of enlightened aristocrats was an amazing piece of good fortune for Whitbread, but it is fair to add that what luck may have begun, his own talents and courage completed.

The coterie of Whigs had, in addition to their political loyalties, a common taste for life in the country. They would all have sympathised with Burke when he wrote 'my barley makes me a little melancholy'.[6] Even Fox who had passed his earlier manhood in a largely metropolitan existence thought later that there was no pleasure to rank with that of lying in the long grasses of summer, reading a novel. His nephew noticed that the country 'gave him an intense enjoyment which those who knew his former life of politics and pleasure can hardly have imagined'.[7] Grey himself, in his letters to Whitbread, was constantly interspersing matters of high politics with the farm — extolling a threshing machine which could be worked by wind or from a little *fillet d'eau*, and referring to a new foreman who was 'as great a fool as Addington'. And Lambton wrote, describing how he had thundered over that strange Durham countryside — the account of his hunt thrilling even the most squeamish urban dweller: 'I have had the most excellent sport and am most satisfied with my hounds which are really good. We had yesterday a run of two hours and thirty odd minutes without a check, and killed our fox fifteen miles from the place of finding. It was very severe, and although the direct distance did not exceed fifteen, the whole run could not be less than 30.' Can we blame him if London and politics seemed very remote from these excitements 300 miles away. 'I begin strongly to suspect they [politics] are made up of inherent villainy, rascality, duplicity and empty ambition, and that we are all without knowing it at the time, neither more nor less than villains, rascals, knaves and fools, sacrificing our happiness and our characters to the vilest, meanest and most unprincipled purposes.'[8]

None of them would perhaps have challenged what Lambton here says, but all would have agreed that in company with Fox things looked different. Much of the roguery of politics was dispersed by the radiance of his personality.

Charles Fox was fifteen years older than Whitbread. He was descended from King Charles II and Louise de Kéroualle: of the

latter Fox's mother was 'violently fond'.* This Gallic strain may
well account for that liveliness and spirit which he showed to
his dying day. The poet Campbell, who saw him often at the
end of his life, said that what struck him was 'the electric
quickness and wideness of his mind in general conversation'.9 It
was not of course for his achievements in legislation that Fox
stands at the head of English statesmen — for he was only in
office for a small part of his career, at the beginning and the
end — it was rather for his adherence to principles which were
subsequently to be accepted by us all. With this went a capacity
to attach men to him which has been often aped by party
leaders since — though rarely achieved. In a sense he led the
Whigs to disaster — and this was particularly apparent when
Whitbread was of his flock — but it was all the more remarkable
that his personal sway was undiminished by misfortune and
dwindling prospects of power. Only superficially was Fox's
career a disaster. Does it not show that loyalty to political
principle may have a consequence — the control over man's
thinking and purpose in the future, which is far more important
than mere transitory power?

No doubt as a parliamentary tactician Fox lays himself open
to the severest strictures. To his faithful, young disciples he
must have often seemed perfectly maddening. A century later
Lord Rosebery was to infuriate his following by declining to
give them a lead, and by speaking of 'ploughing my lonely
furrow'. With Fox it was worse: there was the loneliness but
not even a plough. In 1797 Fox ceased to attend in the House
of Commons and he withdrew his presence as a protest against
the indifference of Pitt and his great majority to the arguments of the Opposition. He enjoyed letting off pleasantries
about the House of Commons — 'ceasing to be a place of much
importance' 'the insipidity of the House of Commons is beyond
conception, and I think it is catching' and Grey, always glad of
an excuse to linger in Northumberland, enjoyed it all vastly.

* The explanation for this extraordinary link with the past rests on the fact that
Louis de Kéroualle lived to be 85.

There is no evidence what Whitbread thought of it all and he perhaps smiled rather wryly when his brother-in-law wrote from Howick 'we must make up our minds not only to exclusion, but must expect still further to be neglected and forgotten.* Have you philosophy enough to bear this ? I think I have.'[10] One consequence of the secession was that the Whig Club became very much more important, as Fox tended to use it as a forum rather than the House of Commons.

But the uncertainty among his opponents after the fall of Addington drew Fox back to Westminster. There was another, more personal reason. He had lived for many years with Mrs. Armistead — one of the most beautiful and charming courtesans of the day. Eventually he married her, but this was not made public, even to his family, till 1802. For one long excluded from the festivities of life in the capital, Mrs. Fox found them enjoyable : she encouraged Fox to be more in London and to take more part in politics. In writing to Whitbread Grey refers to this point, suggesting that one reason for their leader's greater eagerness about politics could be a desire 'to gratify Mrs. Fox who, now that she is more received and taken notice of, may be more anxious to live in London'.[11] And then he adds 'Remember it is only to you, who love and admire him as much as I do, that I speak so freely about him'. Although in private Whitbread and Grey may have smiled over the foibles of their leader — and regretted them — such things in comparison with their love and admiration for the man were of small significance.

Whitbread and Fox were much together in the last few years of Fox's life. There are several allusions to their dining together in London. Creevey records a time when he dined with Whitbread to meet Fox, and let us hope that this was not one of the occasions when the Liverpudlian got 'a little bosky'. Fox regularly spent ten days or a fortnight with Whitbread in the country. In 1804 Fox wrote to Grey who was undecided whether to come from Northumberland 'Come or not come, only remember that on you, and Lauderdale and Whitbread must

* Grey was the only other Whig who strictly adhered to secession with Fox.

now and always be my only real dependence in politics'.[12]
Whitbread, for his part, referred in the House of Commons four
years after Fox was dead to 'my reverence and love for the
authority of Mr. Fox' as 'unlimited'. He attempted to turn his
feelings into verse and these lines will be found underneath the
bust of Fox in his library.

> Live, marble, to speak the patriot's mind.
> His generous heart, embracing all mankind.
> His constant Fortitude, unbroke by Time.
> His thought profound, and eloquence sublime.
> If vain his toil to save a venal age
> If Wisdom's voice be lost in Factious rage,
> He fosters Liberty's expiring flame.
> Her champion he acquires a deathless fame
> He plead's humanity's neglected cause
> And wins from after ages sure applause.

When first written the lines were sent off to Northumberland
for Grey's approval. The comments were severe. Whitbread
had originally written 'He Guards o'er Liberty's expiring
flame'. Grey would have none of this, as he thought there was
no good authority for using 'guard over' instead of 'guard'. He
also said 'my Great objection to them is that there is nothing
original in them, nor peculiarly appropriate, as it appears to
me, to Fox's character.' At the end he adds rather lamely 'upon
the whole they are good'.[13] Even enhanced by their original
setting and all the dignity of capital letters on marble they
hardly hold the wandering eye of the observer. But yet the
kindly critic will not fail to notice the last line; in the earlier
part of the verse the frustrations and sorrows of the Whig are
sung, with the promise that their memory will be wiped clean
amid the applause of future ages. Whitbread was not so much
promising pie in the sky as pie through the nineteenth century.
On the whole events were to fulfil that promise.

In those days men's feelings for politics cut deep: their
affections were warm and their dislikes intense. This explains
why Fox could, with propriety, vote against the wish of the
House of Commons that Pitt should be buried in Westminster

I

Abbey : it explains why Burke at the instant of his breach with his old Whig friends could exclaim across the floor of the House of Commons to Fox 'our friendship is at an end'. This same intensity of feeling is revealed in Whitbread's refusal to tolerate on his walls a famous painting of Pitt. He gave it to Robert Ward,* an able contemporary of his in the House of Commons who was a follower of Pitt, accompanying it with the following letter :

By the permission you gave me yesterday I have sent to your house the portrait of Mr. Pitt painted some years ago by Gainsborough Dupont for my father who, you know, was a warm admirer and strenuous supporter of the whole of his administration. Had I lived at a distance from Mr. Pitt, I should have been glad to have found myself in possession of so good a picture of a man who for so long a period filled so great a space in the world, whose talents and eloquence were beyond all doubt, transcendent, and whose personal integrity no man has questioned.

But having lived in his day, having fought in the ranks of opposition to him under Mr. Fox, of whom and of whose maxims of policy and wisdom my heart and mind are full : and having my house full of memorials of him I can have no satisfaction in the contemplation of the picture of Mr. Pitt, from whose acts Mr. Fox prophesied the consequences we now deplore. To you as his friend and admirer it will be of value and I beg you to accept it as a proof of my respect and esteem. . . .[14]

* He later took the name of Plomer, and as Robert Plomer Ward is known as a political diarist of interest and a political novelist of mediocrity.

CHAPTER ELEVEN

Impeachment of Melville

FOR the Foxite Whigs, as the nineteenth century opened, their old sense of grievance remained. In 1804 Pitt, the principal cause of all their political disasters, was back in office, whereas their leader, the outstanding political genius of the day, was banned from office by a personal fad of the King. Indignant yet wary — because they sensed the strong feeling in favour of the war — the Whigs turned to that most refreshing of all paths for an Opposition in time of trouble — the unmasking of mismanagement and corruption. Along this path Whitbread emerged as a personality of renown. The year 1805 saw the triumph of Napoleon in Europe with the victory of Austerlitz: it also saw, on a narrower stage, the triumph of Whitbread in the House of Commons. He used the word himself, and wrote of 'my triumph'.* He was successful in impeaching one of the leading members of Pitt's Government. Compared with the great oratorical triumphs such as Fox was winning almost day by day or compared with the administrative triumphs achieved by Pitt in the 1790's, Whitbread's was of a different order. It was certainly more spectacular, but less firmly based — owing more to the occasion perhaps than to the personal achievement of the individual. Whitbread's was the success of a skilled marksman who, from a varied armoury, draws out a blunderbuss — and shoots a fox — unexpectedly effective though possibly not absolutely sporting.

From when Pitt took office in 1804, sixteen years had passed since the roaring hall of William Rufus had thrown back the Irish brogue of Burke as he said 'I impeach Warren Hastings in

* To his brother-in-law, Charles Grey (Durham).

the name of the people of India. In the name of human nature itself, in the name of both sexes, in the name of every age, in the name of every rank, I impeach the common enemy and oppressor of all'.[1] The impeachment of Melville in 1805 lacked the sustained splendour of the impeachment of Warren Hastings in 1788 : it lacked too the mysterious setting of the Orient. But, like the impeachment of Hastings, the impeachment of Melville saw the revival of the great criminal political machinery of the seventeenth century — that by which Strafford had perished — to deal with the more matter-of-fact crimes of a later age, peculation, malversation and plundering the public funds. By impeachment the House of Commons could bring to trial any citizen for crimes against the state, and the solemnity of its process drew much of its sombre dignity from the realisation that the sanction behind it was the block and axe of Tower Hill. In the gradual political civilisation of the country, which followed the expulsion of the Stuarts, the headsman and his axe became only a memory from those vivid days. The ultimate penalty had gone, but the machinery of impeachment was left, and the idea of bringing a political culprit before a tribunal of the nation died hard. The same idea was reflected in the constitutions of other countries : it explains why impeachment was written in to the constitution of the United States in 1787 : even as lately as 1919 it found a place in the Weimar Constitution of the German Republic.

Inevitably fame attaches to the last time when any part of the constitutional machine creaks into life and activity. The history books remember that King William IV was the last sovereign to dismiss his government, or that in 1909 the Conservative peers attempted to impede the passing of a money-bill. If Lord Melville is remembered today as the last victim of impeachment, so Whitbread should be among the immortals as the last member of a political opposition to explode this particular weapon against the government of the day.

The ground was carefully chosen. Instead of being tempted to aim at Pitt, Whitbread and the Whigs chose for their target the weakest part of the Ministry. Around Pitt, and protecting him, was what might be called a curtain of coronets. The cabinet was noble. In it were two dukes, three earls, two viscounts and four barons. Whether these noble colleagues were really a strength to Pitt is a matter of opinion, but it was indisputable that among them his weakness lay in a particular individual wearing viscount's coronet. In this war-time administration the Admiralty was in the hands of a viscount — Henry Dundas, Lord Melville. Moreover it was noticed in 1804 that in spite of all these noble stop-gaps Pitt was finding difficulty in filling the lesser posts in his Government. 'Nothing can be more wretched' wrote a shrewd observer 'than the way in which Pitt is eking out his Government with Roses and Dundases'.[2] Both these families came from Scotland, and they descended on Westminster rather as their ancestors descended on the farmsteads of northern England — to direct the flow of milk and honey unto themselves. The Right Honourable George Rose had travelled far since he started life as commander of the bomb-ketch *Infernal*: leaving this lively little ship he had sauntered through politics at the heels of Pitt, rewarded with a great variety of little posts and perquisites. He was Paymaster-General in the government of 1804, and successfully slipped in his elder son as Joint-Paymaster in this well-coffered Government department. The Roses are a familiar portent in English politics: their attachment and competence deserve rewards, but their support, blindly given, repels the independent minded. As Lord Campbell once shrewdly noticed, such politicians are like the sailor who looks for high salvage and prize-money; 'they must be prepared to go out in all weathers'.[3] The Roses were.

The Dundases were more lethal to any government. The then head of the family was Lord Melville. He had been Home Secretary and then Secretary for War in Pitt's first Government, and he became First Lord of the Admiralty in Pitt's second Government.

Loud voiced and rough accented, he had a boisterous, overbearing eloquence : Fox used to say that he always spoke with effect except when, by some strange fatality, he happened to understand the subject on which he was speaking. It is also important to stress that he was Treasurer of the Royal Navy for seventeen years from 1783 — an office which he was able to hold concurrently with ministerial posts. His nephew William was Secretary at War, his son and collateral relatives swarmed behind Pitt. The Dundases were a clan of able, avaricious Scots : their political talents were mediocre but their capacity for manipulating an election was splendid. They were very corrupt. Whether Pitt really liked Melville is difficult to say, but he certainly loved what Melville brought in his train — forty-three out of a possible forty-five Scottish Members of Parliament. Even Orkney and Shetland, which had for a short time won immortality by returning Fox to Westminster, fell before the bawbees of this wily man.* 'The means by which I govern Scotland can not be dissolved by the breath of any Minister' said Melville.4 Brag of that kind breeds unpopularity. For example the country-gentlemen, at that time still the strongest single force in the House of Commons, cordially disliked too shameless a display of political management; moreover they had inherited from their fathers and grandfathers a lingering dislike for the broad accents and frugal habits of those who lived behind the wall of Hadrian. Windham, one of Pitt's former cabinet colleagues, thought that if Melville had remained in power much longer 'they would have given us a Scotch navy'.5 In attacking Melville, Whitbread was not to lack spontaneous sympathisers.

Perhaps the only good thing which Addington did in office — and it was one for which he deserves the plaudits of Englishmen — was the appointment of Lord St. Vincent as First Lord of the Admiralty. This endearing man — he thought it arrogant to take as his own title the scene of his great naval victory, and he refused to do so until over-persuaded by George III — passed

---

* I am grateful to the present distinguished Member of Parliament for this constituency for reminding me of this.

through the Admiralty with all the penetrating force of one of his own familiar sou'westers. He enquired, he exposed, he reformed. In the course of this long spring-clean he published ten reports on conditions in his department. For Melville, his predecessor and for long the Treasurer of the Navy, all ten were damning : the last and tenth was an emphatic verdict against him personally. This was the document which reached Pitt when Wilberforce happened to be with him; he was so eager to read it that Wilberforce noticed that he did not wait for a paper-knife to cut the leaves, but peeped at the crucial passages between the pages. Although many embroideries on what was contained in the Report and many explanations for it can be attempted, the facts are simple. Over a period of years stretching back to the mid-1780s Melville had allowed his paymaster, a Lowland Scot called Alexander Trotter, to take the naval balances and lay them out at interest with Coutts the banker. It is perfectly true that after their spell of usury the balances were all returned intact : the miserable Trotter pocketed the fruits of usury, shielded Melville and in fact lent him money. Although Melville may not have plundered the nation he was clearly guilty of conduct which was indefensible — except for those to whom loyalty to Pitt and his party over-rode all other considerations.

The case against Melville was tersely but accurately summarised by Whitbread :

Lord Melville, in the first place, put the public money out of his own control, and thereby exposed it if not to loss, at least to hazard; in the next place Mr. Trotter, to whom he had chosen to delegate his control, also put it out of his power, by placing it in the hands of private bankers, which was exposing it a second time to loss. To what risk it might have been further exposed after it had been handed over to private bankers, he would not pretend to state.

The Attorney-General, Spencer Perceval, writing to Pitt on this point on 20 April 1805 said :

Upon reconsidering the subject of our conversation the other day I feel great doubt upon the possibility of making Lord Melville answerable for the profits which have been made by Mr. Trotter of the public money — If any loss had been incurred he must no doubt have been held responsible, but I think for the profit made by it nobody can upon any equitable principle be made answerable, who has not had the profitable use of the money.[6]

The additional charges against Melville, which were finally enshrined in ten articles of impeachment, went in great detail over all the financial arrangements on which the naval balances rested. Whitbread described them accurately enough in his opening speech at Westminster Hall during the impeachment. 'He feared he should, in the progress of his duty, fatigue his hearers. He had to state to them a lengthened detail of financial accounts, and a series of dry facts, which, from their notoriety, were deprived of all novelty, but not susceptible of embellishment even from the most eloquent.' There is no reason why the readers of this book should run the unnecessary risk of fatigue through having to go through the sordid evidence of bank-clerks and cashiers. Such matters belong to those who want to whitewash or blacken Lord Melville. Whitbread and the Whigs — and they had no doubt a tolerably good source of information from the Grenvilles who had been in Cabinet with Melville — believed Melville to be guilty of culpable negligence. He was patently guilty, but on the question of personal corruption, after 160 years, we should perhaps be wise to find refuge in the familiar Scottish verdict — 'not proven', though perhaps not overlooking the phrase of Samuel Romilly, one of the fairest minds at the Bar, who was Solicitor-General, and in Westminster Hall called Melville 'the noble delinquent'.[7]

On 6 April 1805 Whitbread opened the matter in the House of Commons with a comprehensive accusation against Melville including the charge that he had himself been a participant in a system of peculation, though admitting that this only rested on suspicion. He ended his speech by moving a number of resolutions which were clearly drafted as a basis for impeachment. Pitt immediately followed Whitbread, saying that he thought it 'not very fair' to endeavour to excite passions on such a charge.

He attempted to move that the question be referred to a select committee of the House of Commons but the vote was taken on Whitbread's motion. There voted for Whitbread 216 : against him 216. To Speaker Abbot, an able and distinguished man, fell the task of deciding the question. He turned deathly pale, paused for some time (one authority says for ten minutes)[8] and then gave the casting vote to Whitbread. Pitt's friends crowded round him lest the Whigs should see his tears. But the heart of the Whigs was not softened, and this was the occasion when a distinguished Welsh baronet, Sir Thomas Mostyn, hurried behind the Speaker's chair and let out a great cry 'View holloa we have killed the fox'.

That may have been the case, but plenty of people were determined that the corpse should not be thrown to the hounds. Debates dragged on through the summer. The King wrote plaintively to the Prime Minister that when a man is fallen Englishmen are naturally 'too noble to pursue their blows'.[9] Such niceties did not afflict the Whigs. Creevey was merrily writing that the Leviathan Melville had given them all famous sport, and Whitbread's radical collaborator William Belsham could write 'Has not Lord Melville been hurled from the pinnacle of power to the lowest pitch of political degradation?' The relish is unmistakable. And Whitbread was quick to urge that the King should expel Melville from the Privy Council. Fox joined in, with sarcasm, to suggest that expulsion from such a body by the King was too good a fate for Melville. 'I find, sir, after a careful examination, that during His Majesty's long reign, now a period of forty-five years, only the late Duke of Devonshire and myself have been dismissed his majesty's councils, and I assure you, sir, we want no such person as the noble lord to be our associate'.[10]

Melville himself appeared in the House of Commons on the 11 June 1805. He was accommodated with a chair, then stood to speak and in his broad, Scots accent he rambled over the charges against him acknowledging that he had appropriated public money for services other than the Royal Navy but

solemnly denying that he had derived any private benefit from
the transaction. After he had left the House, Whitbread made it
clear that the procedure by impeachment was intended not only
to bring down Melville but to uncover corruption on a wider
scale. 'By the foot of Hercules you may judge of his size, by the
finger of a giant you may form an estimate of his strength.' At
the end of his speech, he justified his motives as he was fond of
doing. Though noticing the self-righteousness, readers will
remember that honourable motives in public life were less
tacitly assumed to govern a man than is the case today, and
from George III and Pitt downwards criticism was made of the
vindictiveness with which the Whigs pursued Melville. 'I
trust that on the contrary I can appeal to my own heart for the
purity of my motives. I am conscious on all occasions of having
been actuated by principles of honesty and views of public
advantage'. After this speech the House of Commons voted on
the motion to impeach Melville, and it was lost by seventy-
seven votes. While the vote was being taken Fox took the
unusual step of addressing his followers in the lobby : he said
that they would probably be in a minority on impeachment, but
this would be followed by a motion for criminal prosecution and
'he intreated those who thought with him not to leave the
House'. A criminal prosecution was carried by nine votes.

During June Whitbread made one valiant effort to implicate
Pitt. It transpired that eight years previously Raikes, a
Governor of the Bank of England, had told Pitt that naval
money was being drawn out of the Bank, contrary to Act of
Parliament. (By what was known as Burke's Act, which was
passed in the 1780's, the Paymaster's accounts were to be kept
at the Bank of England and drawings were to be made only for
official purposes.) Pitt allowed himself to be satisfied by
Melville's smooth explanations. 'I do not mean to impute
criminality [to Pitt]', cried Whitbread, 'but great negligence'.
Was he far wrong? But he somewhat spoiled the effect of this
by wandering off into a diffuse account of his views on the
money market, and of all that he owed to his father. He said

that he had a great dislike for the word money-market, and he amused the House by comparing Pitt with the familiar lame ducks waddling out of the Alley. Other markets he claimed to understand for 'they remind me of him to whose indefatigable industry and judicious exertions in transactions with these markets I am indebted for everything I have the happiness to be possessed of'. Alluding to pride of ancestry he said that 'while others pride themselves in their remoteness from their founder, I feel a pride and satisfaction in being the nearest to mine'. If he intended to touch Pitt by memories of an old friendship he was not successful and, replying immediately, Pitt said that he did not think it necessary 'to follow the honourable gentleman with the variety of matter, unconnected with the subject, which he has thought proper to introduce', adding 'His fastidious ear is greatly offended with the coarse term money-market.'[11] Two months before this, the Whig lawyer, Erskine, who sat for Portsmouth, had written to Whitbread 'in every effort to implicate Pitt in the disgrace, and criminality of the transaction, I am persuaded that the *whole public out of doors* will be with you'.[12] That was perhaps correct: but in the House of Commons there was a phalanx of protection for the Prime Minister.

But in those June days Melville's friends suddenly realised that he might be less vulnerable in an impeachment than in a criminal prosecution. They therefore changed their tactics and on 25 June the decision to impeach Lord Melville was taken by the Commons without a division. On the following day Whitbread, introduced by Black Rod, attended the House of Lords. He was accompanied by the flower of the Whig Party — Fox, Grey, Windham, Tierney, Lord Temple, Lord Henry Petty and Wilberforce. Small but conspicuous and (we may be sure) enjoying every moment was a comparative newcomer — Thomas Creevey.* Including Whitbread himself there were

* Originally the Opposition had planned for a Committee of the House of Commons to examine the whole case — as was done (to take a random example from modern history) at the time of the Marconi allegations. Fox sent to Creevey 'to desire that in such an event I would be chairman of the Committee'. (Whitfield, Creevey to Dr. Currie.)

twenty-eight Whig Members of Parliament, and like St. Paul
he must have felt uplifted by seeing that he was compassed
about with so great a cloud of witnesses. As soon as Whitbread
reached the bar he said :

My lords, in the name of the Commons of the United Kingdom of
Great Britain and Ireland in Parliament assembled I am commanded
to impeach Henry Lord Viscount Melville of high crimes and misdemeanours. And I do hereby, in their name, and in the name and on
behalf of all the Commons of Great Britain and Ireland impeach the
said Henry, Viscount Melville of high crimes and misdemeanours. And
I am further commanded to acquaint your lordships that the House of
Commons will, in due time, exhibit particular articles of impeachment
against the said Henry, Viscount Melville and make good the same.

The party then returned to the House of Commons and
Whitbread, advancing to the bar of the House of Commons,
said 'I have gone to the bar of the House of Lords and impeached
Henry Lord Viscount Melville.'

In the House of Commons Fox alluded to the talents which
Whitbread had shown 'so highly honourable to himself and of
such signal advantage to the country'. And praise was not
confined to the House of Commons. At one of the concerts of
Ancient Music, where no music less than twenty years old might
be given and where the front seats glowed with blue ribands
and shone with stars, the eldest son of the royal house bowed a
gracious head and spoke favourably of Whitbread, especially of
his manner of opening and of the way in which he had carried
on the proceedings. Whitbread was also publicly thanked by
resolution of the Common Council of the City of London, and
by the Mayor and Corporation of Bedford. Such personal praise
was more than justified, but there was a shadow across it, for
the reader will bear in mind that the House of Commons, when
party is in hue and cry on these personal issues, does not
necessarily show to advantage. There was the smirching of Pitt,
and on their side the Dundas faction hit back at Fox. Dundas's
nephew reminded the House of the peculations of Fox's father,
when he was paymaster to the Army. Warming to his subject
he pointed out that Fox had gambled some of this money away

thereby squandering the property of the public. One who had been a Member in the 1770's and had served the nation in the highest diplomatic posts remarked of the debates on Lord Melville 'they exceeded in party spirit and savage feeling all that I ever recollected in this country'.[13] For some of this vindictiveness Whitbread must shoulder the blame. All might have been forgiven if success had been complete.

Throughout the winter of 1805 and the early spring of 1806 Whitbread, as manager of the impeachment, was engrossed in compiling the case and in a vast correspondence with witnesses and lawyers. In addition there were the usual flock of carrion crows eager to settle on this unsavoury topic but careful to keep in the heights of anonymity. A typical Edinburgh writer warned Whitbread about a man who was a servant; 'last summer Melvell had him at his cuntree house in the Highlands his Principal business there was sorting papers.' But such things were all considered and kept. Even Lord Holland, who was never sympathetic to him, speaks of the prodigious diligence with which he had made himself completely master of the whole transaction. But it would be idle to pretend that there did not hang over the whole a faint air of make-believe. It was pageantry without reality : a colourful spectacle without authority. The impeachment of Melville had something in common with the Eglinton Tournament thirty years later, in which all the trappings of the medieval tournament were perfectly repro-duced, only the ferocity was lacking, and the polite Victorians looked in vain for the great moment when 'with one stroke Sir Gareth split the skull'. Similarly the solemnity of impeachment was all designed to throw its sombre light on the axe, to herald the ultimate sanction of death. 'It was never accounted either cruelty or foul play to knock foxes and wolves on the head because they be beasts of prey' said Oliver St. John, in the seventeenth century at the trial of Strafford. Times had changed : the life of the fox and the wolf was preserved. The Scotsman's head was not in danger.

Also the death of Pitt on 23 January 1806 softened the whole.

If he had been the ultimate target he had gone beyond the range of his critics. Moreover Fox and the Whigs were, at long last, in office in the Ministry of All the Talents. Some of the political spring behind the impeachment had slackened. But so far as it lay with Whitbread and the Managers they were determined that no particle of the pageantry should be trimmed.

Westminster Hall was fitted up as it had been for the impeachment of Hastings, and on all the days of the trial strong detachments of the three Regiments of Guards were posted at all the approaches to the Hall. The throne was about one quarter the way down the Hall from the great north window, behind it and below the window were tiers of seats for friends of the peers. Facing the throne the observer saw on his left rows of seats for the Commons with a small, individual seat for the Speaker; there was a box at the end on the right of the throne for the representatives of foreign states; on the observer's right were rows of seats for the peeresses and members of the public. These rose in tiers. In the centre of the Hall were the peers mostly facing the throne, though the marquises and bishops were placed at right angles to the throne, parallel with the seats for Members of the House of Commons. The Managers' Box, in which Whitbread sat on the right, was immediately behind the peers facing the throne. Shorthand writers were on his right: then came the witness box; Melville had a box next to the witness-box.[14] There was plenty of room for members of the public in the various galleries. Great puncheons of water were distributed throughout the Hall in case of fire, and sixteen earthen *pots de chambre* were provided for the convenience of the company.

In those days the law courts opened off Westminster Hall, and it was perhaps a pointer that the lawyers did not look on the proceedings as of the utmost gravity when complaints were made that the preparations drowned the urbane utterances of members of the Bar pleading their cases. 'The noise of carpenters and counsel can not go forward at the same time.'[15] The case began on Tuesday, 29 April. The Speaker was seated at ten: at half past ten Members of the Commons moving by

counties, proceeded to their seats. Five minutes later the
Managers moved in, led by Whitbread. They were Fox, Grey,
Lord Henry Petty and the other leading Whigs. Whitbread was
in full dress which meant that he was wearing a velvet coat, lace
ruffles and a bag — that is a wig tied at the back in a silken
bag.[16] The procession from the Upper House then began to
move into the Hall. It was preceded by various dignitaries, by
the judges and by the heralds, and immediately before the lords
themselves came — what might be called the flotsam and
jetsam of their order — the eldest sons of peers and the peers
who were minors. After a pause came the barons, walking two
and two, the viscounts and the bishops. The peerage in all its
aspects was represented, and there was an unfortunate misunderstanding when the bishops in their lawn appeared: they were
thought by members of the public to be the peeresses in their
own right. There was then a long pause of a quarter of an hour
while the public began to wonder what earthly potentate was
coming. It was nothing more formidable than all the earls. Lord
Melville then slipped into his seat from the other end of the
Hall. He was wearing court dress — bottle-green with cut steel
buttons. Then came the highest orders of the peerage followed
by the Archbishop of York, the Primate, the Lord Chancellor
and the Princes of the Blood. The Prince of Wales came in last.
He attended on thirteen out of the fifteen days. All the peers
were in their full robes, and bowed to the Speaker and to the
throne before taking their seats. So many peers attended that
extra benches had to be brought in for them. The Lord Chancellor then explained to Melville and to Whitbread that they
must address their remarks to the peers and not to him, and he
left the Woolsack, the Prince of Wales taking his place on that
uneasy throne. Lord Chancellors are easy targets, especially for
the shafts of their own brethren, and the Chancellor in the
Ministry of All the Talents was to prove no exception. Thomas
Erskine was a warm partisan of Fox, a Scotsman, with such
minor peculiarities as the decision to take Trial by Jury as the
motto for his peerage. Everyone applauded his conduct of the

Melville case, and he made the vitally important decision that the court should sit from day to day until the case was finished instead of (as was the case with the impeachment of Hastings) sitting for a few days in the year as a theatre for rhetorical display. When the case was finished Melville rose in his place and made a deep bow to Erskine, a bow which was interpreted as a striking mark of respect from a political opponent for the impeccable fairness of the Lord Chancellor's conduct of the case.

On the whole, attendance was kept up throughout the hearing of the case, although on the second day there were only 150 Members of the House of Commons present. One spectator, accompanied by her governess, came to be initiated early in the mysteries of constitutional government. This was the Princess Charlotte. She was ten. Her mother, who was to figure largely in Whitbread's life, did not attend. Always eccentric she contented herself with writing to an intimate Tory friend, and asking after the health of 'forever respectable Lord Melville'.[17] Whitbread's wife did not fail to make herself felt. She went every day to Westminster Hall: on one occasion when she was getting out of her carriage she expressed great uneasiness at having left her smelling-salts behind. In the course of the proceedings a commotion was heard — a messenger attempting to reach Whitbread's wife with the smelling-salts for which, despite all his preoccupations, he had sent out.

For Whitbread, who had to open the case, the task was formidable. He had to carry with him his own party zealots, and to convince men as various as Frederick, Duke of York, as Manners Sutton the Archbishop of Canterbury, or Horace Walpole's friend Lord Carlisle. And all the time the occasion demanded what is called in the language of a catalogue of fireworks 'a set-piece'. He had fortunately a sense of occasion. Pausing for several minutes while as an observer wrote 'the splendid assemblage was filled with anxious expectation', he began at 12.15 and sat down a few moments before four o'clock, to a 'general buzz of admiration'. Into the details of what

HENRY DUNDAS, FIRST VISCOUNT MELVILLE, 1742–1811

By John Rising

SAMUEL WHITBREAD, *c.* 1803

By John Opie

Whitbread said it is unnecessary to go. He opened the case against Melville, sharpening with additional evidence the points which had already been made against him in the debates in the House of Commons. An unfriendly observer laughed at the sedulous care with which Whitbread's friends gave him sips of wine, and 'clouts for his mouth and nose': the same observer saw Fox in the managers' box, covered with a grey cloak 'in which I suppose Mrs. Armistead formerly walked the streets'.[18] But Fox praised Whitbread's performance by using a forceful adverb 'Whitbread opened the business capitally'.[19] The Lord Chancellor wrote to him,

DEAR WHITBREAD, Although as you may suppose I do not mean to convey any idea of the impression made upon me by your speech *as a judge to decide upon the impeachment*; yet I can not refuse myself the pleasure of expressing the satisfaction I received from the ability and genius displayed in every part of it. Detailed as it was it appeared to have no details, and full of relief from the dullness of mere business for which it was remarkable. There was no episode or digression but everything connected with and embodied in the subject.

Yours most faithfully
ERSKINE

And it must be confessed that as an exposition of an extremely complex case by a layman it deserved the highest praise. Only once did he apparently show irritation. He was expounding Burke's Act which made it obligatory to pay the naval balances into the Bank of England, when he noticed that Melville's lawyer, William Plumer, was smiling. He turned on Plumer and said that he would be very happy if Plumer smiled because of confidence in his client's innocence, but he was sure that Plumer was not smiling 'from any contempt for those who, with myself, are employed in the service of the public, and who have reluctantly undertaken this great and laborious duty'.

Plumer, who was generally known as the Roaring Bull of the Oxford Circuit, was blessed with opinions which were rugged and reactionary. He was reactionary as a lawyer, and reactionary as a Member of the House of Commons. The managers of the impeachment of the venerable Tory Scot were naturally

K

antipathetic to him. And unluckily Whitbread put himself at the mercy of this sharp-witted practitioner from Lincoln's Inn. To understand this it is necessary to go back to the June day in 1805 when, in response to the Speaker's invitation 'there is a chair, repose yourself', Melville sat down before rising to address the House of Commons in defence of his conduct. In a sense he incriminated himself because at the end of his speech he had said something about a sum of £10,000, the whereabouts of which no power on earth would force him to explain. Speaking of this £10,000 Melville explained that he was the confidential adviser of the Government in everything connected with Scotland. 'Every person must readily perceive the impossibility of being so, without having recourse to the expenditure of occasional sums for the purpose of Government. I think it is impossible for any one to expect that I should enter into a more minute explanation . . . without incurring the charge of a great breach, as well of public duty as of private honour.'[20] But naturally that had to be repeated formally in evidence. Whitbread approached the Speaker and asked him to tell the Court what Melville had said. This, the Speaker said, he could only do with the permission of the House of Commons and, as this could not be immediately obtained, Whitbread mistakenly determined to give evidence himself. Plumer naturally drew attention to this double function, claiming that he was never quite certain if he was dealing with the witness or the Manager. And then he began to enjoy himself. When Whitbread gave evidence of what he had heard in the Commons was he merely listening to what Melville said, or was he listening for the purpose of answering him? Was he watching him with the design to accuse him? Had Whitbread any notes of exactly what Melville said? No, he did not know where to find them, and in an unguarded moment he said that if he had been able to find them he would not have been able to understand them. All this made Whitbread ridiculous, and his failure to prove what Melville said, which was certainly one of the strong points against him, was criticised. The familiar motto about manners has never been

very readily absorbed in the precincts of Lincoln's Inn, and
Plumer went on to describe how the Managers had seized some
of their evidence from a widow's attic and said that Whitbread
had acted throughout in a third capacity as 'a box-porter'. He
meant by that, one who carries the possessions of others, and he
gave the obvious edge to his point by the emphasis which he
placed on the word 'porter'. Such jokes abounded. Lord
Melville was described as Whitbread's 'entire butt'; Whitbread's eloquence was said to have a good deal of quassia in
it — bitter stuff with a bad taste. (Quassia was sometimes used
in the brewing trade as a substitute for hops.) The managers
were likewise described as mismanagers and imaginers. The
most celebrated comment came from the renowned Duchess of
Gordon who, it will be remembered, had not hesitated to
stigmatise her own daughters as bastards. She described
Whitbread's oratorical efforts as 'teaching his dray-horse to
caper'. The true wit of that observation will not blind the reader
to the fact that the Duchess, through her Maxwell relations, was
allied with those who had practised corruption in Scotland, and
were under attack from Whitbread and his Whig friends. The
remark was made by a violent partisan — and a slightly
apprehensive one at that.

Whitbread's closing speech has attracted some ridicule : it
was certainly less effective than the speech with which he
opened, but it is revealing of his character. He began with a
curious allusion to Archimedes, saying that if he could have
discovered the fulcrum by which to throw the world into chaos
he would not have used it : so he, Whitbread, would not
attempt to hurl the moral world into chaos by perverting truth.
He then alluded to the diverse characters in which he had
appeared — manager, witness and porter which he said 'had
excited so much pleasantry in the learned . . . My lords there
are no duties which an upright heart may not fulfil . . . I, under
the lash of the wit of the learned counsel, have anticipated a
glorious reward in the service I have rendered to my country'.*

* But his friend Belsham once wisely wrote to Whitbread : 'It is better, as it

He then referred to the machinery of impeachment, and said that it had been the object of the Managers 'to vindicate the character of impeachment'. He brushed to one side the legalistic arguments of Plumer by correctly pointing out that on impeachment the Commons were not restricted to legalistic forms but were entitled to base the charges 'more generally and comprehensively'. He pointed out that the Managers had been content to prove their case by written evidence, but that Melville's lawyers were not satisfied with this and insisted on cross examining witnesses on their recollection of the business. In illustrating the capriciousness of memory against written proof he quoted the case of a celebrated judge* who had formerly given an opinion which was contrary to a judgment, and consenting to look back to this opinion (of which he had no recollection) involuntarily burst out, 'There it is — as true as God's in Gloucester'. And dealing with the readiness of the lawyers to dismiss evidence because it was impossible he recalled a game of whist played by one he knew who was an indifferent player. He happened to hold an excellent hand and a bystander backed him with money to win. When he succeeded in losing, the onlooker, with some animation, exclaimed 'with such cards it was impossible to lose'. 'That may be so,' replied the player, 'but I have lost it'. Dealing with the argument that meanness was out of keeping with the known generosity of Melville's character he quoted Sallust on Catiline : 'Simulator ac dissimulator alieni appetens sui profusus — satis eloquentiae, sapientiae parum.'

This was followed by one of those unaccountable lapses which Whitbread too easily introduced into his speeches. The day on which Melville had given evidence in the House of Commons was 11 June, and the *Hansard* report reads :

My lords, I could easily remember the date, because the 11th of June is to be a day memorable in the aera† of your Lordships' honour, and

appears to me, that a writer or speaker should be wholly silent as to his intellectual merits.'

* Lord Mansfield.   † Perhaps a mistake for 'arena'.

of the justice of the country.* But there are particular circumstances which lead me to the remembrance of this day ... There are, my lords, in the history of every man, however obscure, certain *dies notandi*. Some, indeed, bring to the minds of the children the gallant exploits of their ancestors, others have their memory impressed, like myself, by more humble events. Now, my lords, the 11th of June is to me a *dies notandus*. On the 11th of June my father set up in business. On the 11th June he annually balanced his accounts : and on the 11th of June his son was required to assist him in this laborious duty. On the 11th of June he knew the progressive increase of his substance, and the generous fruits of his honest industry. On the 11th of June my father died, and the day on which a good man dies is not to be forgotten.

No doubt the psychologist would explain this as springing from remorse for his disagreement with his father in earlier days — heightened in retrospect by the wealth he had received from him. That is of course possible. A more rational explanation was that stung by the gibes about beer (both during the hearing and in general conversation outside) he had attempted to show an honourable pride both in his family and in its trade.

Yet the full text from which Whitbread was speaking has survived, and it gives a fairer picture of why he introduced these personal reflections than does the necessarily abridged report in *Hansard*. He had been twitted by Plumer on remembering nothing of Melville's speech in the House of Commons but on yet recalling the date on which it was delivered.

It is a day, my Lords, henceforth memorable in the annals of this country. But I wish to exculpate the witness [i.e. himself] from any suspicion of having a convenient memory; and to show Your Lordships that the 11th of June was a day likely to be strongly imprinted on his memory.

The Romans had a custom in their great families, the observance of which in the little families of this country might produce admirable effects, of commemorating certain *dies notandi* — days made memorable by the performance of great exploits by their ancestors, and in those days the achievements of their forefathers were held up to the admiration of the children in order to form them to the execution of

* He is here referring to the debate in the House of Commons immediately following Melville's statement which preceded the division in favour of criminal proceedings.

those great duties which they would afterwards have to fulfil. Now the 11th of June happens to be a *dies notandus* in the family of the Witness. On that day in the year 1748 [1742] his Father (with a fortune of about the same amount which Mr. Trotter had when he began the world viz £2000) set up as a Brewer in the City of London. On the 11th of June every year he balanced his accounts, and, by God's blessing, he always found them on the right side; and he early called the attention of his son to that fact; and showed him how, by the great progress of uncorrupted industry, a fortune would gradually accumulate. On the 11th of June 1796 that good man died; I received his parting blessing, and closed his eyes; and they say, my Lords, that when a Good man (as he was) dies even the Angels in Heaven rejoice — that day then was again strongly imprinted on my recollection. On the 11th of June 1805, as I was going forth to the House of Commons, to move the vote of impeachment against Lord Melville, I happened to see the children with which God has blessed me, and I remarked to them the circumstances, that had happened on that day in our family . . . such are the reasons for my remembering the 11th June.

Although the sophisticated — both then and now — can hardly resist a smile the speech reveals the simplicity and other-worldliness of Whitbread.

Eloquence is perhaps a dangerous weapon to employ on a sophisticated audience. Whitbread attempted it. He ended :

My lords, as long as your posterity shall represent this illustrious court of judicature : as long as the events of the country are transmitted to those descendants on the page of history : nay even as long as the radiant orb of Heaven extends his cheering beams over the Earth, I trust will the impeachment be carried down through evolving ages, and I glory in the reflection, that my humble name will appear in the same annals, not on account of my personal merits, but from the blaze of that refulgence by which I am surrounded.

How his speech struck his opponents has been cruelly immortalised for us by George Canning. Canning had been Treasurer of the Navy in Pitt's last Administration.

> I am like Archimedes for science and skill;
> I am like the young Prince that went straight up the hill.*

* See page 9.

And — to interest the hearts of the fair, be it said —
I am like a young lady just bringing to bed. *

If you ask why the eleventh of June I remember
So much better than April or March or November,
'Tis because on that day — as with pride, I assure ye —
My sainted progenitor took to his brew'ry.

That day in the morn he began making beer;
At night he commenced his connubial career.†
That day too he died, having finished his summing
And the angels cried out 'Here's old Whitbread a-coming!'

So that day I still hail, with a smile and a sigh,
For his beer with an e, and his bier with an i.
And still on that day in the hottest of weather,
The whole Whitbread family feast all together.‡

My lords, while the beams of this Hall shall support
The roof which o'ershades this respectable Court,
Where Hastings was tried for oppressing the Hindoos —
While the beams of the sun shall pour in at these windows,
My name shall shine bright, as my ancestor's shines;
Mine recorded on journals, his blazoned on signs.[21]

Canning's wit — at once rapier-like and merciless — cannot
fail to delight the hard-hearted and the flippant. But the
laughter has to be judged by the friends of Whitbread as well as
being enjoyed by his critics. With lapses of judgment and taste
Whitbread, grappling largely on his own, built up a formidable
case against a miscreant: as he himself expressed it 'I have

---

* 'I have not, my lords, been insensible under the mirth I have afforded but, as
there are pains to which the human body is subject, which the most delicate of the
race can endure under the expectation of the promised blessing. . . .' Reports of the
speech are rather summaries than verbatim. From the draft from which he spoke
the words were 'as the most exquisite pangs of the body are supported by the most
delicate and amiable of the human race, not only with forbearance but with exulta-
tion, in the expectation of the delicious and beloved fruit thereof, so I, while
writhing under the keen lashes of the wit of the learned counsel, found consolation
in the indulgence of a fond expectation that the fruit would be indeed that which I
love, Justice to my country.'

† A touch of poetic licence; Whitbread did not say this.

‡ Another touch of Canning's imagination.

hewn the stone and drawn the water'; he may have over-elaborated his case, he may have been too impatient of allies and professional guidance but he was striking a blow for respectability in public life.

Particularly gratifying must have been this further letter from the Lord Chancellor written a day or two after Whitbread's closing speech :

My Dear Whitbread

Still keeping my mind most sacredly open as I said before to do justice according to the ultimate results of my own mind, I have great pleasure in repeating again to you the great pleasure I have received in the very superior mind and genius and ability which you have displayed which is a pleasure that none of your friends can possibly have felt more than

Your most faithful friend
Erskine*

And there was a gratifying if slightly less orthodox tribute to Whitbread's personal success. A lady, carefully concealing her identity, wrote to say that she had daily attended the trial and if she could meet him would consider herself 'the most fortunate of women . . . I shall be in Hertford Street half past 10 o'clock on Thursday evening near Lord Liverpool's door, meet me there'. Poor Lord Liverpool, who lived at number twenty-six was a respectable old gentleman not likely to be using the front door of his house at that time of night; he was nearly 80.

Legal argument followed Whitbread's speech and the court adjourned, reassembling on Thursday 12 June for the vote. It was a lengthy process. Addressing each peer by name the Lord Chancellor asked 'How say you, is Henry, Lord Viscount Melville guilty or not guilty of the first article of charge exhibited against him by the Commons of the United Kingdom ?' The peer then rose and laying his right hand on his left breast said 'Guilty' or 'Not Guilty' — as the case might be — 'upon my honour'. The Prince of Wales did not vote : the royal dukes

---

* The word 'pleasure' seems to have been beating in the mind of the Lord Chancellor.

were divided, the sailor (the Duke of Clarence) and the intellectual princes (Kent and Sussex) generally voting guilty. There were ten charges, and Melville was acquitted on them all. His smallest majority (27) was on the second charge — namely the one which accused him of permitting Trotter to draw the naval balances from the Bank of England and apply them for his own private advantage with Messrs. Coutts and Company.

In a sense the impeachment of Melville was a drawn battle. He was found not guilty on all counts; he was rapturously received in Scotland, and he was restored to the Privy Council at the change of government in 1807. But he never held office again, and it was generally felt that the size of the vote against him on the question of conniving at Trotter's use of the naval balances was a decisive condemnation. For Whitbread himself the case enhanced his reputation, especially with the realisation of all the hard work by which his speeches were sustained. It is true that he had attracted some ribaldry to himself — a Scottish correspondent took the trouble to write and tell him that Paisley was ceasing to sell Whitbread's entire — and there is always danger for the individual who employs elaborate and picturesque procedures to trap an eminent man who then walks away. But his own share in the whole case was always that of a leader, and he never lost sight of the principle which justified all his exertions — namely that the funds of the public should be inviolate from private devices. With the Melville impeachment Whitbread stepped into the van of the Whig Party.

CHAPTER TWELVE

No Place for Whitbread

FOR Whitbread 1806 was the year of destiny. His political career stretched back fifteen and a half years — years of achievement and renown with a leader whom he revered and loved and with comrades who were welded by adversity into a true brotherhood. Only nine years of public life remained for him in the future. They were to carry him away from old loyalties to the company of less sturdy friends, to a parliamentary career, which was indubitably crowned with laurels but marked by a certain erratic extremism disturbing his old friends, and we may fairly guess, causing the ghostly shade of his old leader Fox to knit those famous eyebrows.

The year 1806 was one which saw the death of both Fox and Pitt, and men of all parties would have echoed the famous words of Walter Scott :

> Drop upon Fox's grave the tear,
> 'Twill trickle to his rival's bier

The death of these two men of genius had a kaleidoscopic effect on parties which influenced the course of Whitbread's career.

Pitt's government still supported by the House of Commons and with ministers of the most mediocre capacity, was subsisting throughout 1805, but its head was visibly moving towards death. He died on 23 January 1806, probably from typhus fever imposed on what, in those days, was called an impaired constitution. He left the sight of man in a style reminiscent of a comet which on the verge of extinction bequeathes a shower of lights. No man in the last ten weeks of life has handed to posterity such a wealth of valedictory remarks. 'England has saved herself by her exertions and will, as I trust, save Europe by her example.' After Napoleon's victory of Austerlitz : 'Roll up that map, it will not be wanted these ten years.' And on his death-bed — 'My country! Oh! my country.' 'I think I could eat one of Bellamy's veal pies.' Some of those remarks were doubtless apocryphal. But what he did undoubtedly say was this. 'We can get over Austerlitz, but we can never get over the tenth report. Such is the nature of Englishmen.'[1] And in passing we may notice that that was a remark with which Whitbread would whole-heartedly have agreed. It may well be true, as Lord Holland says, that the impeachment of Melville was mishandled : that is almost inevitable in a legal prosecution organised by amateurs. It is likewise probable that Whitbread, agreeing with Pitt about Lord St. Vincent's tenth report, was bitterly disappointed that Melville escaped from the snare into which he had carelessly run. The Grey family always believed that Whitbread's quarrel with his Whig comrades sprang from the disappointment of his hopes over the Melville impeachment and chagrin over the supposed failure of his speech summing up the case against the Scottish lord.*

But whether that is so or not there was a more fundamental cause dividing Whitbread from his friends. Eight decades later Gladstone was to say that the task of cabinet-making was 'painful, intolerably painful'. So Fox and Grey were to find. When Pitt died, George III, after a brief reconnoitre among the coronets which had encompassed Pitt, sent for Lord Grenville. Laughter rises instinctively as we look back to this Prime Minister; 'Bogey' Thomas Creevey always called him, perhaps because he was too prone to see the dangers of life. He came with his retinue of relations and connexions, and they all expected a generous rattle of danger money for undertaking the ardours of office : the family was thought, according to Cobbett,

---

* The third Lord Grey, Charles Grey's eldest son, who enjoyed looking on the darker side of human nature made a great point of this in some family comments of his which are at Howick. As he was a child at the time of Melville's impeachment, he must have gleaned this from his father.

to have drawn £1,000,000 of public money over the years. Long after Whitbread's time Grenville's elder brother, the Marquis of Buckingham, was coaxed on to the Tory side by a dukedom: the coveted eight strawberry-leaves were to adorn the brow of one, not unjustly called at the time 'a blubber-head'.[2] Grenville himself drew £4,000 a year from a comfortable little post — the auditorship of the Exchequer. Yet these perquisites were not irretrievably lost to the nation; as the public saunters through the Grenville library in the British Museum — those shining shelves of calf and gold — they may fairly remember that Thomas Grenville, who was Lord Grenville's brother, left them to the nation because, as he explained in his will, they had largely been bought with the profits of a sinecure post. Lord Grenville had married a cousin of Pitt. In her home, Camelford House in Park Lane, she and her husband lived a secluded patrician life. He had the reticence of aristocracy, and the wife of Windham complained that she had once been in the same house as Lord Grenville for a whole day, without his saying a single word to her. And yet 'Bogey' has perhaps hardly received justice at the hands of history. Although he could never be called progressive, he seems to have understood politics and to have taken a perfectly firm stand for those causes in which he believed — moderate reform and Catholic Emancipation. It was highly creditable to him (and indeed to any politician) that he absolutely refused to rejoin his old chief Pitt because he felt that — whatever the temptations of office — the division between them over the Catholic issue was unbridgeable. Of him Fox once said 'I like Lord Grenville because he is a direct man'. For those experienced in politics that quality stands high. George III, who in politics was tortuous, quickly experienced Grenville's directness. When he asked him to form a government Grenville replied with five words — 'I shall consult Mr. Fox'. For twenty years one of George III's prime objectives had been to exclude Fox from government. But in 1806 the game was done, and Fox came into the Government.

Grenville and Fox decided to broaden the Ministry still

further by including some Addington men so as to secure the support of their followers in the House of Commons. The Whig Party of Fox, known as the Old Opposition in distinction to Grenville's Whigs known as the New Opposition, found, as all coalition governments must find, that there were not enough places to go round. Of the Foxite Whigs Fox himself went to the Foreign Office, Lord Henry Petty (afterwards Lord Lansdowne) to the Exchequer, Lord Fitzwilliam was Lord President, Lord Erskine Chancellor, Lord Moira Master-General of the Ordnance and Grey First Lord of the Admiralty. Room was found outside the Cabinet for Sheridan, Lord John Townshend and for General Fitzpatrick. The government came into being at the beginning of February 1806 and was immediately dubbed the Ministry of All the Talents — some think the choice of name satirical, but it is more likely to have been a friendly allusion to the capacity of the Cabinet contrasted with the nonentities of Pitt's government. There were obvious dangers in a name of this kind. 'All the Talents' suggests a comprehensive class, and also implied that those excluded failed to reach the necessary standard. Exclusion was a slur. So Whitbread felt — and felt keenly.

There are those who think that there is great honour and distinction attached to a perpetual exclusion from office. The Tories in the first half of the eighteenth century or the Whigs in the half-century before the Reform Bill were virtually in perpetual opposition and could only comfort themselves by feeling that they were martyrs for a righteous cause, murmuring the lines of Addison :

> When vice prevails and impious men bear sway
> The post of honour is a private station.

Such reflections may soothe the mind of a politician, but they do not satisfy it. Romilly, a friend of Whitbread's who was Solicitor-General in the Ministry of All the Talents, said that after removing a public man's ambition for wealth or for a title 'there still remained the more captivating ambition of fame and popularity'. That showed an understanding of the elements of political human nature. Did not even Wilberforce once say 'I feel within me the stirrings of political ambition'? And this was unquestionably true of Whitbread. For wealth or titles drawn from politics he did not care a fig : his fame and popularity on the other hand weighed heavily.

The Ministry was formed on 3 February 1806. Four days later Whitbread was writing to his brother-in-law :

MY DEAR CHARLES,

I am sorry to come so early to you with applications, but you will be perfectly aware how much is expected of my connection with you and how impossible to refuse in certain circumstances to make an effort for one's friends. [There then follow the names of a number of Bedford-shire people including the chairman of quarter sessions, deserving honour from the new government.]

I wish to God you would immediately make your Father an Earl; it is the only thing that could make one of his remaining Days cheerful; you owe it to him not to be squeamish about it but to get it done.

I have returned [from Bedford] more uneasy in my obscurity than I went down. My constituents received me with looks of surprise, and having stupidly supposed that whenever the Turn did happen I should be among the first wanted, conclude from my exclusion that those who know me more intimately and are of course better judges differ from them very widely in opinion as to my usefulness, or that I have made a Bargain about a Peerage.

In short I feel that I have lost all the reputation my Consistency and Effort of fifteen years, added to the triumph of Last Session, have procured for me; which if I had anticipated I should not had acted quite as I have done.* But 'tis my own fault, and I have only to reproach myself. To all others I carry the thing off as well as I can : to you I can not help expressing my Feelings.[3]

Grey replied on the same day, beginning his letter 'Indeed, my dear Sam, the subject which appears to hurt your feelings so much is not less painful to mine.' He adds, what many will feel to have been a sensible comment, that Whitbread's reputation 'already so high' can not suffer with the public 'because your name is not included in the list of the new ministers'.

* He means here that he would not have let it be known that he did not want office.

And here, in order to make the story plain, one point must be emphasised. In conversation with Grey, Whitbread had made clear that if it facilitated arrangements he did not want to be considered for office. But this is generally a dangerous form of self-abnegation. 'Count me out' is a cry which is often heard : and then when it is seen who has been counted in, the cry turns to lamentation because the command was taken literally. Lord Holland undoubtedly records precisely what happened when he writes 'Lord George Cavendish and Mr. Coke of Norfolk refused peerages, and Lord Howick [Lord Grey] somewhat hastily answered for Mr. Whitbread's declining both title and office, an act of friendship which did not strengthen the ties of family connexion or political attachment between them.'⁴ On 7 February Grey wrote again to Whitbread and said 'I certainly had remained ever since our last conversation on this subject under the impression that you felt a great unwillingness to take any office and that nothing but our absolute want of you could induce you to do so.'

The brothers-in-law evidently met on the same evening and the opening sentence of Grey's next letter sufficiently describes what that meeting was like. 'The very few words you addressed to me tonight have hurt me beyond expression, not only as they showed the mortification you suffer, which never can happen without pain to me, but as they conveyed something like a reproach for my neglect of you.' He then went on to say that the only place in the Cabinet which could have gone to Whitbread was the Exchequer, filled by Lord Henry Petty. Certainly Lord Henry, on the face of things, was scarcely qualified to be chancellor of the Exchequer. He was 25. He succeeded Pitt as member for the University of Cambridge defeating Lord Palmerston. The candidates were immortalised by Byron in 'Hours of Idleness' :

> One on his power and place depends,
> The other on — the Lord knows what !
> Each to some eloquence pretends,
> Though neither will convince by that.

The power and place to which Byron alludes are the explanation for Petty's appointment: he was the son of the old Whig Prime Minister Shelburne, and his appointment was gratifying to some senior members of the party. But for all his youth Petty was to prove himself a competent and courageous Chancellor of the Exchequer and to win for himself in old age that agreeable sobriquet — the Nestor of the Whigs. Whatever Petty's shortcomings it would have been quite out of the question for Whitbread to go to the Exchequer. The reason for this was that someone actively engaged in a brewery, or for that matter in trade of any kind, could not possibly have taken the Exchequer without first removing the contamination of commerce. The eighteenth-century holders of the office had all been aristocrats and the fact that some of them, like William Pitt, were in financial straits themselves was of no consequence provided they were not besmirched by trade. In recalling their conversation in the letter already quoted Grey said of the possibility of Whitbread going to the Exchequer 'You yourself acknowledge the objections'. The only other office appropriate to Whitbread's standing in the party was the Secretaryship at War. In those days there were three Secretaryships of State — Home Affairs, Foreign Affairs and the combined office of War and Colonies. But in addition to the last, and generally outside the Cabinet, was the Secretaryship at War: here gouty and genial but comfortably installed was Fox's oldest political crony — General Fitzpatrick. He had held the office almost a quarter of a century before in the days of the Fox–North Coalition. Grey explained to Whitbread the embarrassment of the situation and asked how he could press Fox 'where his oldest friend was concerned' but he had told him that it was a place which Whitbread would like. He ended the letter in a fashion which forces the reader's sympathy for Grey:

'I have not had a moment's happiness since this cursed arrangement began, and I am now going to another sleepless night — I wish to God I could satisfy all discontents by resigning my own office. If I had been aware sufficiently early of the

VIEW OF THE HUSTINGS IN COVENT GARDEN
during the Westminster Election of 1806; Whitbread's hand is on Sheridan's
shoulder

A cartoon by James Gillray

THOMAS CREEVEY

By Abraham Wivell

extent of your feelings on this point, I would have refused to take office without you . . . I am going to bed with a heavy heart'.

Two days later Whitbread replied. He began by apologising for all the vexation which he had caused his brother-in-law. He also made it clear that he blamed himself and not Grey for any misunderstanding of his true feelings. 'Had I seen what I now see I should have been less delicate about myself.' He also makes clear in the first paragraph the force of those potent influences over public men which were epitomised in the words of Romilly quoted above — 'fame and popularity'. 'I can not be easy under the sneers of some, the condolences of others and the conversation of all.' Despite his rugged exterior, despite the rough blows he gave his opponents Whitbread was in reality a highly sensitive man, deeply influenced by what others thought of him.

He went on, 'You must make allowances for Human Passions when dealing with men, and I have my share. You must also make allowances for me more particularly because, having no Family to boast of, I ought to be and am more diffident as to my situation with the Public than if I were nobly born.' Here the reader may think that Whitbread was unduly self-depreciatory. Some of Pitt's Scottish following — the Roses and Dundases — would, so far as lineage went, have hardly stirred the enthusiasm of Garter King at Arms or even of Lyon himself, while Addington both on his own account and with those fearful relatives Brother Hiley and Brother Bragge* showed a steep falling away from the old aristocratic standards of political eighteenth-century England. He went on, 'And although I have at times felt that it would be no unwelcome† thing to the world to see me a good deal advanced, I am easily rebuked, and at other times have felt, as I told you in our first conversation, like a fool for suffering such imaginations ever to

---

* It is true that Bragge was connected with Lord Bathurst, but there was rather more Bragge than Bathurst in the blood.

† This is a conjectural reading as the word is illegible.

enter my heart.' There is a certain unmistakable pathos here — the clear ambition for office, and then the feeling that such dreams were put to flight by the great Brewery in Chiswell Street. He goes on to say that he banished ambitious feelings when first he spoke to Grey

because I thought you felt very strongly my want of Birth, and knowing your Partiality towards me, I conceived that feeling to be in unison with — or rather derived from — those with whom you had conversed. In the sequel of that conversation we talked about trade, which you appeared to think disqualified me for every high situation.* For that I was not prepared: and to your advice to dispose of it [the Brewery] I answered (peevishly perhaps) that it was not a thing to be disposed of in a moment. (I wish it was!) Had I been asked specifically whether to obtain a great object, I could make an immediate surrender of my share in the trade and that office proposed being that specific one with which trade was incompatible, I should have desired a few Hours to consider of it.

He then went on to say that if he had found it impossible to get rid of the Brewery or if he had felt that someone else would fill the office better:

I should at least have had the offer and the world would have distinctly known that Fox and you (for it is that about which I care) thought me both capable and eligible. But I must pay for the peevish manner in which I uttered — what if said in a different Tone — might not have made the same impression upon you and you might have asked me the Question again.

In the conversation I had with Fox I meant to be taken literally: but here again I must say a word. An eagerness to take you literally makes you wish sometimes you had not been so literal; and the quickness with which he told me he should take me literally rebuked me again, and made me feel at the time that in taking me literally he thought he should be rid of a friend rather than that he expected to derive any advantage or assistance from me.

He then repeated how he would have liked the Secretaryship at War and how mortified he had been when he heard that an

* It is certainly difficult to think of anyone directly connected with trade who had, up to then, held one of the Secretaryships of State. Creevey says Burke, Sheridan, Dunning and Barré used to be considered as 'not elevated enough in rank' for the Cabinet. (*Creevey Papers*, ed. Maxwell, i. 162.)

attempt was being made to shift Fitzpatrick but with the idea of placing Lord Charles Somerset there. The letter ended unequivocally : 'I fairly tell you that I claim the offer of the first situation compatible with my credit.'[5]

Few politicians can have ever laid bare their innermost, private feelings as did Whitbread in this long letter. He was not, we may suppose, entirely fair in attributing his disappointment to the Brewery or to his lack of blood. Fox was beginning to fail. His nephew, referring to the beginning of 1806 said 'I had been struck with the change in Mr. Fox's countenance'. In politics he was always susceptible to private friendship — perhaps increasingly so with the decline in his powers — and he undoubtedly felt that men like Sheridan and Fitzpatrick needed the perquisites of office while Whitbread, amply provided for, was independent of such things. There was also the question whether Whitbread could have continued the impeachment as a Minister of the Crown. But whatever the reason and whatever explanation may be offered the fact stands out stark and inescapable. Whitbread was bitterly mortified.

And human nature being as it is there was perhaps a further influence which tended to inflame Whitbread's vexation, and that was the assumption, which seems to have been general among the Whig hierarchy, that high office must be found for Grey. By nature Whitbread was competitive, and he therefore almost naturally was a prey to the commonest failing in politicians — personal jealousy. It is a common and prevailing mistake to suppose that in English politics an association in boyhood, young manhood or social life welds men together in a tight political alliance. Of far greater importance, at any rate in the time of Whitbread's prominence in politics, was the association of men in maturity, drawn by a particular political objective, and symbolising their comradeship by a dinner for men. Lord Holland, looking back to that period, emphasised 'how greatly the strength and union of parties depended on private dinners, tavern suppers, convivial meetings and perhaps intemperance itself'.[6] Whitbread and Grey were not political allies because they were at Eton and Cambridge together, but because they believed, as grown men, in the same causes and associated together in suppers at the Whig Club and in private masculine society. But their long friendship enabled Whitbread to know Charles Grey as no other person in public life knew him, and it is not untrue that jealousy is not diminished by the realisation that public opinion rates very highly the old friend whose foibles and follies come only too readily to mind. Grey was First Lord, but Whitbread would have been less than human if he had been expected to forget those letters from Howick in which Grey cursed the call of public life and was forever saying how he longed to throw it up for the peace and quiet of Northumberland life. In spite of his youthful escapade with the Duchess of Devonshire, Grey had become almost embarrassingly a family man. He had fifteen children, and as Whitbread complained 'the pregnancies are always inconveniently arranged'. He once wrote to Whitbread from Howick 'to leave Mary alone here at this dreary season, with the hollow, wintry wind howling through the passages of this great empty house I feel to be impossible'. Then, as the children emerged from the nursery, his letters are filled with the problem of a governess 'of all animals the most difficult to be found tolerably good'. And even when the governess was found she refused to be left with the children and the winter's wind while the parents enjoyed Whig society in London.

Nor was Grey always at his best after the long journey south from Alnwick. He once complained to Brougham that 'the eternal rattle and motion of the chaise' confused his head.

Then too Whitbread would remember that Grey had once described the House of Commons to him as 'this sink of all abominations'. Was it not naturally a little galling to find this grumbling amateur automatically accepted as candidate for the Cabinet?

In one respect Whitbread was determined to make his old friend work up to the collar. In those days office may have spelt hard work but it also spelt patronage. Whitbread started at once at a fairly high level by urging Fox himself to press the claims of his old friend Monson to preferment in the Church.[7] But unfortunately few vacancies occurred in the hierarchy of the Church during the Ministry of All the Talents. As Lord Holland truly and amusingly expresses it, the clergy 'seemed to live miraculously for the purpose of baffling the Whigs whom they hated. But no sooner were we turned out than canons, deans and bishops began to sing out their nunc dimittis.'[8]

In less exalted spheres Whitbread was more successful. As soon as Grey was safely in the Admiralty he submitted a shower of applications for promotion in the Royal Navy. There was 'the brother to our apothecary at Biggleswade', Mr. Okes, who 'wants to be made a lieutenant. He is son to old Okes of Cambridge to whom we are indebted for early cures'; 'your sister is particularly anxious to recommend someone for an Admiralty messenger's place; Lee Antonie recommends a naval officer and my sister Lady St. John another . . . pray order two letters to be written that I may send an answer to each.' And finally 'Can you do anything for the son of our old roll and butter manufacturer at Eton?'

Whitbread and his wife also took the somewhat hazardous step of recommending a private secretary to Grey. This was a man called Grant who was brother to Mrs. Whitbread's companion, Miss Julia Grant. He was a complete failure, and Grey evidently did not feel able to recommend that his employment in the Admiralty should be continued. The harassment of poor Whitbread from his wife over matters of this kind is only too apparent from the following letter which he wrote on 15 November 1806 :

I do not know anything which gives me more disappointment and mortification than to hear Grant was to lose his Place. Not only because I wished to serve him personally, but because I shall feel the effect of it in a thousand ways and for ever. *Your* sister will be in the highest degree chagrined; and in the present state of *his* sister's health, with our girls at Clifton, I don't know what the Devil I shall do or how to break it to any of the parties . . . surely for a person who has been your private secretary (for his merits or demerits are unknown to others) it would be possible for you to make a push for him somewhere.

Then the Brewery made an interesting claim on the poor First Lord. Sangster told Grant that the tap in Deptford Yard (i.e. Dockyard) which was formerly served by Goodwyn* but then by the new Brewery was much dissatisfied with their beer, and is resolved to change their brewer. 'The consumption is said to be from thirty to forty butts a month.' There is no evidence that Whitbread himself encouraged this little bit of business. Grey writing to him said 'Grant mumbled something to me about Sangster but I did not understand what it was. . . . I can not interfere directly'.[9]

And over the Ministry of All the Talents, throughout the summer of 1806, there loomed the lengthening shadow of Fox's health. Almost from the start of the Ministry he had been afflicted with a disorder of the circulation and by the threat of dropsy. Rumours flew round among the faithful : in July men comforted themselves with the hope that a diet of carrot seeds would help him, and that a turn for the worse was explained by a too eager indulgence in green figs. Hopes rose when he was seen being wheeled in the garden at Chiswick, but only to sink when the news came that he had had to be tapped. Though we may admire Fox's tenacity, for his colleagues the situation was intolerable. Grey in a letter to Whitbread reveals how painfully different the reality was from the confidence expressed by the invalid in July — 'I think I shall do again'.[10] Writing on 8 September Grey says :

He has from the beginning of his illness banished from his mind all subjects which give him any uneasiness. He never enquires, and generally changes the conversation if you attempt to talk to him on the conduct of the war or the progress of the negotiation [with Napoleon]. The whole of the latter has been carried on in his name, without his reading the papers which he has signed . . . I feel that his continuing to hold his office situated as he now is, is not worthy of his character.[11]

* This was the Red Lion Brewery, which belonged to Henry Goodwyn and which, with Whitbread's, had been one of the pioneers of steam power. At this time it was closely connected with Hoare's Bank.

Whitbread's great concern was that the Foreign Office should go to Grey at Fox's demise. On 4 September he had written to Grey 'to yourself and the country you owe it to meet the sad event with manliness, and to make a great exertion that we may not be for ever lost. The fearful situation of the country, the strength which the Party opposed to you have been suffered to acquire, and above all the naturally despondent turn of your own mind are to be met, and contended with, and they will — if you are true to yourself — be overcome. If you withdraw yourself, or shrink in the smallest degree from the difficulties and labours of your situation, all that remains of the Principle which your whole Political Life has been directed to maintain in conjunction with Fox, will be for ever gone.' In reply to this, Grey wrote to Whitbread 'my mind is therefore nearly made up to retire altogether'.

By this declaration Whitbread was horrified. He was at The Barns for the Bedford races and he replied firmly on 9 September 'Would you fly at such a moment? Where would be the Foxite left in Government? Would you leave the country between the Grenvilles and Canning, Castlereagh and Perceval? It makes me sick to think of it. For God's sake rouse yourself from such Dreams. Mischief enough has been done already by the unhappy supineness of Fox, arising from the disease which has been long creeping upon him. But for you to give it all up, and at such a moment, would be inevitable Destruction and ever-lasting Disgrace.'

As a family the Greys were always hesitant about office, though this hesitancy did not prevent them from occupying the best posts which the Government had to offer. On Fox's death Grey moved to the Foreign Office — a little attracted to it because (strange as it may seem to modern ideas) the labour of the Foreign Office was as Whitbread told Grey 'trifling' compared with the Admiralty.

Fox died on 13 September, and the funeral, which took place in October 1806, showed to the world the extent of Whitbread's attachment to his old chief. He died at Chiswick, in the house of

the Duke of Devonshire, and the body was brought from there
to his own house in Stable Yard, St. James's. From there it was
borne in public procession to the Abbey. The chief mourner and
others intimately associated with Fox (including Grey)
followed in carriages. Behind them came the younger mourners
on foot. With the Law Officers of the Crown walked Sheridan
and Whitbread. An observer recorded 'His face was inflamed
with tears'.[12] But the pageant of sorrow was symbolic of a
parting, which was larger and more affecting, than Whitbread's farewell to his old chief. The death of Fox marked the
end of his friendship and association with the hierarchy of the
Whig Party: henceforward he was to walk alone, not always
out of step with Fox's comrades, but something of a solitary,
proclaiming, as he went, that the spirit of Fox went marching
on — but with him not with them.

Wordsworth marked the occasion by his celebrated sonnet
composed on the evening of a stormy day under the shelter of
the Lake hills around Grasmere. As the streams and becks of
that delectable valley roared like the sea they seem to symbolise
the fury of the storm which, with the death of their old friend
was to break out anew between Whitbread and his brother-in-
law. Six days after Fox's death Grey wrote to Whitbread
asking him to meet him at the Admiralty — 'pray wait for me
there — you can write your letters or do anything else there as
well as in Dover Street'. Though it is not absolutely easy to
piece together what was said at this interview, Grey evidently
suggested that Whitbread should consider the Secretaryship at
War and that William Windham, the Secretary of State for
War and Colonies, should be urged to go to the Lords. This
would have given the Secretary at War in the Commons a
rather magnified position. Whitbread evidently declined the
suggestion with some warmth. Grey wrote: 'I am sure you did
not mean to be unkind to me; but surely, my dear Sam, the
grounds of your refusal, and above all your tone and manner in
the whole of the conversation were not kind.' Grey went on that
the only reason he could divine for Whitbread's refusal was that

the ministry 'was exposed to more difficulties'. Whitbread answered two days later, and he made plain where the truth lay 'Were it offered to me upon the terms on which Windham held it, I would gladly accept it; upon any other I should certainly injure myself . . . and consequently my power of doing you service if I took it.' Before he was Secretary of War and Colonies Windham had been Secretary at War in Pitt's earlier government and he had held the office with a seat in the Cabinet. This was the point of Whitbread's ambition and he continued in his letter 'The addition of a Foxite [to the Cabinet] at this crisis, would I suppose give great satisfaction. . . . However I have only unburthened my mind to you. I mean not to press or even ask for anything. But I must adhere to what I have said, or render myself completely ineffectual to your assistance. While I am as I am I may afford you at times some small service, whenever it can be it shall be, as it has been, with all my heart and soul.' He ended with evidence of all the old attachment 'To yourself I could never mean to be unkind, and the manner of both of us is, I suppose, so decided* as to call at times for mutual forgiveness. I ask yours, and assure you you need never ask mine for I am always most affectionately yours.'

Grey replied with a firm but friendly letter on the same day. He told Whitbread that he could not at present press his inclusion in the Cabinet 'with any chance of success'. He urged him strongly to be content with the Secretaryship at War without the Cabinet because he would naturally advance from there to a higher place in the Government. The only result of his refusal would be that when Fitzpatrick went, his place would be filled by a follower of Lord Grenville 'that branch of the administration, which you think is possessed of too much influence already'. After asking for three days to think matters over Whitbread wrote on 26 September :

* A friend of Grey's once wrote that 'his Hotspur blood was boiling in his veins'. He had in fact no Hotspur blood, but shared the fiery characteristics of that famous house. *The (Two Duchesses*, ed. Vere Foster, 1898).

As I have made up my mind, I will not delay my communication; neither will I detain you by going into the grounds of my present determination.

Simply then, as it appears from what I can expect, that it would be satisfactory to poor Fox's friends in general that I should give some unequivocal testimony of my cordial approbation of the new arrangements and that you are anxious upon the subject I will accept the Secretaryship at War whenever Fitzpatrick chooses to resign it.

An exchange of letters between Grey and the Prime Minister, Grenville, shows that Grey fought resolutely for his friend. Commenting on Grey's proposals (which included Whitbread's name as Secretary at War) Grenville wrote on 18 September : 'in all these arrangements in favour of Fox's friends we not only most willingly consent, but I am sure for one I can say that there is not anyone of them in which I shall not feel sincere pleasure.' Two days later Grey had to write to say that Whitbread had refused 'I hope however that this refusal may not be conclusive and whenever the Secretaryship at War, or any other office not less in rank, shall be opened, it will be most gratifying to me to have it again proposed, with any such additional inducements as can with propriety be held out to him.' This final clause could have meant a peerage for Mrs. Whitbread, on the same principle by which the elder Pitt's wife was created Baroness Chatham five years before her husband was made a peer : or the clause could more probably be interpreted as a very broad hint about Whitbread's inclusion in the Cabinet.[13]

There, in the future, the matter rested — a reward hereafter but not today, a promise unfulfilled. Whitbread was never to hold office in any government. To an extent Fitzpatrick was the bother. Though, as his friends anxiously remarked, his constitution was somewhat shattered he lived on till 1813 remarking as he was dying, in his strong, determined voice *La pièce est finie*.[14] He was loved by all — Whitbread included — and seemed like some apostle to echo the spirit and reality of Fox whom he had followed with distinguished faithfulness. Whitbread himself was largely responsible for persuading him to sit for Bedfordshire from 1807. Fitzpatrick represented too much of the soul of the Whig Party to be unceremoniously plucked from office to make room for a more vigorous War Minister. The civilised government of the Talents, even in the throes of the life and death struggle with Napoleon, would never have thought gout and debility good reason for moving Fox's friend from the direction of armies.

At the end of September Whitbread was writing cheerfully to his friend Lee Antonie 'I have consented to accept the Secretary-ship at War whenever Fitzpatrick shall think proper to resign it, which will probably be the case at no very distant period'.[15] Then came an autumn election which was followed by a sharpening of the political differences between Grey and Whitbread. The negotiations started by Fox with Napoleon had foundered, and during the election the battle of Jena was fought and threw Prussia at the feet of Napoleon. Whitbread had asked his brother-in-law to announce the arrangements about the Secretaryship at War before the election. This was not done and thereafter there was some deterioration in the relations between the two men. Whitbread's difference with Grey and the orthodox Whigs over the negotiations with Napoleon put his inclusion in the Government out of the question. The Ministry of All the Talents fell in March 1807, and Grenville was writing to one of his junior ministers 'pack up your awls'.[16] They were not to be needed again for a quarter of a century.

The interest of the exchanges between Whitbread and Grey lies in the revelation they give of the inner feelings of a public man at that time. The old friendship and relationship between the two men enabled Whitbread to speak with complete frankness to the person who happened to have the distribution of the offices. He made it clear in conversation and by letter what he wanted and what he thought he deserved. Normally such things are reported back to the Cabinet-maker by a third party or in an interview there is a hint of dissatisfaction — a shadow of disappointment. 'I make it a rule never to open my mouth on such subjects' says Taper in *Coningsby* 'a nod or a wink will speak volumes'. Whitbread preferred to speak volumes, and if what he has to say seems too egocentric, too concerned with his own career, the reader will remember that those are the occupational disorders of public life. In only a few cases are they revealed with the starkness of Whitbread's correspondence with Charles Grey. Naturally the relations between the two men were strained, and they were never to return to the easy familiarity of the day when Fox was still alive. But as was true of the whole of Whitbread's public life he spoke his mind, he hit hard but he never bore resentment. Rather it was his brother-in-law and the Whig hierarchy who after the events of 1806 marked him down as difficult and tiresome. For his part Whitbread was invariably generous in his allusions to Grey. Writing to Creevey and alluding to the loss to the party in the Commons when Grey went to the Lords he expressed his feelings in three words, 'it is irreparable'.[17]

CHAPTER THIRTEEN

Elections and Temper

THE death of Fox, we may surmise, was felt in the Whig Party — that is, not only the hierarchy, not only on the green benches of the House of Commons, but among his supporters in the constituencies — with the same blank despair that struck the common sailors when, on the evening of Trafalgar, they looked to *Victory* and saw that no admiral's lights were burning. Nowhere was the sense of loss more keenly felt than in Fox's old constituency of Westminster. The democratic force of the people of England at this time was, like the population in a later age, concentrated in the county of Middlesex. It embraced three constituencies — the county which forty years earlier had reverberated to the campaigns of Wilkes, the City of London and the City of Westminster. Each constituency returned two Whig or radical Members of Parliament, but Westminster had a wider franchise than the others because every man who could point to himself as owner or occupier of house or hovel was able to vote. Fox dearly prized the excitement and villainy of a Westminster election, and glowed with pleasure at the moment of triumph when he was borne through Covent Garden shoulder high in a chair, gilt without and crimson plush within. The leading electors, as is shown by the following exchange of letters, would have liked Whitbread to succeed Fox :

The Committee appointed by the electors of Westminster at a public meeting held at the Crown & Anchor on Thursday the 18th instant — having, this day assembled at the Rainbow Coffee House, King Street, Covent Garden, in pursuance of their directions to consider of and select a proper person to represent them in Parliament by filling that vacancy occasioned by the irreparable and ever to be lamented loss sustained in our late worthy member the Right Honourable Charles James Fox.

Have resolved that at a most respectable and numerous meeting of the electors of Westminster held at the Crown & Anchor as above described, it was by them determined that Lord Percy was not a fit and proper person to represent them in Parliament, and Mr. Sheridan having, at the said meeting, been put in nomination and declined becoming a candidate — it appears to the Committee that Samuel Whitbread, Esquire — as a firm, able and independent Patriot is highly proper to be proposed to the electors of Westminster at their adjourned meeting to be held at the Crown & Anchor on Friday the 26th inst. as their representative in Parliament.

Resolved that the Chairman of the committee do forthwith transmit the above resolution to the said Samuel Whitbread, Esquire, who is hereby respectfully requested to afford the electors of the ancient and respectable City of Westminster (by becoming their candidate at the ensuing election) an opportunity of once more evincing their spirit and independence and their resentment at being considered either the tools of Party or subservient vassals of any administration.

Resolved that the said Samuel Whitbread, Esquire, be requested to honor the Committee with his answer addressed to their Chairman as early as convenient.

Resolved that these resolutions be signed by the Chairman of the Committee.

JAMES GIBBONS, *Chairman.*

The following is the draft for Whitbread's answer :

Dover Street, September 21, 1806.

SIR,

I have received the resolution which you have been so good as to send me by the direction of the Committee of the Electors of Westminster, appointed by the meeting held at the Crown & Anchor Tavern on Thursday last.

It is my first duty to express my grateful acknowledgement for the high honour you have conferred on me by the selection made of me as a person worthy to be put in nomination to succeed that truly great man who has been just taken from amongst us to the deep and lasting affliction of his friends and to the irreparable loss of his country and the world.

But, Sir, duly sensible of the consequences which the representation of the City of Westminster must give to any man who shall be so fortunate as to obtain it, most especially after the manner in which it has been filled for so many years, there are motives of a private nature which would induce me to decline the offer proposed to me, were there not others of a public nature also which preclude the possibility of my appearing as candidate for the seat so unhappily vacant.

I am so firmly attached to that respectable and independent body of constituents who have returned me to Parliament at three successive elections and who have four times previously distinguished my family by the same token of their confidence and approbation, that the representation of the City of Westminster itself could not tempt me from their service.

Further having duly weighed all the circumstances of the present crisis as it relates more particularly to your situation, and my own as one of your body I have determined to give my vote to Lord Percy; and it is with great concern I find that any part of the Westminster electors have resolved that he is not a fit person to represent the great city in Parliament.

I am perfectly certain that neither I, nor any of those persons who have acted in unison with your late illustrious member, during the whole of our political lives, should support Lord Percy could we for a moment suppose that by that support we were instrumental in making either you or ourselves the tools of Party or the subservient vassals of any administration.

The electors of Westminster in their choice of Mr. Fox triumphed over all the tools of Party and all the vassals of power; and such is the estimation and love in which his memory is held, that could his wishes be consulted I am sure they would decide the object of your choice.

Under this conviction then that if his valuable life had been spared in a state of health to have prevented him from again offering him to you, he would have recommended Lord Percy as his successor, I, and I believe most of Mr. Fox's immediate and personal friends, feel bound to assist his cause, to which however nothing could urge us were we not impressed to believe that in Lord Percy will be found a young man of principles as independent as the name he bears is noble and great, and the one who is desirous of treading in the political paths of Mr. Fox. I have the honour to be sir, your very obliged and obedient servant.

S. Whitbread.[1]

In spite of refusing to be the Westminster candidate Whitbread took a prominent part in the very delicate electoral business which was now agitating the streets and dairy farms of

Westminster and Middlesex. Now Sheridan, regarded by his Whig associates with a mixture of indignation and reluctant admiration, had long coveted Westminster. He rightly thought that a popular constituency lent some of its strength and individuality to the Member representing it. Creevey gives an amusing picture of him just after Fox's death listening simultaneously to the talk of his cronies about the prospects of his standing for Westminster and to the opinion of his doctors about the likelihood of his surviving a particularly heavy bout of drinking. The Whigs were determined that he should not step in to Fox's shoes, and they brought forward Lord Percy, a stripling of twenty-one. Whitbread, on the hustings in Covent Garden, proposed Lord Percy, who was elected without opposition and was then chaired down the Strand to Northumberland House. In later life Lord Percy was described as 'an absolute nullity — a bore beyond all bores'. Queen Victoria concurred in this description, but possibly if she had drawn him out about the moment of glory when he was carried in Fox's golden chair she might have found that after all there had been something in the nullity. But the moment of glory was almost literally a moment. He was elected on 7 October. In a little more than a fortnight Parliament was dissolved.

At the General Election Sheridan, in one of his frequent fits of folly, put himself forward as the Whig candidate. It was a double-membered constituency, and Sir Samuel Hood, the distinguished sailor, who had lost an arm in the West Indies the previous year, was the other Whig candidate.* Grey, with a nice sense of what was likely to appeal to the voters, said 'He will silence all opponents with his *stump*'. The Duke of Northumberland was so vexed by Sheridan's intervention that he removed Lord Percy from the fray and made him stand for Cambridge University where he was unsuccessful. Whitbread, feeling perfectly secure in Bedford, was in charge of the Whig campaign in Westminster and in order to understand what happened it is necessary to take a look at the contest in Middle-

* He was a cousin of Lord Hood (1724–1816), the famous admiral.

sex. Here the Whig champion was George Byng who was to sit for that famous constituency for fifty-six years, being returned at sixteen successive elections. A lukewarm Whig stood with him, for it was, like Westminster, a double-membered seat. Into the fray at Middlesex sprang that young aristocratical demagogue, Sir Francis Burdett. Behind him and manipulating him, as all the world knew, was that alarming survivor from the great days of Wilkes, the Reverend Horne Tooke who, as has been well said, enticed others into scrapes and kept out of them himself.[2] And a scrape this indeed was — for between them the clergyman and the baronet fought the wildest contest based on radical doctrines of reform and shrill attacks on all who enjoyed any places of profit under the Government. Whitbread's partner, Timothy Brown, was a fervent supporter of Burdett — support which was perhaps to be expected, but was not without embarrassment to Whitbread. He took a leading part in the contest which he called an attempt to 'rescue this Metropolitan County from the degradation of becoming a Rotten Borough of the Treasury'. The atmosphere must have been decidely frosty when the two partners met in Chiswell Street. In his address to the freeholders of Middlesex Sir Francis said, alluding to the fusion of parties on which the Talents rested :

Whenever the Leaders of contending parties and factions in a State unite, the history of the world bears evidence, that it never is in favour, but always at the expense, of the People; whose renewed and augmented pillage pays the scandalous price of the reconciliation. . . . The watchword of one party is — The best of Kings. The watchword of the other is the best of Patriots. But neither of these parties will . . . inform you what the best of Kings, and the best of Patriots have already done or will hereafter do for you. What they have done for themselves, we know, and feel. . . .

He went on to say that he stood independently of any party 'I will not distribute, nor consent to the distribution of a coin or a single cockade : nor will I furnish, nor consent to the furnishing of a single carriage.' He was not elected.[3]

At the same time these firebrands encouraged James Paull, the opulent son of a Scottish tailor, to carry their blazing torch into

M

the very citadel of Whiggery — Westminster itself — and to stand against Sheridan and Hood. Burdett contributed £1,000 towards his election expenses.

The hustings of a popular constituency such as Westminster were in complete contrast to the dreary decorum of modern electioneering. On the platform were placed the three candidates — the two Whigs and the radical; with them were their influential supporters. Each candidate spoke, debated with and interrupted the other speakers. The hustings were a valuable introduction to the stern realities of the House of Commons at its zenith. Although Whitbread's private feelings were in conflict with his public support for Sheridan for Westminster, he was always to be seen on the hustings behind Sheridan during the later and more violent part of the campaign. The hustings stood in Covent Garden and all the rowdies and bullies of that not very salubrious part of London stood at the foot of the platform, jeering, interrupting, bellowing and emphasising their disapproval with what was called 'their ejected rheum'. Conspicuous among these worthies was a broad-faced gentleman, who was a publican and delighted in shouting down Sheridan. Once when Whitbread was speaking he had to stop because of a burst of laughter and cheering caused by this heckler who called out 'Mr. Whitbread's insolence is much stronger than his porter'. Whitbread took this good-humouredly, and said that he would like to talk to them over 'some pots of my porter, for the more you drink of it the better'.[4]

In the evening after the poll was closed for the day, the leaders and candidates adjourned for dinner and speeches at one of the taverns round Covent Garden or in the Strand. At one of these celebrations Whitbread in his speech, alluding to the charge that Sheridan was a placeman, said that if a place were offered to him [Whitbread] where he could put out someone less qualified he would certainly accept it. The words were curious and were possibly aimed at poor Fitzpatrick. Paull, on the hustings in front of Whitbread, said that he hoped the reports of a place for Whitbread were unfounded : 'I should be very sorry indeed to see that gentleman, sunk as he already is, go to the Hospital of Incurables.'

A final touch of unpleasantness had to be faced. Abraham Hewlings, who dealt in feathers and was an ardent supporter of Paull was mistakenly named by Whitbread as a supporter of Sheridan's. As he was not supporting Sheridan he demanded an apology from Whitbread. The letter lay at Dover Street without being forwarded to Southill and Hewlings wrote to Whitbread : 'the arrangements of your establishment must be of the most singular nature and your servants the worst set of *varlets* that ever a gentleman was served with.'[5]

At that time voting was spread over several days — a count being taken at the end of each day. In the opening stages Paull did extremely well. It was decided correctly that the only chance of stopping Paull was for the two Whigs to amalgamate their forces (Hood was a Grenvillite). As it was a two-member constituency, voters were thus encouraged to give a party vote for the two Whig candidates instead of a 'plumber' for one. Sheridan became, according to the easy witticisms of the day, 'hooded'. Sheridan and Hood were comfortably elected. Whitbread had to appeal for funds and two replies have survived. Lord Buckingham, the eldest brother of the Prime Minister wrote 'I have sent Whitbread £100 for his committee and would gladly have given more — not to bring in Sheridan but to keep out Paull'.[6] General Fitzpatrick, drawing from his slender resources, sent Whitbread £20 with the following letter 'With the utmost reluctance I enclose a small subscription which is, however, infinitely too large considering the purpose to which it is to be applied'. He added that he would have gladly doubled his subscription to give Sheridan any other seat 'than that which your efforts have procured him' and that he did not think that he and Whitbread would differ as to the advantage Sheridan would be to the government. He went on :

He has had a pretty severe lesson, and I shall not grudge my £20 if it leads to any amendment in his future conduct; I heartily wish it may, since with all his sins upon his head, I have a sort of unjustifiable

kindness for the Dog, which I can hardly account for. Not that upon
this consideration I would contribute a single penny to his election, it
is merely in support of the government that I am so *magnificent* in my
subscription. I can easily conceive how much you must have disliked
paying to help him out of the mire and the shove you gave poor Sir
Francis to plunge him into it must have been much more satisfactory,
both his and Sheridan's folly are equally incorrigible.[7]

But, as Whitbread was to find, young and ardent baronets are
not to be pushed in the mire without some retort to those who
push. During the Middlesex election Whitbread wrote a letter
to Burdett repelling the charges he had made against the Whigs,
and explaining why he was going to vote against him.[8]*
Burdett savagely attacked Whitbread on the Middlesex hustings, which were held at Brentford and replied insolently and
offensively in a published written statement, after the election.

To the FREEHOLDERS of Middlesex.
GENTLEMEN,
The moment before the commencement of the late Election for
Middlesex, Mr. Whitbread, in a manner most unbecoming his station,
connections, and character, inserted in the public newspapers the
following passage, signed with his name, addressed, indeed, nominally,
with dissembled respect, to me, but intended as a political electioneering manoevre against you.
'I do not perceive in your present address (says Mr. Whitbread)
any allusion to an opinion promulgated by you on the late Election for
Westminster, which is, "That a person holding an Office under the
Crown, however otherwise estimable, cannot at any time become the
fit Representative of a free, uncorrupt, and independent people." If
such opinion be founded in truth, which (continues Mr. Whitbread) I
utterly deny, a law ought to be passed to exclude all the executive
servants of Government from seats in either House of Parliament. I
have not heard that it was in the contemplation of any one to propose
such a measure, and if proposed, I am sure it would meet with resistance from all descriptions of persons, who have the power or the will
to reason upon its consequences. The people, by the acceptance of your
doctrine, would reduce themselves to the hard necessity of being
governed by the worst of mankind.'
These, Mr. Whitbread's sentiments, have likewise been recently
paraded by Mr. Windham, Secretary of State; by Mr. Tierney,

* Whitbread would vote in Middlesex by right of his house in Dover Street.

Chairman of the Board of Control; by Mr. Sheridan, Treasurer of the Navy; and are now held, I presume, as the political creed of the whole party.

Gentlemen, in that Act of Parliament (12 and 13 Will. III) which gave the throne of these kingdoms to his present Majesty and his family, entitled 'An Act for the further Limitation of the Crown, and better securing the Rights and Liberties of the Subject' it was wisely and honestly thus enacted; 'That no Person who has an Office or Place of Profit under the King, or receives a Pension from the Crown, shall be capable of serving as a Member of the House of Commons.' But Mr. Whitbread, it seems, never heard of this provision, 'for better securing the Rights and Liberties of the Subject.' And, because, after a melancholy experience of the necessity of such a provision which our honest ancestors only foresaw, I maintain the opinion of those from whom his Majesty holds his Crown; I am represented, by those best of Patriots, as an enemy to the Constitution; and, by some of their place-holding and place-hunting party, as a traitor to my country. The worst of traitors to their country are those who eat up its resources. Mr. Whitbread's judgment upon us who hold this opinion, is indeed something milder : he only concludes us to be either fools or rogues — 'either we have not the power or the will to reason upon its consequences.' I have reason to believe, that Mr. Whitbread himself possesses both the will and the power to obtain speedily a lucrative office under the Crown, without much embarrassing himself with its consequences to the public.

Gentlemen, when the last additional taxes for the present year were lately imposed upon the people by these best of patriots, it was undisguisedly and tranquilly acknowledged by them, without the least compunction or commiseration of the people, that the necessary effect of these taxes would be to drive the inhabitants of a house into lodgings, and the lodgers of the first floor into the second. Here indeed they stopped : leaving us to complete the miserable picture of national calamity : viz. That the lodgers of the second floor must mount up into the garret; the garreteers descend into the cellar; whose former wretched inhabitants must be thrust out upon the pavement; and from thence transferred to the workhouse or the grave. And this process is to be repeated *toties quoties*. So that the best provided amongst us, cannot tell where himself and his family may be found at last. This is a hard lesson for Englishmen to hear. It is harder still to hear it enforced from the mouths of those who themselves are all the while creeping forward from their original garrets into palaces. Such unfeeling insult as this could never have taken place but amidst placemen and pensioners. Had they been really the Representatives of

the people, they would have felt something for the people : and, instead
of incessantly calling for fresh sacrifices, and telling us gaily that we
must 'retrench even part of our necessaries,' they would surely now at
last have held out to us some prospect of consolation and redress : they
would no longer continue to gorge upon the vitals of their country,
but would think themselves too well off, if they were not justly
compelled to disgorge their past infamous swallowings. . . .

Your most obedient and respectful humble servant,

FRANCIS BURDETT.

The story can now be carried on in a letter from Whitbread
to Burdett written from Southill on 2 December 1806 :

SIR, Ever since my entrance into public life as a Member of Parliament, it has been one of the first wishes of my heart to divest political
differences of all personal animosity : and I have been at all times
ready to concede to others with regard to myself, the liberty I have
assumed towards them, of the fullest and freest discussion of every part
of my public conduct. But there are limits beyond which it is not
possible to step without injury to the party who may happen to be the
subject of animadversion, such as he must be compelled to resent.

It is with pain I am forced to say, that I feel myself so injured by
some passages contained in your advertisement to the Freeholders of
Middlesex published in the Statesman of yesterday.

In the face of the people of England you tell me, that by the
publication of a letter addressed to you in answer to a printed circular
letter addressed by you to me, as one of the electors of Middlesex, 'I
have acted in a manner unbecoming my station, connexions and
character.' and after the account I gave you privately on the hustings
at Brentford respecting the letter in question, which was, that it was
written without concert or consultation with any person whatever, that
I began it within half an hour of the receipt of your circular letter and
address; that it was out of my hands before four o'clock on the same
day and that it was entrusted to the revision of one friend only* (and
that not till after the copy addressed to you had been sealed and
despatched) in order that he might see whether from the haste in
which it was written it was not too inaccurate in point of language for
Publication. You say that I addressed that letter nominally, and with
dissembled respect to you : but that I intended it as a political
manœuvre against the freeholders of Middlesex.

I did not dissemble, sir, in any part of that transaction, and I

* Lord Holland.

unfeignedly, as I told you, felt respect for you at the time I wrote that letter: if you are possessed of those feelings with which I am still willing and desirous to believe that you are actuated, you will find that it is impossible for me not to demand reparation for the injury my character must sustain from a patient acquiescence under such imputations as you have most unprovokedly thrown upon me: and such reparation I demand at your hands. Mr. Brand has been so good as to undertake to carry this letter and is the only person who is acquainted with the circumstances of its having been written.

He will state to you what my demands are.

The letter ends with the statement that it is not the time for Whitbread to point out the general fallacy in Burdett's advertisement or the personal injustice implied in it for 'you are certainly not so much in my confidence as to entitle you to tell the people what my political views are'.[9]

The bearer of this challenge was Thomas Brand, afterwards Lord Dacre, a young man with unexpectedly wild opinions among the thoughtful family of Brand, who was to be known on this account as 'Firebrand'. He sat in Parliament from 1807 for the adjoining county of Hertford and was Whitbread's neighbour living at the Hoo near Welwyn. He has been described as 'all gentleness and courtesy — the very opposite of Mr. Creevey'.

With the challenge young Brand had his instructions. Any reparation must be public as the original insult was. 'It is my earnest wish to avoid all extremities. This may be done by the publication of my letter of which Mr. Brand is the bearer and any proper answer Sir Francis may chuse to write. Mr. Brand is possessed of the alternative, and I repeat my earnest wish to avoid it.'

Whitbread still occasionally hunted, and if Burdett chose to accept his challenge the early start could have been disguised from his wife as a happy day with the Oakley. On the day after his letter to Burdett he wrote to Lee Antonie: 'If you hunt anywhere within reach of my horse from Southill next week I will (*deo volente*) take a last look at you.'[10]

To Brand he wrote explaining what he wanted done if Burdett

accepted the challenge 'Our party to hunt on Thursday morning will afford a good excuse for my early departure with you from Southill, and you will have the goodness to fix some place which may be reached on horseback from hence. The arrangement of other matters I leave to you, and need not enjoin secrecy. I know you too well. Thank you for this friendly act.'[11]

Burdett's apology, written in his fine, sensitive hand, was published; it was complete — not to say abject.

Piccadilly Decr 3rd 1806

SIR

Nothing could have been more distant from my intention than to introduce into the advertisement which I thought it necessary to address to the freeholders of Middlesex any expression which could be construed into personal disrespect to yourself; and I take this opportunity of assuring you that every interpretation of its contents, which may be $\frac{perverted*}{construed}$ into a sense personally disrespectful to you is contrary to my meaning and intention.

I remain Sir

Your most obt hume st

FRANCIS BURDETT

P.S. Mr. Brand thinks it necessary to give publicity to this correspondence to which I can have no objection.[12]

Grey wrote to Whitbread three days later, in reply to a letter from him, saying that after reading the insult he himself could not have lived five minutes without taking action — 'Nothing can be more perfect than your conduct has been throughout . . . I think it the meanest and most humiliating thing I ever saw, and I can not state my opinion more strongly than by saying that if the situation had been reversed, I should have preferred seeing you shot to your signing such a paper upon such a requisition.'[13]

* construed is struck out.

CHAPTER FOURTEEN

The Rebellious Whig

THE intricacies of the Middlesex and Westminster elections obscured but did not heal the deep divergence between Whitbread and Grey. Almost inevitably their personal disagreements were followed by political ones. The latter were close behind. Within a month of the elections, Whitbread was in rebellion against what he regarded as a betrayal of the peace negotiations with France started by Fox earlier in 1806. The course of those negotiations had been devious. In the spring Fox had written to Talleyrand to warn him of an attempt against Napoleon's life, ending his letter by subscribing himself 'with perfect attachment'. This rather strange cordiality between the representatives of two nations engaged in a bloody war was explained by Fox's acquaintance with Talleyrand when he was in exile in England during the Terror. Fox then followed this up by asking for the release of certain English travellers who had been seized by the French and imprisoned by them in Verdun when hostilities broke out after the rupture of the Treaty of Amiens. Among them was Lord Yarmouth, in later life Lord Hertford and making an aristocratic but distasteful appearance in the pages of *Vanity Fair* as the Marquis of Steyne: with his wife, the reputed daughter of the Duke of Queensberry, 'Old Q', he led a life which was French rather than English, lurid rather than decorous. He and his wife were released, and into the hands of this choice pair Fox entrusted the task of opening the negotiations. Though by day Lord Yarmouth was somewhat handicapped by lack of diplomatic training, at night he and his wife were more favourably placed for finding those inner secrets hidden from more conventional members of the *corps diplomatique*. The possibility of peace rested on the principle of *uti possidetis* which could be explained by the armorial motto of a later Foreign Secretary 'Let Curzon have what Curzon holds'. In addition to agreeing that each belligerent should keep their conquests Napoleon was prepared to hand back Hanover to the King of England.* The English Government was also insistent that any serious negotiations should be held in conjunction with Russia. As the summer of 1806 began to assume hints of autumn, two serious hitches developed. The French signed a separate treaty with Russia, and a difficulty developed over Sicily which was possessed by the British but strongly coveted by Napoleon's brother, Joseph, who for two wild years had reigned in the Neapolitan half of the Kingdom of the two Sicilies. In August the English decided to send out Citizen Maitland (Lord Lauderdale) to give the negotiations a more workmanlike appearance. He immediately took his stand on *uti possidetis*; but over Sicily Napoleon would not yield; and after dragging on for eight weeks the negotiations collapsed amid the thunder-clap of Jena and the fall of the Prussia built by Frederick the Great.

Fox died while the negotiations were still active though probably, as we have seen, he was too ill to be really familiar with what was happening. He told his nephew, 'It is not Sicily, but the shuffling, insincere way in which they act that shows me they are playing a false game'.[1] But against that must be set the view of many French historians that Fox sincerely wanted peace though his colleagues did not. 'Fox's death was one of the fatalities of my career,' said Napoleon at St. Helena. The question of the sincerity of either side can be asked and debated, but it can perhaps never be answered. The answer is buried with Fox, with Grenville, with Grey and in the splendour of Les Invalides. Moreover whatever the intentions of both sides neither was defeated in battle : the dream of peace must have seemed a shade less real to Fox as news came in of naval victories and of the surrender of yet another Caribbean island.

* 'Hanover is as dear to us as Hampshire' — a saying of Fox (Lord Broughton, *Recollections of a Long Life* (1909–11), i, 206).

Peace with Napoleon was the hall-mark of the genuine Foxite Whig: it distinguished them absolutely from Pitt and his followers, and it stamped the difference between them and the Grenville and Windhamite Whigs. It lay rooted in the past, back thirteen or fourteen years to the time of Louis XVI's imprisonment, when the Duke of Brunswick, in command of an allied army, threatened Paris with 'an exemplary and never-to-be-forgotten vengeance'. In the debate in the House of Commons at the beginning of 1793, which followed, Whitbread said of the Duke's manifesto — and gave lively satisfaction to the historian Gibbon by doing so — that 'it breathed the spirit of Attila of whom, in the emphatical words recorded by Mr. Gibbon, it had been said Where Attila's horse sets his foot, the grass never grows'. From that time forward the possibility of peace with France had been the first tenet in Whig policy.

At the time of the Peace of Amiens Fox had shocked conservative opinion by saying that that peace was glorious for France and by asking the rhetorical question 'ought not glory to be the reward of such a glorious struggle?' Whitbread's speech on this occasion in the same debate echoed Fox. Whitbread's radical guide, Belsham, thought that most of Fox's friends had shown themselves on this occasion little better than Windhamites 'Yourself excepted' who 'seconded his efforts in the true and genuine spirit of his wise and admirable policy'.² The most thoughtful of the Whig leaders at this time, Shelburne, objected to the war with Napoleon on the grounds that it was 'a metaphysical war declared against France on account of her internal circumstances'.³ The twentieth century has grown accustomed to metaphysical wars but to the civilised mind of an Englishman in the Augustan age such struggles were irrational and horrible. Whether Fox in the plenitude of his powers would have gone deeper into the negotiation with France throughout 1806 must remain a matter of opinion. We can certainly say that if he had done so it would not have been inconsistent with what he had ever preached in opposition.* Whitbread was convinced that in

* In the final exchange between Talleyrand and Lauderdale, after Fox's death,

allowing Lauderdale to make a stand on *uti possidetis* and thereby
to break the negotiations, the Foxites in the Ministry of All the
Talents were breaking with the spirit of Fox. For the remaining
years of his political life Whitbread was to stand out as the
unrelenting opponent of the war, and, at any rate in his own
opinion, to be the stern, unbending disciple of the master he had
buried in Westminster Abbey. He had perhaps evidence of this
particular discipleship between himself and Fox in words of
praise and approbation from the master : we know it from a
letter, published four decades after Whitbread's death, when
Fox in reference to one of Whitbread's speeches in favour of
peace with revolutionary France said 'Whitbread did very well
indeed'.[4]

The full correspondence between Yarmouth, Lauderdale and
the French Government was published in the middle of December 1806. Whitbread at once wrote to Grey :

I could wish you had told me that a great part of Lauderdale's share of
the Correspondence had been forged. I confess I have read it with
astonishment and disapprobation and there must be a great deal indeed
to be produced in the Publication you will give to the World to
reconcile me to the manner in which L. conducted himself. I am
the more astonished and disappointed, because you have repeatedly
mentioned his conduct in such high Terms. I wish I had been for the
time a Man of Rank and Consequence to have tried my hand at the same
game. I am sorry to the greatest degree for the Impression which the
Papers given by the French have made upon me from the moment of
Lauderdale's arrival.*

emphasis was laid on the wishes of Fox, Talleyrand saying that Fox 'had nothing
to add to his glory, except the reconciliation of the two nations'. In reply Lauderdale
said that he had no authority to mention the subject but from twenty-six years
intimate connection with Mr. Fox he was convinced that he would have given him
the same orders as he had received from the Government based on the conviction
that peace was impracticable.

    * Durham. Since Whitbread evidently felt that he was debarred by lack of rank
from the highest political influence it is fair to point out that Lauderdale was the
grandson of a silk mercer; he married 'a nice, little painted doll' — the daughter of
a Post Office official. His own manners were described by an aristocratic observer
as 'coarse'. Although most of Fox's intimates were men of rank, Whitbread was
mistaken in thinking that rank unlocked the door to political power for the Whigs :
it was rather private friendship — at any rate so far as both Lauderdale and
Yarmouth were concerned. It also seems possible that Whitbread was considered

In his reply Grey said:

I shall deeply regret your taking a part if you should feel yourself compelled to do so, in which I really believe you will not find yourself supported by the opinion of any one man whose opinion you would think worth having.[5]

For Whitbread the risk of being in a minority was never a deterrent: rather he regarded this as one clear call for action. He accordingly made his speech on 5 January 1807, and it fills thirty-four columns of *Hansard*. His chief point was that the English plenipotentiaries had made a mistake in rupturing the negotiations on a general basis (*uti possidetis*) without moving forward to more precise details and finding out exactly what the French were prepared to yield or to hold. He spoke of the time when Fox was really too ill to handle the negotiations as 'the political death of Mr. Fox'. He began by emphasising the pain he felt in separating himself from his political friends — 'my known love and enthusiastic veneration for the dead: my close connection with, and affectionate friendship for the living [Grey]'; but he went on that his private feelings only revealed his motives, which he described on this occasion as 'unmixed and sacred duty'. To Lee Antonie he wrote: 'I very much wish you to hear the sentiments I shall have to express upon that occasion if my powers are not wholly overcome by the mortification I feel in differing from those I so dearly love'.[6] He said that he had particularly rejoiced when the Ministry of All the Talents was formed because 'it opened the way to a pacification with France'. As always in his speeches there was sound sense reinforced by experience and knowledge of human nature.

SIR, I am upon principle, as well as from feeling, in all transactions of life — public as well as private — an enemy to perpetual and endless suspicion . . . there is such a thing as for a man to become the dupe of

as a possible negotiator by the Government and that the objection was not rank but the pull of Lady Elizabeth. Writing to Lord Grenville in August 1806 Grey said: 'Whitbread certainly would do extremely well, but the state of my sister's health is such, that I am sure he would not on any account leave England.' (Historical Manuscript Commission, (Fortescue), vol. viii.).

his own distrust, and that is in my opinion the most disgraceful as well as the most fatal of all kinds of dupery.

Then he burst out,

Good God if peace be not the issue of the contest, whither are we hurrying? Contemplate, sir, if you can with composure those two mighty empires exerting their utmost efforts, each for the destruction of the other; and think upon it, if you can without horror, that before the contest be ended, one or the other must be destroyed. Sir, this is a catastrophe I can not bring my mind to anticipate without sensations of the deepest anguish.

And perhaps from the drift towards the dark, taken by the world in the Twentieth Century, we should recognise the force of the two sentences which follow with a vision of wars only to be ended by unconditional surrender.

It is a prospect which, I do not think, with the blessing of God, it is necessary, even in the present disastrous state of the world to look forward to. If it be, how trifling are the woes and calamities, already suffered by mankind, to those which are yet to come.

Whitbread admitted that his views were peculiar, but he did not divide the House and confessed that he would be content if it were recorded in the journals of Parliament that there were some, however few, who held such opinions. Canning, always a dangerous foe of Whitbread, shed crocodile tears at Whitbread's plight 'left alone in opinions which he had held for so many years in common with those who sit around him'. The Secretary of State for Foreign Affairs refused to be drawn : Grey did not speak. William Roscoe, the Liverpool radical and slightly pompous historian of the Medici said of this speech 'Whitbread seemed while delivering it to be inspired'.[7]

In this same session of Parliament, within six weeks of his speech on peace with France he embarked on a great speech advocating domestic reform which showed at once the sincerity and benevolence of his mind. With the experience which he had gained in Bedfordshire and with the help of his friend Wilshere he launched a far-reaching scheme for the reform of the Poor Laws. The Elizabethan conception that the able-bodied poor should be compelled to work (if need be in some kind of communal enterprise in the workhouse) and that relief from the locality should be paid for the aged and impotent still prevailed. In his speech Whitbread pointed out that the total population in England and Wales — excluding those serving in the Army and Navy — was 8,870,000 in 1803. Out of those almost one in seven were receiving parochial relief. The cost of this was £4,267,000 which was almost double the amount which was paid in the 1780's. The spread of relief on this scale was partly caused by war distress and possibly (as Whitbread hinted) by a wave of helplessness which had weakened the independent spirit of the labouring poor. He denied that in the proposals, which he was putting forward, he was a 'visionary perfectionist. I know the laws of God to be immutable, and bow to their uncontroulable force. I believe man to be born to labour as the sparks fly upwards : that a certain portion of misery is inseparable from mortality : and that all plans for the lodging, cloathing and feeding of all mankind, with what may be called comfort, are quite impossible in practice'. He thought that people who believed this could be compared to some of the convicts in New South Wales who laboured under the unaccountable delusion that next door to where they toiled was a land where earth brought forth her fruits without the aid of man.

He included in his measure some sensible proposals for reforming the assessment for rates and one, which roused the antagonism of Cobbett, to give a plural vote to those assessed at the top scale. He defined his objective as being 'to exalt the character of the lower classes of the community'. To this end he advocated the establishment of schools in every parish; attendance at them should not be compulsory but they should be organised on the principles of Lancaster's school in the Borough Road which had attracted the favourable notice of the Whig aristocracy and especially of the Duke of Bedford. Lancaster's innovation lay in children being taught by monitors or pupil-teachers. He then urged that the labouring poor should be given the chance to taste 'the sweets of ownership'. He supported the idea, which was then attracting attention, that the countryman should be given the chance of part ownership in cows. He also urged that savings banks, under the Post Office, should be established for the labouring classes. He was critical of the friendly societies, which in those days partly filled the need for encouraging the people's savings. His objection to these was interesting for a brewer: he thought that their meetings always in a public-house were too frequent. 'I do not wish that the temptations to indulgence, in which the head of the family can alone partake, should be multiplied.'

Whitbread was never the man to shun an innovation because it was unorthodox. Mr. J. L. Hammond says that his proposals for stimulating thrift were a strange medley of enlightenment and childishness.[8] Among the latter was the suggestion that magistrates could give rewards (up to £20) with a badge of good conduct for labourers who had brought up their families without parish help. The magistrates were also to be allowed to give a meritorious labourer the present of a hat or of a parchment certificate to hang in his cottage. Mr. Hammond does Whitbread considerable injustice when he accuses him of proposing that a labourer refusing to work or denied work through misconduct should be branded with the emblem 'criminal poor'. In his speech he alluded to a provision of Edward VI by which anyone found idle was to be branded by a red-hot iron with the letter S — standing for slave. He called this an enactment of such atrocious cruelty that those who had not read it could not believe it. His own proposal (though odd) was not in line with the savagery of the Tudor boy-king's advisers. The criminal poor were to wear a badge on their clothes which stated the parish to which the man belonged and the crime of which he was guilty.

In opening his speech he said that he was attempting a solution of one of the most difficult of all political problems; namely to reduce the sum of human vice and misery — a problem which he called 'one of the most interesting propositions which ever occupied the attention of any deliberative assembly upon earth'.

Much of the foundation of facts, on which the speech rested, was prepared by his friend and neighbour William Wilshere: he alluded to this — 'in every part of my task I am under the greatest obligation to a very valuable friend'. In May 1806 he had told the Commons that he hoped to introduce a measure of this kind — 'I have had a plan of this nature in contemplation for some years past, which has occupied much of my attention, but I found it extremely difficult to reduce it to a shape, in which to offer it for the consideration of Parliament.'

He wrote to Grey two days before he spoke. He said that he had told no one of what he planned to say (except those who had helped him) 'because I know how flat the subject is. . . . All I ask of you and your friends is a patient and candid hearing. I have laboured much at it. . . .' He did not think a discussion between them would have been useful 'standing as I do. I am sure that neither you nor your colleagues would have found time to have entered thoroughly into the subject with me'.[9] Grey was primarily interested in foreign and political issues, and seemingly little moved by social and economic ones. The contrast between him and Whitbread is illustrated by the attitude of the two men to Malthus. This clergyman believed that all the mischief of the times derived from the increase in population, and that any increase in productivity would be followed by a rising birth-rate — that 'revolting ratio' as it was called at the time. Malthus had also proposed that within a year after the passing of an Act to reform the Poor Law no child, born in wedlock, should ever be entitled to parish assistance and that in the case of illegitimate children the time should be extended to two years. Whitbread rejected this, but in his speech he paid a warm tribute to Malthus, though he thought that any man reading him ought to 'place a strict guard over his heart lest it become hardened against the distresses of his fellow creatures'. Two years later Malthus went to stay at Howick and Creevey told Whitbread that 'a better man than Malthus does not exist' but that he had been perfectly shocked at the opinions he heard delivered by Grey.

N

'He could not have believed it, had they not been delivered to himself. What infatuation so to expose himself to such a critic!'[10] Replying, Whitbread wrote: 'If the sort of opinions which our friend suffers himself at times to utter are genuine it is fatal — if they are not it is very foolish.'[11]

The fate of Whitbread's Bill was settled in August 1807 when it was thrown out in the House of Lords on the motion of the future Prime Minister — Lord Liverpool. Whitbread had written to Grey that he was well aware of 'the tiresome trial' to which he exposed himself 'in an encounter with all the country-gentlemen in the House'. But in fact the country gentlemen — in particular Spencer-Stanhope from Yorkshire and Bathurst from the west country — spoke strongly in favour of Whitbread's proposals. After the Second Reading the Bill was printed, and sent to quarter sessions for the consideration of the justices. In the *Annual Register* Whitbread's performance was described as 'very long, elaborate and animated'. And he who arraigned Melville must have been singularly gratified by receiving a warm letter of compliment and congratulation from the Scottish lord's predecessor in affliction — Warren Hastings.[12] One unexpected consequence of the speech was a stir among the gaitered clergy. In his speech Whitbread had contrasted the inadequacy of education in England with the far better system prevailing in Scotland. The Archbishop of Canterbury sent a circular letter to all the bishops asking them to find out from the beneficed clergy in their diocese the number of schools in which the poor were taught to read. The Church had a responsibility (though not an exclusive responsibility) for such voluntary education as existed. But otherwise Whitbread's Bill (though a herald of the future) fell with that flatness which he had expected.

And now unhappily the Government of All the Talents was plainly drifting towards extinction. The Cabinet seemed incapable of making an effort; it lacked the will to live. In an effort to soothe the Irish and to satisfy their Whig following the Cabinet decided to make a gesture to the Roman Catholics.

By the Catholic Relief Act of 1793 Pitt had allowed Catholic officers to serve in Ireland with the Army: it was proposed to extend this concession to those serving outside Ireland, and to extend it upwards beyond the rank of colonel. The King, almost blind, did not immediately spring to arms when the paper with these proposals was laid before him. However Addington, now Lord Sidmouth,* with the treachery engendered by all coalitions, went to warn him. The King then demanded a written undertaking from the Cabinet that they would never again raise the question. All was over. George III told Grey that he might explain to the House of Commons that 'in consequence of what had passed the King had sent for persons not in the number of his present Ministers'.[13] Indignation against this intervention by the Crown was general in the House of Commons. Lord Temple wrote: 'the country gentlemen and the saints [Wilberforce and the devout evangelicals] are now with us but if Easter is suffered to intervene [before they are given a lead] their anger will cool.'† Easter came and went but no lead came. Instead the new Government under the Duke of Portland, elderly and ailing, showed unexpected vigour by dissolving Parliament in order to catch the horrible wind of 'No Popery'. It was a disgraceful manoeuvre, ranking with the tactical elections of the present century.

In those days of rotten boroughs and constituencies where the personality and reputation of the candidate could carry the day (as was the case with Bedford), 'snap' or tactical elections were less lethal to the House of Commons than, say, the Coupon Election of 1918. The election of 1807 did not sweep the Whigs out of Parliament but it gave them some heavy knocks. Grey himself was one of the victims of the field of battle in Northumberland and, wealthy as he was, Whitbread felt the strain of

* Though Sidmouth threatened to resign, the King ordered him to stay.

† In those days the opinions of the Members for county constituencies carried a little more weight and influence than Members for boroughs. The support of these county Members meant something more than a mere tally of numbers. As some trifling indication of their distinction they alone were allowed to wear spurs in the House of Commons. (Lord Colchester, *Diary and Correspondence* (1861), i, 45.)

two elections in such rapid succession. To a relation who owed him money he wrote 'This sudden and unexpected dissolution of Parliament puts one so much to one's trumps in every way, that one is obliged among other things to look out for money to buy ribbons etc.'[14] Bedford electioneering was a little more expensive than Whitbread's airy allusion to ribbons might imply. The headquarters of the Whigs in Bedford at election time was at The Swan Hotel and bills for the festivities leading up to Whitbread's return have survived. Scanning the one for 1802 the reader may be reminded that as the crow flies Bedford is not far from Eatanswill. There were three days of what might be called roistering, when the faithful wearers of the buff and blue enjoyed meat, fowls, ducks, ham, tongue, plum puddings, fruit pies with port, sherry, spirits, cider and 136 gallons of porter. Eighty-one wine glasses were broken, and it is perhaps surprising that the bill was not more than £250.* Although Whitbread had no difficulty at Bedford (he was always returned there unopposed throughout his life) the Church opposition could have been disagreeably formidable. Even though a contest was not held, great importance was attached to the preliminary canvas, which Whitbread called 'an irksome labour'. In the 1806 election he told Lee Antonie that there would be 567 visits to pay which he described as 'two good days work for those who are not bunglers'. Even the most ardent electioneerers of the twentieth century would have to salute the exertions of these candidates from the early nineteenth century. Lord John Russell, a boy of fifteen during the 1807 election, was told that in Bedfordshire county the Tory polled no fewer than seventeen divines on one day, and General Fitzpatrick only narrowly saved the seat. The clergy, who were the best-educated professional class in the country, were strangely narrow in their politics. They were the type of men who began any formal dinner with two toasts : the first 'Church and King', the second 'The Two Universities'. Whitbread was able, through his friend Garrard, to detach one clergyman from the Tory side. In 1807 the

* See Appendix 2, p. 317.

election in Yorkshire was fought on a prodigious scale costing Lord Harewood, the father of the Tory candidate, £100,000 and a similar sum was spent by Lord Fitzwilliam, the father of the Whig candidate. The latter limped to victory by a few hundred votes out of a poll of 23,000, thanks to the support of the West Riding. Garrard's brother-in-law, Thomas Gilpin, wrote grandiloquently to Whitbread that as a result of a letter from Garrard 'I attended at the hustings, accompanied by the eldest son of Sir William Milner, and gave a *plumper* for Lord Milton in right of my freehold — the Vicarage of Kirkby-upon-Wharfe.'[15]

The cry of 'No Popery' was still capable of travelling over the British Isles with the blind fury of fire among the stubble. As the twentieth century found a label for the Coupon Election of 1918 and the Red Letter Election of 1924 and the Bankers' Election of 1931 so the election of 1807 might be called the Establishment Election. The King's name was freely used: the protestant character of the deity was emphasised on every Tory husting. Especially offensive was the campaign of Spencer Perceval, the little, chauvelinesque person who was Chancellor of the Exchequer and the leader of the new Government in the Commons. He sat for Northampton, and told the electors that 'it was a peculiarly sacred duty of His Majesty to defend the established religion of his kingdom'. Against his copy of this, Whitbread has written: 'Madam, 'tis all a plan. He made the giants first and then did kill them.'[16] The election infuriated the Foxite Whigs but discomfited them. Thomas Grenville, in his peculiar, hypochondriacal way, expressed views which were general 'little as my health can now bear the attendance of Parliament, my indignation may supply to my constitution more strength than naturally belongs to it'. He had explained that he could only attend a long night's sitting at the cost of a week's illness. (He lived to be 91). The Whigs, as has been said, were not routed, but they returned to Westminster from the general election in some disorder. Anger and indignation are seldom the best binding material for an opposition: their temper availed them little as they watched their opponents guiding the Government with some competence through perilous seas which attracted many a waverer on to their side. Moreover the overriding issue of the day was the war with Napoleon, and as the Whig Party was now broadly speaking in agreement with the Government over the war, there was no commanding issue on which the Opposition could rally themselves against the Government. Their ranks were not completely shattered by the election of 1807, but their spirit had gone.

CHAPTER FIFTEEN

Creevey and Num-Num

I N Parliament the next five years, from 1807 until the murder of Perceval in 1812, were for the Whigs the years of lost opportunity. As Byron wrote in *Don Juan* :

> Nought's permanent among the human race,
> Except the Whigs *not* getting into place.

If we accept, as we must, that the existence of Portland's Government and Perceval's which followed it, rested on terror of Napoleon and the feeling that a change of Cabinet might weaken the nation's resolve for battle we have to admit that the Government completely lacked the air of a warlike administration. The Prime Minister was incapacitated by illness from attending to business; as Lord Holland amusingly put it, 'he had left a couch of pain' to preside over the Government. His Cabinet was an amalgam of Pittites, Canningites and Addingtonians kept together not by leadership but by fear. They made the most appalling mistakes and their crowning folly was the expedition against the Scheldt, commanded by that strange, slothful Pitt — Lord Chatham. The disgrace of the whole enterprise led to a duel between Canning and Castlereagh and put the extinguisher on the flickering life of poor Portland. Perceval, who succeeded him, was rather a churchman than a statesman. Does he not still raise an indulgent smile for his comment on attending the anniversary service, when Parliament implored God's forgiveness for the execution of King Charles I, 'the attendance is discreditably thin' ? Though never a man of shining talents, he rallied the Government after the fiasco of the Scheldt. In a sense the strength of the Governments of Portland

and Perceval lay in their very weakness. The Opposition, with good reason, thought that their feebleness must make them turn to some new combination of men, and that the moderate Whigs might after all find themselves called to Whitehall as part of a new coalition. Just as the Government was held in place by the nation's fear of Napoleon so the Opposition was confirmed in its feebleness by fear — fear that too assertive an Opposition would alarm the country, engrossed by Napoleon, and might block the path to office in any new combination which might evolve. The distant lure of office dulled the sparkle of Opposition.

For the Whigs the problem of leadership was immediate and insoluble. It was immediate because Whitbread's father-in-law, Lord Grey, died at Howick on 14 November 1807 and Charles Grey moved to the muted splendours of the Lords, 'where there was just enough light to make darkness visible'.[1] A whole decade later Lord Holland was lamenting, with ample reason, his departure from the Commons, 'his place has never been adequately supplied'. Apart from his gifts as a debater and orator, Grey's strength rested on the confidence both of the Grenvilles and the Foxite Whigs. Now it is obvious that for prominence — there were the impeachment and his speeches on peace and the Poor Law — Whitbread had no competitor for the position as leader in the Commons in succession to Grey. He had long been a Member of Parliament : he had no rival in the faithfulness of his attachment to Fox. He was scarcely considered. Lord Holland, in reference to the possibility used the harsh adjective 'obnoxious', though it must be remembered that in politics people tend to become obnoxious to their colleagues when they grow popular. Whitbread had certainly achieved popularity in the newspapers and with the public at large. Holland went on to say that for independent-minded and well-educated men Whitbread was too vain, too rash. Thomas Grenville wrote to his brother Lord Grenville about Whitbread 'I must fairly say I think the unpopularity and impracticability of the man to be such as would render it quite impossible to act

with him'.² Of course it could be argued that, although Whitbread would have antagonised the sober elements in the Party,
his very violence and relish for battle might have been
generally stimulating to the cause. Those, who believed this,
could certainly look backwards to Fox, to whom timidity and
caution were unknown words.

But the problem cut deeper than any mere choice of an
individual. Grenville did not think that their army was
sufficiently united 'to proceed to the choice of a new general'.
Although blistering in his comment on Portland's Government
'whose system I abhor and whose talents I despise' he expressed
what was uppermost in the minds of many Members of both
Houses of Parliament at that time 'I am alarmed beyond all
power of expression at the state of the country, both internal
and external'.³ Possibly in those circumstances the Opposition
might have been sensible to choose no leader, but they did what
was almost inevitable — they compromised. They appointed an
able but colourless man to the lead. George Ponsonby was an
ill-kempt, hunting gentleman from Ireland, related to Lady
Grey. He had that slovenliness which is attractive in Ireland, but
is noticeable outside it. In the House of Commons he used to sit
on the front-bench, cross-legged and displaying conspicuously
dirty boots. He wore the customary tall hat but it was old and
unbrushed, and he had all the air of a Georgian farmer. As the
editor of *The Times* remarked, Ponsonby would have done more
service to the common-weal by killing a fox in the county of
Kildare than by leading the Whig opposition.⁴ The best to be
said of him was noticed by Lord Holland — he was a 'handy'
speaker.⁵ He had been Lord Chancellor of Ireland — an office
which carried a comfortable pension of £4,000 a year, but
otherwise fortune had not favoured him : a clumsy man, he once
had to write to Whitbread and say that he had been knocked
down in Clifford Street by the pole of a coach and thrown under
the horses. 'I am a good deal hurt but not *very* much.'⁶ To
Creevey he was 'the old drone'.⁷

> And Ponsonby leaves the debate when he sets,
> Just as dark as it was when he rose.*

Poor Whitbread to be harnessed to such a leader! But as Lord Holland (who understood human nature) implies, he may have been comforted by the feeling that his own abilities would shine more clearly with a nominal than with a real leader. As soon as the obsequies of the old general at Howick were complete Grey was writing to London 'Whitbread has just left Northumberland and is very intently determined upon some measure in Parliament for peace'.[8] There was no political reconciliation of Whitbread and his brother-in-law beside the open grave of the general.

Two people attempted to improve matters. The Duke of Bedford had written a month before the general's death saying, 'I can not bring myself to believe that there is any *political separation* between you and Grey'. We can hardly fail to admire the aristocratic straightforwardness of the duke when he said that if he had differed from Whitbread on any political issue they had differed but yet saw the point in question 'from the same unswerving patriotism, the same ardent zeal in the cause of your country and the same attachment to the genuine principles of liberty and the English constitution, he felt that as it was with him, so it was with Grey.[9]

The other pacifier was more unexpected — George Tierney, who long ago had exchanged shots with Pitt, and had then disgraced himself in Whig eyes by serving under Addington. The Foxite Whigs were said to have given vent to their feelings by calling their dogs Tierney. As was also true of Whitbread his origins were commercial, and he was rich; this was supposed to explain why the Whig hierarchy viewed him askance, when he returned to the Whig fold. Creevey always called him old Cole or Mrs. Cole — after an old lady in one of Foote's farces fond of proclaiming her respectability. Creevey once wrote to Whitbread to say that at a convivial gathering at

---

* A parody of Thomas Moore's 'Believe me if all . . .'.

Southill the Whig hierarchy believed that a number of impious jokes were in circulation about Whig personalities and 'that we did not scruple to libel the purest and most genuine of all the Whigs by calling him 'Mother Cole'.[10] Like Ponsonby 'Cole' was Irish, but he was able, sarcastic and perhaps in consequence mistrusted. Brougham noticed that he lacked fervour and thought that this made his consistent opposition from 1807 onwards the more remarkable and commendable.[11]

He wrote to Whitbread on 16 December saying in his sarcastic way 'I begin to think Geo : Ponsonby will succeed to the high and lucrative post of leader to the opposition.' He and Whitbread had evidently discussed the whole question previously in Dover Street — especially about Whitbread's feelings for Grey. After this Tierney wrote to Grey saying 'I have seen Whitbread and all I need *now* state of a very long conversation is that he has authorised me to declare he will support G.P. as he did you, that is reserving his own right to express his own sentiments on points whereon his opinions are fixed.' G.P. is Ponsonby, and the point of his underlining *now* was that he was reserving till they met an account of why Whitbread still felt aggrieved with Grey. In his reply Grey went over all the old ground with which we are familiar, the early friendship — the relationship — the distress which he felt because Whitbread thought that he had been remiss in 'pushing him forward'. Then he adds 'Nothing would have given me so much pleasure as to see him succeed me, but I felt that it was impossible from many communications I received on the subject — and nobody knows better than you how hopeless the attempt would have been.' Tierney told Whitbread that he recognised the danger of passing on the contents of a private letter. 'I have done it because I have felt it to be the surest method I could adopt to satisfy your mind. . . . When you next meet I trust it will be as it was in old times.' The letter was written on the day before Christmas — the eve of goodwill.[12]

Whitbread replied to Tierney in a Christmas letter of temper.

MY DEAR TIERNEY,

I have received your letter, and am highly gratified by the friendly disposition you manifest towards me, and the pains you take to smooth the little political roughnesses there are between me and Grey. As to personal differences there can be none, for I have the greatest possible affection and respect for him, and so I am sure has he for me. What I complain of is that he does not understand my feelings upon subjects of this sort, and of course can not enter into them. I want not to be Leader of his party — If he in the warmth of his heart, and an estimation of my fitness far different from what he has, had pressed upon me to take his place, and pressed upon his friends my adoption, I am so well aware of the sort of reasons which prevail against me, and of the difficulties attending upon the situation itself, that I declare to God I would not have accepted it, if indeed there is anything to accept. But I am mortified in supposing that he, above all other persons, questions my capacity; and I am disappointed because he does not show at any time (except in very particular emergencies) any belief that I could assist him. I can not have a stronger proof of his misconception of my feelings than his letter to you furnishes. He imagines I want him *to push me forward*. I neither wish him to do it, nor has he the power. I shall find my level and always have found it without his assistance, and my estimation with the country I would not change for his, however I may and do acknowledge his superiority in many respects to be very very great.

I need not elucidate my meaning to you; when you know that he thought a peerage would be an acceptable thing to me : and he was so good as to say that he had talked to Fox about it, and that in time after the impeachment it might be managed. I could not but be indignant at the offer especially so made : and I was immediately convinced that as an active friend he could have no opinion of me at all, or he would not have dreamt of disabling me, and disgracing me. . . . His manner too has been so unlike poor Fox's. . . .[13]

Poor old 'Cole' could only lament that he had made matters worse, assure Whitbread that he had misunderstood Grey's feelings and add that Whitbread's hostility to Grey was plainly of long standing and deep rooted.[14] Perhaps the psychologist would see in this antagonism to Charles Grey, some hurrying shadow across the mind — some hint of the cloud which was to obliterate reason. But attempting an explanation which is more straightforward we may suppose that Whitbread felt deeply chagrined at being passed over in favour of a man like George Ponsonby. It is perfectly true that he had agreed to serve under him, as Tierney says, but was he wrong to think that the friend of his boyhood might have struck a stronger blow on his behalf? Did he perhaps also feel, as he heard Tierney explaining that he was 'not acceptable', that Grey — applauded by the Foxites and respected by the Grenvilles — had only won those encomiums by sacrificing the basic principle of Fox — peace.

Whitbread was not slow in distinguishing himself from his new leader — and indeed from his brother-in-law. At the end of 1807 Austria had somewhat unexpectedly sought to mediate between Napoleon and England through her ambassador at St. James's, Count Starhemberg. If this deserved the description of a move for peace it was effectively blocked by Canning, the successor of Grey at the Foreign Office, who denied that any tangible overture had been made. Parliament met on the last day of January 1808, and in preparation for this Lord Grenville gave a great dinner for his followers and comrades. Camelford House, which he had acquired through his wife — the great house looking across Hyde Park from Park Lane with its memories of Chatham and the Cornish remoteness of the Pitts — was one of those fine, aristocratic establishments thickly peopled with men-servants and maid-servants and with great boilings and roastings downstairs which made it easy to give a political dinner with the numbers undetermined. Invitations were haphazard. Guests arrived knowing more or less who was expected and who would be welcome. There was some apprehension lest Sheridan — never averse from the white and the red both in food and drink — might appear forgetting that he had made some insulting allusions to the Grenville sinecures in the House of Commons. The new leader, Ponsonby, did not make a very good impression by assuring one of the principal guests that he had met Sheridan in a drunken carouse at Brooks's: Ponsonby had cautiously avoided drinking, and then had gone home and written down what Sheridan had said of politics. Although the members of the Whig hierarchy were

always nervous of Sheridan, their generous nature was repelled
by Ponsonby's rather underhand methods of pitting sobriety
against conviviality. On this auspicious day Whitbread had
come up from Southill and had chanced to meet Sheridan who
said 'you have a fine field open to you about your peace'. He
then spoke of the Austrian negotiation, shed a few tears over
'the poor Danes', who, in the previous September had sur-
rendered their fleet to the English, after the bombardment of
Copenhagen, and cheerfully added 'we shall all be ruined in less
than eighteen months and I am now going to dine at Carlton
House'. (After the death of Fox, Sheridan was the rather
uncertain link between the Whig Party and the Prince of
Wales.) When Whitbread got to Dover Street he found on his
table a card of invitation to dine with Lord Grenville that
evening, and a note from Grey pressing him to go. 'I dressed
myself as fast as I could and arrived before dinner was served.'*
The company was the usual Whig hierarchy with both Ponsonby
and Tierney attending. 'We dined cheerfully and comfortably
and it was not till some time after dinner that any conversation
of importance took place.' Lord Grey then animadverted 'in the
most peremptory tone' against a demonstration which had been
held at Leeds. 'The terms and the manner employed were both
of a nature calculated to excite me, and I told him, after such a
declaration, I should think I did not treat him — or the company
present — well if I were silent, and allowed any of them to
suppose I agreed in the doctrine of Lord Grey.' Whitbread
stated that he thought that it had been proved in earlier times
in the political lives of some who were present and older than
himself that petitions were productive of the best results.

* This, and what follows, is taken from a letter written by Whitbread which is at
Chewton. For some reason Whitbread seems to have been at pains to conceal the
recipient of this letter. His secretary has carefully obliterated the name, which
makes the text here and there difficult to decipher. As it begins 'My dear Sir' the
letter can not have been written to an intimate or to a peer. It was possibly written
to Creevey or Brougham, who were now coming into Whitbread's confidence; a
much more likely suggestion (though it can only be a guess) is J. W. Ward — the
future Lord Dudley. He was a young Member of Parliament moving at this time
uncertainly between the Whig Party and Canning.

Whitbread of course meant here the pressure of outside public opinion on Parliament. The host, Lord Grenville noticed Whitbread's violence of view and expression with some distaste.*

Earlier in the letter he had given his reasons for trusting Starhemberg and for believing that the French were serious. All was destroyed by Canning; his part in disrupting the negotiations Whitbread called 'a compound of insolence, rashness and folly'. He went on to describe how later that evening he met Grey and told him that there was a necessity of 'maintaining a clear distinction between the Foxite part of the Party from the Grenvilles'. Grey on the other hand spoke of 'the propriety of merging the distinction at which I expressed my abhorrence'.[15]

On the day following the dinner Whitbread with the ex-Lord Chancellor Erskine and George Tierney went round to see Lord Hutchinson. He was a mixture of diplomat and general who had fought the French, knew the northern capitals and was in the offing at Tilsit when Napoleon and the Tsar had come to terms on the raft. He was a myopic bachelor, as slovenly in his dress as Ponsonby, and perhaps Creevey had no great cause for alarm when he described him as Mrs. Creevey's 'chief flirt'. But for all his personal defects he was a direct and forceful man who understood Europe. As soon as the three men were ushered in to see him he began 'There is but one sound man among you by God! and that is Whitbread'. Erskine chimed in 'Damme I always thought with him and everybody knows it'. Lord Hutchinson then went in detail into the position of England 'which he truly views as deplorable' and showed how vilely the fortunes of the country have been sacrificed.

Such words were not lost on Whitbread. In the House of Commons on 3 February he said of the attack on Copenhagen 'the English have behaved like shabby thieves'. Of Canning, at whom the description was particularly aimed, he said earlier that

* Lord Holland, *Memoirs of Whig Party*, (1852), ii, 242. Grey, describing the scene to his wife, wrote: 'Grenville seemed quite dumb-foundered. . . . You may guess I was on thorns, as the vehemence of his manner was more particularly applied to me.'

he was 'little calculated from his temper, his feelings and the whole tenour of his political life' to guide the nation into the path of peace.

A few weeks later, in an allusion to Canning's over-elaborate style of wit and oratory, he described him as 'the gilt ginger-bread on the other side of the House'. On 29 February he made what was perhaps his most powerful speech in favour of a negotiated peace. It occupies fifty columns of Hansard. He began by admitting that he was by nature sanguine in the face of political difficulties, and he thought that no one should embark on public life unless he was determined never to despair of the public welfare. All Portland's cabinet was comprehensively and scathingly attacked. They were, he thought, expressly designated for the consummation of the nation's doom. Canning received Whitbread's sharpest blows, and Whitbread spoke scornfully of the smartness and satire in all his despatches. 'I deny the insane proposition that peace is more dangerous than war. I am convinced that in everlasting war we must find our ruin.' He stoutly denied that there was anything miraculous about Napoleon's successes : they were merely the consequence of a man of extraordinary talents taking advantage of the follies and blunders of the rest of mankind.

> 'The lucky have their moments, those they use
> The unlucky have their hours, and those they lose.'

He paid a powerful tribute to Fox — 'I willingly acknowledge myself his true and genuine disciple . . . would to God I could feel myself as I have often done, secure under the impenetrable aegis of his eloquence . . . I am not the apologist of France, I am the advocate of England.' But the advocate of England could only muster 58 votes in the lobby against 217. Almost alone of the leading Whigs Sheridan supported him *in toto*.

His exertions for peace brought him a strange admirer. The Duke of Queensberry, 'Old Q', watching the world go by from the corner of Piccadilly and Park Lane, looking back on a long life of debauchery and pleasure, was paying the price for these indulgences with a severe accumulation of infirmities. He was blind in one eye, deaf in one ear, toothless and physically a ruin, relying for continued existence on the ministrations of a friendly Piccadilly chemist. But all who met this remarkable man agreed that for all the disintegration of his system his mind was unimpaired. After he had seen a letter from Whitbread to Lord Holland about the state of the country and the chance of peace he wrote to Whitbread : 'I agree entirely with you in every word, and in every opinion, but I am particularly pleased with what you say concerning this being the very moment for proposing peace.'[16] This duke's lasciviousness may have become proverbial but he seems to have combined it with some fairly sound political sense.

As Whitbread opposed the war so he opposed the brutalisation of warfare which, after a time, is the inevitable vulture on the field of battle. The inclusion of jesuit's bark, or quinine, in the embargo on goods going to France aroused his particular indignation. In the House of Commons he said that such an embargo meant 'war with the helpless, the sick and the hospitals — one at which the feelings of all mankind would revolt. It was reviving the savage practices of remote antiquity, and substituting them for that modern civilisation which rendered even war itself less horrible'.

The choice of Ponsonby for the lead and the realisation that he was 'obnoxious' to many of his comrades had the inevitable consequence of strengthening Whitbread's radical independence, of turning him away from what he called the Whig 'grandees' to association with wilder men. Rather strangely that engaging, quizzical man Thomas Creevey emerges from this period for the remainder of Whitbread's life as his closest friend. Creevey as letter-writer and diarist is so diverting and entertaining that the more serious side to his character is overlooked. At this time he was more political than social : mischievous certainly but with strongly held radical opinions. By his enemies he was called the Joe Miller of the House of Commons. (Joe Miller gave his name to an eighteenth-century

o

jest-book, and his name was used to imply a purveyor of stale jokes.) His wife was a Northumbrian, widow of William Ord and daughter of Charles Brandling, both Members of Parliament. These origins probably explain her intimate friendship with Lady Elizabeth Whitbread (which dated back before her marriage to Creevey) and with Whitbread — to both of whom she was Num-Num (or Nummy). The sparkle of Creevey has possibly blinded later generations to the charm of Mrs. Creevey's letters : those which have survived show her to have been full of perception and gifted with a humorous tolerance of life. She was much admired by the Prince of Wales and had been greatly in the confidence of Georgiana, Duchess of Devonshire. The duchess is understood to have given the full story of her relations with Charles Grey to Mrs. Creevey.[17] From 1810 onwards her health gave anxiety. 'She labours under a painful relaxation of the muscles of the neck, which makes her head droop. He is all attention and kindness.'[18]

Creevey held a minor post in the Talents — he was secretary of the Board of Control — the body which supervised the East India Company. After the fall of that Government he joined Whitbread as one of the critics of the Whig leadership. Creevey, with his house in Great George Street, his membership of Brooks's and his easy manner in political society, was singularly well placed to know everything that was afoot. Whitbread, immersed during the recesses in Bedfordshire affairs, used Creevey both as an informant and a counsellor. As early as the impeachment of Melville he was writing to Creevey from Southill for help on legal precedents — 'I have no light of my own to shine by and want to borrow some rays of you'. Thereafter he regularly writes 'tell me everything you hear', 'Pray, write, write, write'. And those familiar with Mr. Creevey's calligraphy will understand the full force of Whitbread's gratitude when he wrote that the letter was 'not the less acceptable because it was *legible*'.[19] Creevey, with his wife and step-daughters, were constant visitors to Southill and after one visit we may picture Creevey's somewhat Liverpudlian taste in food. After thanking Whitbread for the visit, he says: 'let me present my particular thanks to Lady Elizabeth for all the pork chops, Irish stews, bubble and squeak she so graciously ordered for me'.[20] But, alas, the time was to come in Creevey's life when even these plebeian dishes were to pass beyond the range of his encumbered purse. Although it was not the cause of his embarrassment, a fine of £100 at Lancaster Assizes for libelling the Inspector of Taxes was an unpleasant burden. He had published one of his speeches in the House of Commons in which he accused this public servant of being paid a salary to screw up persons' assessments to the extent of his own imagination. No doubt he was not the first person to have such unworthy suspicions. At the same time he owed £5,000 to a fellow Member, Squire Western, or as he often playfully calls him 'Stiff-rump'. He also contrived to owe his grocer — Gray of Charing Cross—£450. 'Stiff-rump', with the help of Creevey's solicitor, found a total indebtedness of £7,000 and virtually no assets except Mrs. Creevey's £2,000 a year 'on the full extent of which he is living'. Whitbread stepped in handsomely and in addition to earlier gifts gave him £1,000 and an annuity.[21] From Brighton where he was living to economise, Creevey wrote to Whitbread on 20 January 1813:

MY DEAR WHITBREAD,

. . . Although I began by saying you should learn nothing of myself, I cannot let this occasion pass without expressing my hopes that you have not interpreted my silence, in the midst of all your goodness to me, into any want of feeling of everlasting obligation to you — The more I think of your conduct to me, the more I am convinced that no one would have behaved with such true generosity to me and, above all, I am convinced that no other human being but yourself would have accompanied his munificence with such affectionate and kind-hearted manner as you have shown to me. You may well suppose I am inspired by every possible emotion to struggle against the storm in which my carelessness has involved me, and believe me none can operate more strongly upon me than the gratitude I feel to you and the wish I have to prove worthy of your most valuable friendship.[22]

The important part of this letter is not the gratitude but the acknowledgment of the sensitive way in which Whitbread had helped his friend. Those who might — from his public career — think that Whitbread was coarse-grained will recognise that in one of the most difficult transactions between equals he showed true feeling and understanding of human nature. So far as it is possible to tell, there was never the slightest ruffling of feeling between the pensioner and paymaster. When the over-throw of Napoleon opened Europe to English travellers it was with the Creeveys that Whitbread and Lady Elizabeth went to France. A cheerful letter from Creevey, on their return, has survived.

Brighton Aug. 25 1814

DEAR WHITBREAD

I am very much delighted to hear that my fellow travellers remain in such force, and very grateful to you for telling me of it. But I am somewhat jealous that you should all be so much better than poor Num-Num and me. We have been at a considerable discount ever since you left us; sleep, sleep, sleep is all the exertion we are each of us equal to. Whether it is Beef and mutton, and port wine in opposition to French living or whether it is the early rising and little sleeping of last week I don't know but Nummy and I have not even yet a single word to throw at a dog.[23]

A little later he was writing : 'And believe Nummy and me to be ever devoted to you all.'[24]

Whitbread's intimate friendship with Creevey and the iden-tity of opinion between the two men explain why he unburdened himself to Creevey with particular frankness. In 1808 Whit-bread showed those first symptoms of illness which were to concern his friends. Just before Christmas he wrote to Creevey to say that he had renewed hunting to the great benefit of his health and 'the complete fugitation of all critical deposits' resulting from high living. But now 'the frost has come and locked up my Playthings' — a twist of nature which left him time to turn to politics. He told Creevey how much he valued his guidance because 'you are interested in my Reputation' because 'you mix more with the world than I am enabled to do from particular circumstances'. (This last is an allusion to Lady

Elizabeth's health.) He would approach the session of 1809 with confidence because of the praises of Creevey and other friends for what he had achieved in 1808. He then said that he began the session of 1808 when he was 'piqued'. He explained that he had not been anxious to lead the Opposition in the Commons especially as it would have meant being 'a slave to a Party in the Lords'. (That is probably an allusion to Grenville not to Grey.) But his 'ambition had been disappointed' by the person who had before held the place 'with so much dignity and reputation'.[25] That is of course Grey. 'We shall all find our level' were the words which he had used to Grey and he admits that in the session of 1808 he was anxious to show that 'my level was not very low'. But having satisfied himself on that score he adds 'I am no candidate for the lead'.

This letter was in reply to one from Creevey who had written 'you succeeded in showing yourself to be the strongest man in your own party and the most to be feared by your opponents'. He then went on 'but you are not aware of the perfect apathy and indifference with which all reasonable men look upon the proceedings of the House of Commons'. After alluding to 'my adoration for poor Fox' Creevey went on that the indifference of the public to what went on in the Commons derived from the great blow given to public opinion by Fox's coalition with North a quarter of a century before, and what was almost a death blow — the coalition with Grenville. (This is possibly an ungenerous comment from one who served, in minor office, in that Government.) He thought that these events had staggered the best men in the country so that Perceval, Canning and Castlereagh, 'the vapouring villains', had been able to seize power. He therefore urged Whitbread not to devote too much of his talents to 'common party questions' but to concentrate on such things as 'the frightful increase of the influence of the Crown . . . that can select the damnedest fools in England for the most important commands . . . the whole is favouritism and job in this leading article of national character and defence, the army of the country; stick to subjects like these. Your character will be a sufficient certificate of the purity of your views : you have an advantage over all other public men in never having been in office.'[26] In commenting on this Whitbread said that it was advice 'I will certainly attend to with assiduity'. In a further letter urging him to an open assault on corruption Creevey says 'it will be too mortifying if the person who in all England could make this attack with the most advantage to his country and the most honour to himself should from any over-fastidious feeling of delicacy leave so great a work to inferior and undeserving artists'. This letter reached Whitbread at Woburn 'in the midst of routs, festivities and masquerades'. Creevey replied that he had been enjoying stag-hunting with Lord Derby at The Oaks, near Epsom, and added 'Do then dear Whitbread lend yourself upon this occasion to this poor insulted country and its constitution; if fame is your object I am sure it is the road to it and if you are in pursuit of power I do from my very soul believe it the only road to it also.'[27] Replying to this letter Whitbread says : 'My object certainly is fair Fame. Neither Place nor Power I hope. I am not quite sure of the way of the former, the two latter I never expect to possess.'[28]

CHAPTER SIXTEEN

A Royal Mistress

At the very moment that this advice was being dropped into Whitbread's ear, the country had one of its periodical fits of morality, one of those obsessions which have been dubbed ridiculous by Macaulay. About this particular fit there was plenty that was ridiculous, plenty that was comical but coloured as such things generally are by murky shadows and indeed here and there tinged with pathos. The facts can be briefly told. Frederick, Duke of York, the King's second son, had the soldierly qualities of his house. George III was a civilian though a courageous one, but his uncle the Duke of Cumberland, his grandfather George II and his great-grandfather George I were all fighting men. The Duke of York had commanded in Flanders and had been made commander-in-chief of the Army in 1798 when he was in his middle thirties. All agree that in this office he showed himself popular, very industrious and efficient. He was a large, handsome man, addicted to pleasure and with his father's rather spluttering, incoherent speech. He was a conservative. His marriage, though not disastrous, was uncomfortable as his wife, niece to Frederick the Great, liked the rather insipid hills of Surrey and the society of a retinue of pet dogs.

The simple-minded believe that a prince has but to shoot a glance at a lady and she is his for the asking. The reality is different. Princes, in this respect, are curbed by notoriety : often they must rely on the good offices of their friends for any gratification of their desires. So it was that the Duke was introduced to a renowned and amusing courtesan Mary Anne Clarke. He installed her in Gloucester Place in some style,

fitting her up with — among other extravagances — plate
which had belonged to the Kings of France. After a few years of
bliss in Gloucester Place Mrs. Clarke found that her illustrious
(though not exclusive) lover had driven away. She was given
£1,000 a year so long as her behaviour was 'good' — that
adjective would have to be interpreted by the moralists as
meaning not indiscreet. However, whether through her indiscretion or the Duke's financial embarrassment, the money was
not completely forthcoming. Like some expert horsewoman,
who just touches up the leader to remind him of who is in
control, Mary Anne Clarke decided to let the duke feel her power
and above all to enjoy herself. She therefore let it be known that
while she was under the duke's protection, she had sold
commissions in the Army and, needless to say, had gratified the
desires of her applicants in less nefarious ways. The duke had
certainly had no part in these transactions, and it was most
unlikely that he had the slightest idea of what she was doing. For
light relief she had also tried her hand at a little ecclesiastical
patronage.

The first indication that the firm, robust figure of Whitbread
was stirring this savoury pot was apparent at the end of 1808.
He then received a letter from a fellow Member, who had been
at St. John's with him, Colonel Gwilym Lloyd Wardle. The
letter was written ostensibly to enlist Whitbread's help in
securing a contract to provide the Bedfordshire militia with
clothing. He ends the letter 'I have the satisfaction of informing
you that I am now possessed of a variety of *facts* respecting the
sale of commissions etc etc that must fully expose the corruption
of H.R.H. the Commander-in-Chief; as soon as I hear of your
arrival in town I shall take an early opportunity of laying them
before you, in the meantime I shall observe a strict silence on
the subject.'

Poor Wardle — he was one of the human beings just touched
by pathos as the case slowly unfolded. He was colonel in
Wynn's Lambs (a troop of dragoons raised by Sir Watkyn
Williams-Wynn) and had the limitations of a colonel and the

easy habits of a soldier. He conducted the case against the duke
in the House of Commons tolerably, and after the duke's
resignation he was a national hero in the high summer months
of 1809. But alas! in the autumn his popularity vanished when it
was found that he was sued by an upholsterer for furnishing a
house for Mrs. Clarke — though whether he himself joined the
furnishings history does not precisely record. His end was
dismal, and he tried a little farming in Kent. Mrs. Clarke, who
knew the social distinction between a colonel and a farmer, said :
'Oh! the wretch. He has taken to selling milk about Tunbridge.'[1]

When Colonel Wardle outlined the charges in January 1809
it was decided not to submit them to a committee of the House of
Commons, but that the enquiry should be before the whole
House. In the weeks immediately following the British Army's
heroic exploit at Corunna the House of Commons gave itself up
with glee to Mrs. Clarke and what Sir Walter Scott once called
'her various profligate associates'. Mrs. Clarke, who was not
an actress, but was one of the most brilliant women witnesses
in history, gave an unrivalled display in which modesty and
persiflage were cunningly mixed. The professional possibilities
of this examination by hundreds of members of the opposite sex
were never far from her mind. Perhaps the lowest depths were
reached when a Member complained that Mrs. Clarke's
footman, who had given evidence, was 'drunk at the Bar' (of the
House). This unconscious witticism was received according to
the official report with 'loud and general peals of laughter'.
People's characters were freely spattered. Mrs. Clarke, for
example, referred to a friend of hers who had lived with a
carpenter. She then corrected herself and said that she had not
ment to say carpenter — he was a clergyman. The unhappy
man, whose name was given, was a clergyman-schoolmaster at
Merchant Taylors'. And even Whitbread had to apologise to the
Archbishop of Tuam — a domestic divine with ten sons and six
daughters — for saying that a letter from him to Mrs. Clarke
had been found.

The enquirer would possibly be justified in supposing that

the dark waves of scandal and innuendo would, by themselves, have swept the Duke of York from the Horse Guards. That may well have been so. But it is also possible that without the support of Burdett and Whitbread, Wardle would have found that the Government had succeeded in turning the attack. Mrs. Clarke herself wrote of Burdett and Whitbread: 'Of both these gentlemen I am bound to speak in the most grateful terms, and to express my admiration of their private worth and great abilities.' She had every reason for gratitude. Their support lent weight to the attack. This explains a sharp exchange between Whitbread and Canning. The latter asked 'what would be said if there was a person who had secretly advised — and had secretly been consulted by Wardle?' Whitbread rose and with great warmth demanded that this person should be named. For half a minute there were loud cries of 'Name, Name'. This was one of those occasions when the watermen on the Thames, carrying their passengers across the river, lay on their oars marvelling at the shouting which came across the water from St. Stephens. Whitbread went on to say that the right honourable secretary by direct insinuation, by his gestures and looks, had pointed him out as the object of attack. Mr. Fuller, the respected Member for Sussex, jovially brought matters to an end, by calling out 'You had better all go home and to bed'.

The speech which Whitbread made in support of Colonel Wardle's motion for an address to the King asking for the removal of the Duke of York was perhaps the most powerful he ever made. It was enormously long and occupies eighty columns of Hansard. A fierce and somewhat reactionary general — Gascoyne, the Member for Liverpool — suggested at the end that the two figures on St. Dunstan's clock should be brought into the House of Commons to remind the speaker of time and by its strike to stir the slumbrous. But to those who endured it — and to some who enjoyed it — the speech carried conviction. It was fair. Spencer Perceval had thrown out the suggestion that adultery should be made a crime. Whitbread dismissed this rather wild suggestion in a sentence, but he complimented

Perceval on what he called 'one of the best speeches which he had ever heard from any living Member'. He firmly rebutted the idea that because Mrs. Clarke was a prostitute she was ineligible as a witness. He probably summed up the views of many Members when he said that in all her evidence there was just 'a scintilla of credibility'. His whole examination of all the tawdry evidence revealed the common-sense which ever distinguished him and made him, in this speech, strive to make Members ashamed of the hypocrisy and humbug which together hold the floor on such topics. He finished with an attack on corruption which he gave as the explanation of the vigour with which he had attacked the duke. 'The passing moment is big with danger. The plague is amongst us. Bring incense quickly. The House alone can effectually interpose : alone can stand between the living and the dead, and slay the plague. Bonaparte is a flea bite, compared to internal corruption, and if we do not prevent its spreading we are a lost nation.' Wardle's motion was defeated by a large majority of 241, but the Commander-in-Chief — perhaps wisely — resigned. In Whitbread's life this case, this mirror of London life, was doubly important. It marked decisively his difference from the Whig leadership. Grey said at Devonshire House 'I disliked and disapprove of the whole business : I think that the means of bringing it about were shabby and dirty, and the manner of conducting it indecorous and hurtful to the greatest degree'.[2] The Whig hierarchy took no part in the proceedings. Whitbread's friend Ward expressed an opinion which was general when he wrote 'My friend the Fermentarian is running out of the course terribly'.[3] But naturally Whitbread was supported to an extent by the ordinary rank and file members of the Whig Party. The other important consequence of the Duke of York's affair was that Whitbread tasted the joys of being on the popular side. The leadership may have escaped him : Lords Holland, Grenville and Grey may have looked askance but his name was reiterated in the newspapers and acclaimed at gatherings of the people outside the House of Commons.

Nor was it altogether unpleasant to find himself the target for abuse from countless Tories and from all the conventionally minded. After a narrow escape from having to fight a duel with his comrade on the left, Sir Francis Burdett, it was not disagreeable to be threatened by a general from the Right. General Clavering, who was serving in Ireland, evidently thought that Mrs. Clarke could help him professionally. He had written to her, when she was under the duke's protection, saying that he was to be at the Prince of Wales's coffee house and would she send him word whether she could receive him 'in boots' at six o'clock. Clavering had given evidence in an attempt to impeach orally what Mrs. Clarke had said. His evidence was refuted by Mrs. Clarke's discovery of his letters which Whitbread said in his speech left Clavering 'as black as Erebus'. To an Irish correspondent Whitbread wrote 'I was not aware that anything which had passed between General Clavering and me had been made public'. This was in reply to his correspondent's statement that 'General Clavering had had the audacity to challenge you'.*

Yet the case of the Duke of York was perhaps grounded on something more solid than appears as we move back, through the laughter, to those distant years. A young Whig lord expressed things well when he said 'we have for once the people in full cry against the Court, and we are fools if we do not ride up to hounds'.[4] In the House of Commons the defenders of the duke complained of a concerted attack, amounting to conspiracy, being made against the royal family in the newspapers. Canning referred to them as 'the systematic calumnies of a set of unprincipled libellers'. In passing, it may be noticed that they were, in some cases, feeding on the thoughtless indiscretion of a member of the royal family. Many of the stories of the family of King George III — a lot of them still believed and spread in the twentieth century — came from the busy tongue and the

---

* It is clear from Whitbread's papers at Bedford and Chewton that Clavering had sent him a challenge. But a parliamentary debate was a privileged occasion and in not meeting the challenge Whitbread was justified.

love-lorn mind of the Princess of Wales. 'How much happier am I than the Duchess of York. She and the duke hate each other.' From such an authority these things were believed — and spread : they were widely circulated in society and the official world. Whitbread himself had a source of information close to the duke himself — his military secretary.

In those days the Government service was staffed by a sediment of permanent officials — clerks who were hardworking though without inspiration; on these foundations rested a less permanent and more forceful assortment of men — principally serving officers and friends of ministers. In those happy times tiresome restraints on the talkativeness of officials, such as the Official Secrets Act, were unknown. Men in Government service had the inescapable vainglory of wishing to show their friends and relations that they were in the know, but the best of them talked for other reasons. They wanted to explain — and perhaps justify — to reliable people the reasons behind Government action. Occasionally they might wish to justify a point of view of their own which had not found favour in their department. By such means an Opposition was by no means ill informed. No doubt it was all very haphazard, but it was broadly governed by the good sense of all concerned. James Willoughby Gordon was an interesting example of this kind of Government servant. He had served in action with his regiment, becoming military secretary to the Duke of York from 1804 till 1810. He was thereafter in charge of the commissariat in the Peninsula, and became Quarter-Master General at the War Office, holding his office until almost 80 and until the verge of the Crimean War. He crossed Whitbread's path because he had married the sister of R. H. A. Bennet — one of Whitbread's earliest friends. The information which he distributed gained in vividness because of the pithy style in which he expressed himself. When his sister-in-law — the grandmother of Algernon Charles Swinburne — came to stay with her family he described it to Whitbread as 'an irruption upon the South with numbers amounting to a northern hive'.[5] He thought that 'a chimney-sweep had a better chance of controlling the Commons than had Spencer Perceval'.[6] He sent a great deal of what was then classed as secret material on the Army and recruiting to Whitbread. When he left the Duke of York for the Peninsula commissariat he wrote to say that compared with his work with the duke the labour was light.

I shall be gratified in answering your queries upon the subject of it, and indeed flattered that the thing is of importance enough to attract your notice . . . It certainly deserves your attention as a Member of Parliament. [Later in the same letter he alluded to his time with the Duke of York] for nearly six years, under a pressure of business, and at times the most unexampled, I was never absent from my duty one half day, not even the day I married . . . I could not again undertake the same office, no, not for £20,000 a year, nor any other depending in any manner upon the discretion, or public conduct of any of the [Royal] Family; I could not say this if I could discover in them anything like talent, judgment or capacity for public affairs. . . .[7]

In a previous letter to Whitbread immediately after the duke's case he said — and this is probably perfectly correct — that 'if the Law Officers had done their duty, every part of that unpleasant business would have been avoided, and the exposure of the nonsensical letters prevented'.* He then made a reference to the *Plain Statement*. This had been published in 1808 and with a good deal of scandal about the duke mixed the suggestion that he was the chief of a conservative cabal which was the secret overlord of all Governments. Gordon told Whitbread that the duke always thought the *Plain Statement* 'the worst libel of the whole, and had urged the prosecution of it accordingly'.[8] In his speech in support of Wardle, Whitbread said in reference to the *Plain Statement* 'the fact charged by the greatest characters of the present reign† that there does exist an internal cabal, controlling the operations of the executive servants of the Crown and thwarting their measures, is there directly avowed : and the Duke of York is named as the head of that dark and dangerous cabal.' There is certainly no clear evidence for the

* These were the Duke's letters to Mrs. Clarke, freely sprinkled with 'Darling'.
† He means Chatham and Fox.

existence of this idea but there was this shred of support
for it : the King had behaved capriciously in dismissing Pitt over
the Catholic question, in resisting the inclusion of Fox and in
changing the Ministry of All the Talents. The duke, in a
position of great influence and authority, was the King's
favourite son and a strong Conservative in politics. There was a
further small pointer. Sir James Pulteney-Murray had been
appointed Secretary at War. He was not perhaps an outstanding
politician : he was immensely rich and repulsively ugly. But as a
younger man he had been a comrade-in-arms of the Duke of
York in the Low Countries, and was regarded as his mouthpiece. A Member of Parliament who was a follower of Lord
Grenville observed, when the appointment was made, 'the
Army given up *in toto* to the Duke of York'.[9] This was no
exaggeration and, in this connexion, Whitbread raised, right at
the close of the debates on the duke when, as he said, the House
was *lassata et satiata* with such topics, a question about a meeting
of general officers of the Army, of which he had almost certainly
learned through Gordon. He understood that 'the Right
Honourable Secretary had attended the meeting' and it was
proposed to present an address to the Commander-in-Chief
'couched in terms of affection and approbation'. He went on : 'In
the moment of deliberation are the Commons of England to be
subject to the interference of the Army ? Shall we henceforth be
compelled to hold our deliberations under terror of the bayonet ?'
At this possibly too-rhetorical question *Hansard* records that
there was a violent tumult in every part of the House which
lasted some minutes.

Exaggerated perhaps : violent perhaps : too heedless perhaps
of the natural chivalry of human beings for a comrade in
misfortune but it swept up all the tarnished gewgaws of Mrs.
Clarke and her associates revealing an issue of principle, an
issue of politics. Whitbread lent respectability to Wardle :
Whitbread's closing shot lent some respectability to the whole
enquiry. Above all it emphasised for Whitbread the delights of
baiting princes, the glory of standing up in the Commons as the

champion of those simple rules on which the people of England reposed their lives. On the other hand, Whitbread's part in the attack on a member of the royal family made him unpopular in those powerful circles where conventional opinions are paramount. The Duke of Richmond, who had once fought a duel with the Duke of York was at the time of the hubbub Lord Lieutenant of Ireland. Attending a dinner in Dublin he found that the toast of the duke had been omitted from the proceedings. He rose and gave the toast in his own forceful words 'The Duke of York, and may God damn all those rascals who have persecuted him'.[10]

CHAPTER SEVENTEEN

The Radical in Bedfordshire

OF all political mortals Whitbread was perhaps one of those most inclined to be inflamed by the buzz of London politics, by the plaudits of his party friends by the jeers of his political enemies. On the other hand as a countryman in Bedfordshire, as patron of the arts, as host at Southill, and as a friend he displayed gifts of sympathy and understanding which are so varied from those which he exhibited in the House of Commons that the reader might be forgiven for thinking that Whitbread was compounded of two distinct personalities. A political friend was also conscious of the difference between the Dover Street Whitbread and the Southill Whitbread : when he heard that Whitbread was quiet in the country, he dryly remarked : 'there are many horses quiet enough in the stable, who kick and plunge and play the devil when they get out with the hounds'.[1] Farington, a shrewd observer, also noticed the difference between Whitbread the politician and Whitbread in ordinary life when he spoke at the dinner of the Artists' Benevolent Society in 1814. A devoted Tory, Charles Long, who sat for Haslemere, even then a town which sheltered a well-satisfied and contented little community, was in the chair. Whitbread, after alluding to the clashes between himself and the chairman in the House of Commons, said that on that particular evening 'they had but one mind, drawn together by the love of Art'. He contrasted Wellington's care for the treasures of Spain with the plundering habit of 'the usurper of France' as he rather surprisingly called Napoleon. He spoke with his accustomed energy; 'his speech produced an electrical effect upon the meeting and their applause was unbounded'.[2]

P

This, the more human side of Whitbread's character, was seen at its fairest in Southill. The same bustling energy which marked the Westminster politician was certainly uppermost, but also apparent were a reasonableness and a sense of neighbourliness which smoothed the rougher edges of his character. At Southill the fermentarian left the seething frenzies of advanced politics behind, and became pre-eminently a Bedfordshire man. In the last election address of his life — in the autumn of 1812 — he wrote 'The season of profession from me to you is past. The connexion between us, so honourable and gratifying to me, has too long subsisted to leave me anything to hope from professions, if my conduct has not secured for me your esteem. As a Member of Parliament I have been too long before you and the public : and in all the other relations of life I have acted too immediately under your eye to have left any part of my character unexplored by you. . . . You have it in your power to bestow upon me the proudest distinction I shall ever covet.'*

The county was less safe for 'the good old cause' of Whiggery than Bedford itself. But Whitbread was indefatigable in building up the progressive strength of Bedfordshire, in which he was of course an influential voter. In 1810 he wrote a revealing letter to Lord Bute about the fortunes of the Whig Party at the general election of 1807. Lord Bute, the son of the Prime Minister, was a somewhat half-hearted Whig but, as the owner of Luton Hoo, he was a great electoral force (in the county) towards the Buckinghamshire border. Whitbread wrote : 'so large a part of the success obtained at the last Election, if not the whole, was owing to the Countenance your Lordship was pleased to give to us'. He went on to say that ever since that election he had placed agents in different parts of the county collecting any information about changes in the ownership of freehold property thereby compiling 'an immediate

* He was anxious that in the event of his premature death he should be succeeded in the representation of Bedford by his eldest son, William Henry Whitbread. Eighteen months before his death he asked the Duke of Bedford to use his influence to this end. 'Be assured that the interests of your son shall never be forgotten by me' was the reply (Bedford).

reference to every freeholder in the county . . . the whole has been done under my direction . . . and all has been carried on in my Name; although my personal views will never extend beyond the Town of Bedford'. He asked Lord Bute to instruct his agents to help in this return and in a following letter wrote : 'In the event of another struggle, please God to spare my life and health, there is no one upon whom the burden of the fight would fall more heavily than myself.'[3]

When he wrote to the Bedford electors that he had 'acted too immediately under your eye' to leave any part of his character unknown he was certainly not exaggerating. In an age which was just emerging from a primitive existence when movement of persons or goods was an adventure and was liable to be disrupted by any frown from the heavens Whitbread's work for road building, for the development of canals and for the re-building of the bridge in Bedford itself was widely approved. The county of Bedford in the opening years of the nineteenth century was like an alert cripple : the top was active but the body was shuffling. Whitbread, Woburn Abbey, Lee Antonie and the leading citizens of Bedford provided the county with an enlightened and progressive head. Below them were the clergy and what might be unkindly if truly called the squires of low degree, who were frightened by change and alarmed by progress; from the labouring classes in the county at this time there was occasionally a sporadic outbreak of feeling but nothing concerted or organised. As Whitbread grew more deeply into Bedfordshire and as his radical utterances were spread more widely he stirred some feeling among the county conservatives. He was perhaps first aware of this in 1810 when he wrote to the duke complaining that the Russells, who were much in London and Devonshire were neglecting the county Replying, the duke said 'You have a fair right to grumble'. He also said — and he is almost certainly referring to politics and not to his personal position 'I feel the importance of not losing by neglect the advantages we possess and which by a little judgment and policy we can not fail to keep'. Rather unexpectedly in a father he deplored the failure of his eldest son to attend the races at Bedford. 'I agree with you — he is very idle.' The duke regretted two weak links in the Whig chain of power — Fitzpatrick 'our worthy county Member "the Spartan General" is, I fear, in these matters incorrigible' and Lord Ossory, the lord-lieutenant, 'whose neglect of everything that has the least affinity to duty is proverbial'. In one year the general was commanded by the Duke of Bedford to attend Bedford races and by the duchess to attend her Christmas ball at Woburn. To Whitbread he wrote: 'It requires the fortitude of Algernon Sidney to endure all these evils for the sake of the good old cause.'⁴ These feelings came to a head over the rebuilding of the bridge over the Ouse at Bedford. The medieval bridge dated back to the thirteenth century and had become a dam to the flow of horse-drawn vehicles into the town. Both the duke and Whitbread contributed £2,000 to the new bridge: the duke accompanied his gift with the wistful remark 'as a lover of antiquity I shall regret the demolition of our ancient bridge'. Whitbread, too, was a lover of antiquity, but in his case love grew cold confronted with the bright lights of progress. The bridge-building started in April 1811 and was finished by the winter of 1813: it was financed by loans on which interest was payable. Whitbread was as active in whipping up money for the bridge as he was to be in securing money for Drury Lane. Partly owing to political feeling the contributors hung back, and Whitbread had to ask the subscribers to give up their interest, and to subscribe further. The reply from Lord Ossory was typical of the kind of thing with which Whitbread had to contend: 'I will not enter into a reasoning upon the subject *after dinner*; all I can say at present is that I rest my oars.'⁵ But although lords, clergy and Tory burghers may not have pulled their oars the bridge was built and stands, in the words of a neighbouring lord at the time, as a monument 'to the rare if not unprecedented public spirit of Whitbread'.⁶

Simultaneously with the building of Bedford bridge Whitbread was active over the project of constructing a canal from Bedford

which was to join the Grand Junction close to Newport Pagnell.
Golden dreams filled the minds of the canal promoters:
Bedfordshire corn was to glide northwards to Birmingham and
Manchester, while the 'back carriage' was to provide the
county with coal, iron and manufactured goods: nor was it
thought impossible that, turning south on joining the Grand
Junction, the produce of Bedfordshire farms might journey
quietly to the capital. Moreover speed lured on the enthusiasts.
Goods, going by waggon on the roads moved at one mile an
hour: by canal it was calculated that the speed might be
doubled. But against these rosy prospects had to be set the
selfishness of the country-dweller, the parochial vagaries of
Bedfordshire personalities. One lady seriously wrote to
Whitbread to say that she would gladly subscribe to the canal
if its planned route could be diverted within three miles of her
house, since it would make her coals cheaper than if they were
sent by road from Bedford. Then there was Henry Hoare, who
was described by his opponents as 'an artful man'; in fact he was
a country gentleman and a reactionary, he led the opposition
partly because he argued that the commercial waters of the
canal would sully private property and partly because he
believed that they were to be placed under his drawing-room
windows. He organised a protest meeting which he somewhat
rashly held under the nose of the Duke of Bedford in the inn at
Ampthill. He was sharply rebuked by the duke for referring to
the promoters of the canal as 'a few burghers of Bedford
indulging in visionary and extravagant schemes'.[7] Whitbread
started as a neutral observer in this warfare: he declared that
as a Member of Parliament he would carry out the directions of
his Bedford constituents, adding that if, after examination, the
scheme was found to be beneficial to the community 'I shall
support it with all activity'. He consulted with John Rennie —
the great canal builder through the difficult country of the
north-west of England; Rennie told him that the cost would be
in the region of £10,000 a mile. Whitbread subsequently
announced that he was a warm supporter of the canal from full

conviction. He subscribed in the names of his sons* but the chief promoter of the canal in Bedford was obliged to tell him 'there is a prejudice against us among the gentry'.[8] That was indeed the case; the canal was never made, and the visionary burghers of Bedford had to wait until deep in the railway age before having their link with Birmingham and Manchester.

The building of roads and their maintenance was another matter in which Whitbread's influence was widely felt. Bedfordshire roads were enclosed in the fork of Watling Street and Ermine Street — two paragons of straightness to which the other roads did not conform: these latter reflected exactly what Chesterton had in mind when he wrote 'the rolling English drunkard made the rolling English road'.

For the most part parishes were responsible for maintaining the roads in their area, and it was the duty of magistrates to 'present' or fine a parish if it was lagging in its duty, which would be carried out by farmers and agricultural labourers. On the question of roads all human beings are improvers but, with the psalmist, they are disposed to pray that the improvement shall not come nigh them. Perhaps one of the greatest difficulties which Whitbread had to face in Bedfordshire was forcing his friends and neighbours to do their duty over roads. He not only had a local responsibility as magistrate but he was also commissioner for several of the county turnpike-trust roads for the whole county. To Sir Montague Burgoyne, a cavalry officer and the squire of Sutton, just to the north of Biggleswade, he wrote that it was 'preposterous' for him to have attempted to repair the road with mud. Then there were the pathetic pleas of gentlemen, who felt themselves aggrieved by the proposed route of a new road, epitomised by the plea of an immediate neighbour, the Reverend D. S. Olivier 'Pray, pray, pray be so kind, so very kind as to transfer your injunction a little more westerly'.[9] We see something of the hazards of Bedfordshire roads after a journey which Whitbread made with Lady

---

* Had he personally subscribed, he could not have advocated the project in Parliament.

Elizabeth to Lee Antonie's house, Colworth, in the north of the
county. 'Pray make my best love to Madame' he wrote 'and tell
her as I value both her life and yours very much, there are two
or three most dangerous passes between Colworth House and
the turning coming from Bletsoe, which I mean to have altered
or rendered more safe or one or both of you will inevitably be
overturned some day or night or other. The first is . . . where
there is an open drain with a large flat stone laid across the
mouth of it, into which people are much more likely to drive
than to go along the road itself.' Then there was a new bridge
'which I think of all the positions of a bridge I ever saw in my
life is the very worst — standing immediately at right angles
with the road, and so placed that it is impossible to make a good
approach to it, and will never be otherwise than dangerous'. He
said that, as a road-commissioner, he would try to attend the
next meeting about the roads in that area 'but it will certainly
be a great deal better if you will take up the cudgels yourself
and lay about you for these misdemeanours'.[10]

To Mr. Morris, a brother-brewer at Ampthill, he wrote
firmly about over-heavy wagons sent to satisfy the thirsty
citizens of Bedford. He began that he was writing about 'a
matter of great public concern wherein I individually take great
interest'. Owing to the weight of beer imposed on Morris's
wagons 'the turnpike road from Ampthill to Bedford was so
entirely destroyed that it became necessary to erect a weighing
engine in order to protect it from utter ruin'. To avoid the
weighing-machine the wagons were using a fresh route through
the parish of Maulden close to Bedford. 'The consequence must
be a fresh presentment [to Maulden] and a fresh fine : your
gain will have been very small — if any; and that purchased at
an enormous loss to the occupiers of land in the parish.'
Whitbread ended on what he called 'the higher ground that
Morris would not wish to gain at the expense of your less
opulent neighbours'. In his reply the fellow-brewer called the
reproof 'just', said that the fault would be corrected and that no
man had greater admiration than he had for Whitbread's 'zeal

and vigilance'[11] in caring for the roads. In all these matters Whitbread exercised an authority over his neighbours which sprang partly from position but chiefly from strength of character.

At the beginning of the nineteenth century it was possible for an individual to exercise, in a smaller area, the kind of sway enjoyed by thane or earl at the dawn of English history. With the Duke of Bedford, Whitbread enjoyed powers which might well have been envied by a modern county council. But that power was accompanied in Whitbread's case by a personal knowledge of people and events in his neighbourhood, so that in return Bedfordshire people grew to believe that his clear mind would dispel the smallest personal difficulty and that nothing was too much trouble for his personal surveillance. When the lunatic asylum at Bedford was put on a civilised foundation in 1812 it was Whitbread who found the time to enquire from St. Luke's Hospital in London about the best kind of beds, of grates and fire-guards, of kitchen equipment, of blankets and coverlids for the patients, and linen for the superintendents. He interviewed the possible superintendents, paying especial attention to their wives, 'one of whom was not such as exactly pleased me'.[12] He was always anxious that matters of this kind should be settled by practical men and not arranged by the clergy — always a formidable and reactionary squad at any gathering of Bedfordshire magistrates. Whitbread was a churchman rather by tradition than by conviction: he called Perceval's Government because of their narrow views on the Roman Catholic claims 'one pure unadulterated lump of bigotry'. His beliefs rested, as he explained in the House of Commons, on the writings of the Evangelists and owed little to the strengthening structure of churchmanship. A Bedfordshire friend asking Whitbread's support in an application for a prison governorship wrote: 'I am 38 years of age and am a member of the Church of England'. The last three words were underlined, and evidently stirred Whitbread's ire. Replying he said, 'I am surprised you should have thought it necessary to state so prominently that you are a member of the Established Church. I know of no office or station in life which more urgently requires that he who fills it should be in word and deed a good Christian, but it would not have occurred to me to have enquired whether you were of the Established Church or not.'[13]

Horace Walpole has assured us that the country is the worst place in the world in which to find solitude. He adds 'questions grow there'.[14] The questions which afflicted Whitbread were not so much the great controversies of the day, which Walpole had in mind, but the trifles of a neighbourly life, the helpless squeals of those powerless to help themselves. Applications for his help, of all kinds, abounded. There was the doctor, treating a cancer case, who wanted him to get oxide of bismuth from the Apothecaries' Hall in London and thought that Whitbread would be able to spare the time to get it for him. Poor Sarah Hobby — whom he had recommended to the Middlesex Hospital — could he find out if the surgeons really thought her case hopeless? What should be done with Sarah Stone, a lunatic who had run away from the asylum, and presented herself on the door-step of Dover Street? Then what ought to be done about Sarah Brown who murdered her baby and told her friend, while they were weeding corn on the day the child had been born, 'it was so black it was not fit to be seen, and it was not much bigger than a cat'? And would he kindly advise the rector who was asked to christen the illegitimate child of Mr. Butlin with the name of Niltub? And then there was the clergyman who begged Whitbread to do something about the madman Old Joe, who 'disturbs us at night with dreadful shouts and hollowings and frequently strips himself naked before us'. All these and countless similar rubs of Bedfordshire life were paraded before him as though, before the magic wand of Whitbread, unruliness, madness and murder would flee away. Doubtless he was gratified and doubtless accepted much of it as a legitimate burden of magistracy, but these questions did not offer a real relaxation from the larger agitations of Westminster.

Chiswell Street was fortunately not among his agitations,

although there was a serious development in 1810. 'Equality' Brown was always a difficult partner in the Brewery and his personal pepperiness was enhanced by the risk that if his banking-house ran into trouble the creditors of that establishment might have been able to pursue their claims against the Brewery. What happened is described in a letter from Whitbread to Grey, a guest at Southill at the time; in the letter Whitbread apologises for suddenly having to leave Southill for London while his guests were still there. The letter was written on 3 August 1810:

I was then under considerable anxiety respecting the issue of a disagreeable business, which according to the appearances of the moment might have lasted for years; but which according to my presentiment, rather than any reasoning I could support myself by, was cut short; and terminated to my wishes.

Mr. Timothy Brown has never been a very pleasant partner to me but I have always kept him so much at arms' length as not to be annoyed by him. Some circumstances however occurred in the course of the last Autumn affecting his banking house which made it desirable to be rid of him. Having accorded him very great assistance and saved his concern we desired him to withdraw, upon the payment of his capital in the month of July; a step he had often proposed to take, when dissatisfied or out of humour and to which his distresses would have compelled him, if we had not released him. This request, however, he peremptorily refused to comply with; it became then a trial of strength between us, and I gave him notice to withdraw under an article of the partnership which I conceived he had violated. He resisted and filed a Bill in Chancery. We put in an answer, and all the horrors of a long Chancery suit were opening upon us. I left London* with a direction to say that if he should show a disposition to come to terms, I would undertake for the payment of the balance of his capital £50,000, on the seventh day from the day on which I should receive notice of his intention to accede to my proposal. Fortunately a run upon his banking house occurred which induced him to offer to withdraw if he could have his money within 24 hours. The time was short, but the thing was effected. We paid him £50,000 before 3 o'clock the next day, and he is entirely gone. The riddance is great even during my life, and in the event of my death the difference is incalculable.

* He means when he left to spend the parliamentary recess at Southill, from which he was hastily called back to Chiswell Street. Parliament was prorogued that year on 21 June.

After the removal of Brown Whitbread's thoughts evidently turned once again to the possibility of extricating himself from the Brewery. In a letter to Grey nine days later he made this abundantly plain :

I thank you for your kind expressions respecting my concerns. There are reasons why I should like if it were possible to discharge my mind of all concerns in trade.* The riddance of Brown has taken away one very material one but with so large a stake and so much depending upon my name and continuance, it is very difficult. There are temptations of interest too, which are something, for things are prosperous, and the management exceedingly easy. I find a want of time to give quite as much attention as it requires and I cannot oversee any longer. All things of every description are more or less uncertain, but nothing in the way of trade can possibly be reduced nearer to a certainty than a regular trade of this sort, supported by capital more than adequate, as ours has long been through its management and rooted so deeply as it is.

Still as you will have heard me say I should on the whole be glad of the opportunity of being out altogether. That opportunity has not yet presented itself. To seek it might be to remove it. Events may produce it. . . .

In the dispute with Brown Whitbread had the benefit of John Martineau, a fellow-brewer, as arbitrator. Two years later Martineau and Bland of Lambeth joined Whitbread's, the partnership was reformed and one of Whitbread's recurring anxieties was happily removed.

* The reasons were chiefly political, but partly health.

CHAPTER EIGHTEEN

Farmer and Soldier

A progressive-minded man, owning land and living within a stone's throw of the great sheep-shearings at Woburn, could have scarcely excused himself from an interest in farming. Whitbread owned a considerable number of farms and himself farmed a moderate acreage. He was a pillar of the Bedfordshire Agricultural Society, winning a silver trophy in 1803 for the ploughing of half an acre, with a double plough without a driver in 2 hours, 4 minutes; in 1814 for the ploughing of half an acre with two oxen in $3\frac{1}{2}$ hours and in the same year for showing the best two shearing, short-woolled, fat wethers.

When he sent his farm bailiff, Barnes, into Norfolk to learn something of how things were done in that famous farming county, Coke of Norfolk told Whitbread: 'out of all the bailiffs that have been here at different times to view the state of agriculture in Norfolk, yours pleased me the most.'[1] Whitbread was anxious to keep abreast of the swift changes in farming pushed forward by the war. He was one of the pioneers of merino sheep, being encouraged by his Cambridge friend, Lord Somerville, who in 1807 sent him a cut of merino mutton from Somerset. In the following year he wintered a merino ram and ewe for Grey. Sir John Sinclair, the eminent Scottish agriculturist, stayed at Southill and after his visit wrote to his host with his particular type of Scottish bluntness: 'I had a glance at your dairy cows, and I did not think much of them.' The reason for this observation was that Sinclair hoped to persuade Whitbread to experiment with Ayrshires. Although landlords and agriculturists are not generally regarded as the buttresses of progressive causes they were cherished by Whitbread for that

very reason and he could have pointed to most of them — the
Duke of Bedford, Coke of Norfolk, Lord Fitzwilliam, the Duke
of Norfolk to name some, though not of course to the greatest
of them — George III — as supporting his claim. He was
greatly shocked when Sir Francis Burdett at a Westminster
meeting in 1809 said that 'the great land owners disgraced
themselves politically by attending to fat cattle *only*'.[2] To
Creevey Whitbread unburdened himself 'I can not say how
much I was surprised by Burdett's unprovoked attack upon the
great agriculturalists, who are, almost without exception, real
friends of Liberty and Reform — none more so than the head of
them the Duke of Bedford, who thinks Parliamentary Reform
indispensably necessary to our existence. . . . A more wise and
innocent relaxation for a politician can not be conceived nor a
more beneficial pursuit for a gentleman who is not a politician.
Agriculture is in Science the second, in amusement the very
first.'[3]

Whitbread had an enormous success at the Norfolk shearing
at Holkham in June 1811. That great barley-growing county had
been agitated earlier in the year when the Government had
proposed to change the duty so as to benefit those distilling
from sugar rather than from malting barley. Whitbread voted
in the customary minority against the measure. At dinner, after
his health had been drunk with three times three, Whitbread,
replying, said : 'I shall give as a toast the greatest personage in
the country — one who was born and bred in Norfolk — one to
whom you and myself in particular were under the highest
obligations, and who to the last moment of his existence never
failed to make them contented and happy. I shall now proceed
to name that personage, and shall give as a toast Sir John
Barleycorn.' A simple joke maybe, but at a Norfolk dinner it was
received, as the local paper wrote : 'with a burst of approbation
which lasted several minutes'. The Duke of Bedford expressed
some surprise at Whitbread's Norfolk sympathies, and wrote in
the following year to urge him to come to Woburn sheep-
shearing beginning with the remark 'I am not apt to *bore* people

to come to my sheep-shearing'.[4] In the closing weeks of his life he spoke in Parliament of the great services of the landlords to agriculture, illustrating this by pointing out that all the bogs between Bedfordshire and London had been drained since the time that General Oglethorpe shot snipes in Berkeley Square.* He explained that he was personally opposed to what was called old English hospitality towards the labouring classes in the country — what he called 'the cutting up of barons of beefs and the swigging of barrels of ale'. But those classes had greatly gained through the residence of landlords among them. These were possibly rather strange arguments for a radical, but he sustained them.

He also laid himself open to some criticism from his political cronies from his attachment to sport. Hunting — not then a target for the darts of the comfortably-housed urban dweller — stirred some hostility among the farmers but political criticism had not raised its head. This was not however true of shooting where there was political objection to the Game Laws. Whitbread preserved at Southill, as the following pathetically querulous letter from his keeper Thomas Delahay shows. It was written in 1812.

'I have not gaint 3/– by your Plase and has laid ought many cold Nights in your Woods and Plantations wen the Rest of your servants were a Bed and doing so I have decayed my concitution for the Percivation of your Game. I have never had a pleasant word from you in the three last years.' Poor Delahay was dismissed after this effusion. His successor was murdered by poachers.[5]

A farmer wrote with frankness to tell Whitbread that, however much people admired him as a statesman, they were 'hurt at your proceedings concerning the game, as Mankind in

---

* This was an eighteenth-century jest. General Oglethorpe, the distinguished soldier and the founder of Georgia, was extremely secretive about his age. In order to vex him his amiable friends put about the story that he had shot over the fields on the north side of Piccadilly before buildings appeared there at the end of the seventeenth century. This would have made him well over 100 at the time of his death.

General think they were ordained from the beginning free for anyone who could overtake them'.[6] Replying, Whitbread took the trouble to set out his views in some detail. 'I think it my first duty as a Magistrate to make an example of the common poacher because I know his trade in the first instance makes a miserable family and a worthless lot, and leads eventually to the most atrocious crimes — no less than robbery, burglary and often to murder.' He went on, 'if by a trifling punishment I could convert him into a good labourer, I do good to the Society in which I live and this course I shall pursue until I see that it is faulty, let the unpopularity be to me what it may'.

There remained the more subtle question of the gentleman-poacher. Whitbread said that he never in his life refused an application for a day's or more shooting — even from poor Obadiah Bennett of Norfolk Street, Strand, who had no other claim on his generosity than 'I had the honour to sing at your election at Bedford'. But he said that it was from such people 'professing the greatest regard for him' that he had had his servants induced to betray him and his game destroyed.[7] Particularly obnoxious in this respect were some of the clergy. The rector of Sutton near Biggleswade, a doctor of divinity but a warrior who punched his sexton in Church and his squire outside, shot all over his squire's estate. Whitbread, as J.P., issued a warrant for the detention of a basket of game which the rector had sent to the Swan Inn at Biggleswade for despatch to London.[8] These were among the hazards for popularity to be faced by a country radical.

His exertions in the Militia can not have endeared him to such fellow-radicals as Belsham : nor are they perhaps altogether easy to reconcile with his views on the French War. He would possibly have argued that foreign politics led him into an ideal and visionary world and that at Southill the world of reality pressed heavily around him. In the autumn of 1803 the invasion of England seemed probable. Whitbread wrote to Grey confidently predicting 'the French will be in the island'. Replying, Grey said that the Army commander in the north-east had told him that an invasion on the Northumberland coast was contemplated by the French, and that their plans were nearly complete. Grey's reactions to this warning were those of a loving husband and father 'My first object will be to get my family into a place of safety if any such can be found in this country; and then I suppose I must expose myself to the chance of being shot somewhere or other.'[9]

Whitbread's soldiering was more serious. In reply he told Grey that Fox had been staying at Southill : 'he is nauseated with the system of volunteers'. The objection to the system was that the Government lacked men to train the volunteers or any equipment. Moreover there was no means of preventing people more suited for the Army or the Militia from joining the volunteers. Whitbread went on : 'here it is quite impossible to keep out of. Happy those that can. It destroys all comfort and occupies all time . . . by taking out of their sphere all persons in a responsible situation of life, from the D. of Bedford down to the master-carpenter and the farmer, it must produce incalculable confusion. . . . We have only 100 stand of arms for 430 men . . . so that none of us yet knows the smell of powder.'[10] Whitbread himself was colonel of the volunteer battalion and his fellow-Member of Parliament, Lee Antonie, was major. When Whitbread said, 'it is impossible to keep out of' he probably meant that political opponents would have officered the battalion. (There was more than a dash of politics in these questions; it was only ten years earlier that Pitt had refused to allow Francis, Duke of Bedford to take command of his tenants and arm them on the grounds that it would have been 'dangerous for the State'.) Four years later Whitbread was writing that it was planned to merge the volunteers in the Militia, and that he would be 'glad of this opportunity to throw off my red coat' but he understood that if he did this his political opponents intended to take control of the new force. It would be wrong to suggest that Whitbread's duties were very arduous : sessions of Parliament, the hay and corn harvest always loomed a little larger than Napoleon's flat-bottomed fleet in Boulogne. But his military duties went on almost to his death and the days in camp must have been testing. In 1812 he was writing to Creevey from camp 'Up before 5. Breakfast half-past 5. Drill 6 to 8 and so on throughout the day.'[11] Both Brougham and Creevey used playfully to address Whitbread as colonel, and in that same summer Creevey wrote 'And now my dear Colonel permit me to ask you how you endure your military life during these political convulsions in the Capital? Do you never call out "Mr. Speaker" instead of "March"?'[12]

Right at the end of his life he was linked through the Bedford-shire Militia with Lord John Russell, who was to have his ear pinched by Napoleon I at Elba and to live to see the eclipse and death of Napoleon III. Always a shade lackadaisical Lord John wrote to Whitbread from Badminton asking to be excused a February parade — 'the weather has made the journey very inconvenient and disagreeable'.[13]

Lord John's elder brother, Lord Tavistock, who was second-in-command had to face something far more disagreeable, far more disturbing to the soul of an advanced Whig. Private Collington had to be court-martialled and it was feared that he would be ordered to be flogged, though in the decorous ranks of the Bedfordshire Militia no one was found capable of administering a flogging, and Tavistock summed it up : 'what the effect might be on a corps like this I know not'. In fact he behaved with mature judgment — paraded the regiment, read out the sentence and then pardoned the man. This happened in 1808 when Tavistock was 20. Four years later, as the country was preparing for a general election, the press hinted that Whitbread, although an opponent of flogging, allowed it in his own regiment. Replying, Whitbread stated exactly what had happened in 1808, also saying : 'Not a stripe or a blow has been inflicted on any one man of the Bedfordshire local Militia which I have the honour to command from the time of its being first embodied down to the present moment and I trust there never will.'[14]

Possibly the Militia taught Whitbread one lesson — the sorrows of an idealist, the tribulations of a reformer. He issued a

Q

not uncharacteristic order — all non-commissioned officers
were to learn to read and write, paying for this themselves at a
cost of eight pence a week. Sergeant Warden was overheard
saying to a fellow sergeant 'Damn your eyes, Jack. Don't give
up. Don't yield. Don't go to school because I'll be damned if I
do.' For such contumely he was lodged where Bunyan was
lodged — in Bedford Gaol. Aided and abetted by political
enemies of Whitbread the sergeant brought an action for false
imprisonment against the Militia officers, and showed himself
one of the earliest victims of compulsory education.

CHAPTER NINETEEN

Hospitality at Southill

ALL the zeal and energy which he showed in countless directions
in Bedfordshire have to be set against the peace and tranquillity
of his life at Southill; like some homing pigeon which for all its
convolutions and soaring flight is in instinct never far from
home, so he found Southill the centre of existence, the mainspring of his energy. Although public affairs naturally intruded
he was generally able to enjoy the calm of Southill from high
summer to the turn of the year. (The House of Commons
generally had no autumn session then.) In addition he was able
to enjoy breaks from London for the recognised Christian
festivals.

The house itself was virtually untouched between its completion in 1800 and Whitbread's death: the years merely
brought embellishments. In the library was the small collection
of books formed by his father, but the great bulk of the books are
Whitbread's. The library at Southill is not the place to bring a
gleam into the tired eyes of a bibliophile : rarity and beauty had
to yield shelf-room for usefulness. The most handsome book in
the library is probably the Baskerville Horace, bound in red
morocco and given to Whitbread when he was at Eton by Dr.
William Langford, of whom more hereafter. Books of travel,
history and contemporary literature are noticeably strong
sections. A curious sideline for a great peace propagandist is the
history of war of which there is a striking collection. But the
individuality of the books is shown by the ephemera — some
190 bound volumes of tracts and trials. There are several
hundred which are still unbound. Many of them are inscribed
to Whitbread by the authors and a number of the earlier ones —

especially those dealing with the war against France—are heavily
scored by him. As Dr. A. N. L. Munby says: 'the collection
covers all the vital questions of that momentous quarter of a
century'.[1]

Although the flower garden was largely the concern of Lady
Elizabeth, Whitbread in 1812 introduced a great deal of
garden statuary. He bought all that was left of John Cheere's
yard; Cheere was a conventional eighteenth-century sculptor
eclipsed in fame by his brother, Sir Henry Cheere. The subjects
were principally classical — the Rape of the Sabines and Venus
and Adonis — and are believed to have caused averted glances
among the best county families of Bedfordshire. Whitbread's
neighbour, Lord Ongley, who was never one to miss a jest at
the expense of the opposite sex, wrote to him: 'I make no
doubt the ladies of the country will shortly *inspect* them.'[2] He
also formed in the house a bird gallery, and it was thought
sufficiently momentous to disturb him with the news, when he
was in the midst of London politics, that one of the American
sparrows (really, in spite of its name, a kind of bunting) had died.

Within, Southill was a beautifully appointed home: it was a
country house with all the appurtenances thereof. His wine was
stored in Chiswell Street and then distributed to Dover Street
or Southill as it was wanted. At the time of his death his cellar
was valued at £3,500. There was little spirit (4 dozen of rum
and 3 dozen of brandy): it was mostly port (76 dozen and 7
pipes) madeira and claret, but there were some of the less well-
known French wines — and Côte Rôtie, for instance, and
Spanish mountain wine. Port was sent down by the pipe to
Southill by road. His wine merchant was Adamson in John
Street, off Berkeley Square. Squalid inventions of the twentieth
century like economic warfare were not allowed to disturb the
war-time drinking habits of our forebears. In 1812 Adamson
wrote that the Government would permit the import of wine
from France provided there was first an *ad valorem* export of
British goods, and he offered Whitbread two hogsheads of
claret.[3] The table maintained in the house was on a not less

lavish scale than the wines. Even the Duke of Bedford, who entertained in princely style (in 1809 Whitbread describes a dinner party at Woburn of about 200 altogether), was glad to take advantage of the skill of the Southill kitchen. The duke, learning that Whitbread was to have company, asked that he might send over a man from Woburn to acquire a knowledge of trussing under Whitbread's poulterer. There is ample evidence that the political and private friends of the Whitbreads loved their time at Southill. Here is the end of a letter from his political friend and neighbour, Lord John Townshend, written in 1813 when he was planning a summer visit to Southill:

'We may take three of the girls' said Lady John grandly 'and perhaps Fox.'* 'Everyone' said I 'there are only nine of us, and these won't be too many. Audrey must pluck up courage and mount a donkey, Lizzy scamper all over the country with Lady Elizabeth, full speed through all the hunting gates, Jenny play at Blindman's Buff with Tom Adkin, and Fox take a political lesson every day and perhaps hold an argument even with Sam himself. Now for the signatures. J. Townshend. Yes, dear Mr. Whitbread, Audrey Harriet. Yes, dear Mr. Whitbread, Lizzy Frances. Yes, dear Mr. Whitbread, Jenny — again as deputy for Fox — Jenny.'[4]

Rather earlier, in 1808, Lady Holland — rightly renowned for the flow of wit and reason which she stimulated at Holland House — gives a less favourable picture of the company at Southill. 'With the exception of the Trevors† for one day, the rest of the company was *remplissage* of the very worst sort, fulsome flatterers and disgusting dependents.'[5] That is a charge which can often be aimed at a rich man and, in Whitbread's case, was perhaps not incorrectly aimed, though it must be remembered that part of the reason for Lady Holland's remark was that the flatterers led Whitbread astray from the conventional paths of respectable Whiggery. Against this can be set the views of other members of the Whig hierarchy — Lord and Lady Essex, 'Bear' Ellice Whitbread's brother-in-law, who wrote in 1813: 'I must say I never enjoyed a visit more than ours'

* Fox Townshend — the founder of 'Pop' at Eton.

† Almost certainly the diplomat, afterwards second Viscount Hampden and his wife.

and sent Whitbread a keg of Loch Fyne herrings as an expression
of enjoyment, and Lord Jersey and his terrifying wife, the Queen
Sarah of London society, who were delighted with their stay at
Southill and could not believe that any place could have been so
improved since they remembered it in the old days of the
Byngs. As always, Creevey, after a visit to Southill in 1809,
leads posterity towards the truth. He describes the stay of
himself and Mrs. Creevey as a very happy time. He then notices
the flaws in his host, 'rough in manners', 'entirely destitute of
all taste or talent for conversation', and 'almost tyrannical in his
deportment to his inferiors' : but he sets these criticisms against
the praise 'a man of the very strictest integrity with the most
generous, kind and feeling heart'.* (This was written in 1809
some years before Creevey was in receipt of the annuity from
Whitbread.)

The proof of his feeling heart lay in the examples of his
generosity to old friends. The misery and degradation of the
poor in the early nineteenth-century is a familiar theme to
historians; the evidence for their sufferings has been well
thumbed. The misfortunes of the *bourgeoisie* (though touched on
by novelists) is a less frequented (though no less heart-rending)
corner of history. For these unhappy misfits in an ardently
competitive society Whitbread, in his own sphere, showed
uniform sympathy. Then there was no welfare state, but for
numerous genteel unfortunates Whitbread showed that there
was a welfare man.

First and foremost there was Tom Adkin. No doubt the
moralist would tell us that it was wrong to keep this useless but
amusing inebriate in comfort and security from the bailiffs.
'Silver', as Creevey always called him, has not grown less
amusing or less bibulous than when first he came into Whitbread's life. He dispensed humour and attracted it. In 1813,
when he was on circuit in York, Brougham wrote to Whitbread :

---

* *Creevey Papers*, i, 110. The reader will not suppose that Creevey means to
imply that Whibread had no taste. He means no taste for conversation — naturally
a heinous fault in the eyes of Creevey, whose happiness rested on talk.

'Tell T. Adkin that there is in our calendar here this entry "Thomas Adkin aged 22, unmarried, ravishing Matilda Somebody against her will".'[6] Adkin had a curious knack of producing accurate information at most unexpected moments. Whitbread describes an occasion when he took him into Bedford for a dinner when the duke was present. 'Notwithstanding the awful presence of the Duke and the other Lords he had got very drunk'. He insisted on telling a story 'which he prefaced as usual by saying that he had a *fact* to relate'. This fact was that the King had written to the Prime Minister, Perceval, threatening to dissolve Parliament if the House of Commons did not support Perceval's Government. The next morning the company was amazed to find that what was said by Mr. Adkin 'in that wild way' was perfectly true.[7] His London habits did not differ greatly from his Bedford ones, and Lady Elizabeth, when Whitbread was at Coke's shearing, wrote 'T.A. had dined in New Street, and was a *little* in his *usual way* but not disagreeable. We [i.e. she and her daughters] took him home.'[8] Lord Broughton, who from his close friendship with Byron might have been expected to sympathise with those discarded by the British social system, called poor Adkin 'a bald-headed buffoon' a 'pensioner on the bounty' of Grey and Whitbread, and 'a fine warning against such folly'.[9] Creevey thought exactly the opposite. He told Whitbread 'his jokes and pleasantries are to be found in every part of the United Kingdoms and his very name produces mirth and good humour the instant it is mentioned'. Creevey went further; after detailing the long years of Tory misrule he added with pleasantry 'I therefore for one am ready to depose upon oath if necessary after a near and careful inspection of four succeeding administrations in this country, my conscientious opinion is that had it pleased providence to put the whole and uncontrolled power over their dominions into the hands of Mr. Adkin the situation of this Empire and of the world at large would have been infinitely better than it now is and that our latent posterity would have had reason to bless such an event'.[10] Even across the years we feel

inclined to make a bow to Whitbread for preserving for the
delight of his friends a wit otherwise doomed to that twilight
life of sponging-house and debtor's prison.

A more pitiable figure than Adkin was Mr. Frederick
FitzRoy — one of the fifteen ill-endowed children of the first
Lord Southampton, and brother to the General FitzRoy with
whom Princess Amelia fell in love. Whitbread was on close
terms with the family — possibly through their connexion with
Sir Charles Culling-Smith, who was the purchaser of Bedwell
after the death of Whitbread's father. FitzRoy was on the staff
of the Bengal Civil Establishment and Whitbread lent him
£500 on starting. This was repaid. Before long he returned
from the East with three half-caste children and a diminutive
pension. Whitbread contributed handsomely to the salvation of
what he called the 'hopeless and hapless' children and with the
help of the family made up a purse of £400 a year for his friend.
Writing to Lord Southampton (possibly a shade too bluntly)
Whitbread said of Frederick FitzRoy 'he has a great deal of
family pride to overcome, when he looks round at the prosperous
situation of his connexions and falls back on his own poverty and
helplessness'. FitzRoy had that indignation of the suppliant
which, even to the generous-hearted, is the most intolerable
form of begging. Whitbread paid up over and over again for
him. From prison FitzRoy wrote : 'as I am not able to endure
this sort of confinement I think it my duty to inform you that I
may be baled out. . . . There is a mistake which it is my duty to
myself and to my friends to explain away.' And a few months
later, 'Let me ask, sir, what fault or outrage have I committed?
Is a trifle of debt so heinous, so irretrievable? Is the debt so
immense when in its aggregate mass it only amounts to £400 or
something less?' And when the allied sovereigns were visiting
London in the summer of 1814, poor FitzRoy felt out of
things. 'You have had, he wrote, 'princesses, duchesses,
princes, dukes, Russians, Prussians and all ranks of great folks
to dine with you, and to sup with you for all I know, but that's
no reason you should forget me. Send me some money, pray

do.'[11] Alas! for poor Frederick. Within a year his benefactor was dead and how fared the debtor then ?

Perhaps the most painful case of all was that of the Reverend William Langford, D.D. He was Lower Master at Eton when Whitbread was there and gave him the splendidly bound Baskerville Horace. He held the position for more than a quarter of a century. He was Canon of Windsor and one of the chaplains to the King. From these emoluments he was supposed to have earned £3,500 a year. Early in the nineteenth century his affairs became involved — principally because of the extravagant folly of his children. He is believed to have experienced a debtor's prison for a short time : he certainly absconded from Eton and at one time sought sanctuary from his creditors within the precincts of Holyrood House. Whitbread helped him unceasingly and with Lord Holland and the King's Printer (Reeves) he was trustee of what could be scraped together. The shopkeepers of Eton and Windsor drew up a list of their claims against Langford, perhaps rightly taking credit for the fact that they had 'never molested the doctor'. Forwarding this to Whitbread the Vice-Provost of Eton said 'I hear from every quarter of your kindness and liberality to poor Dr. Langford'.[12]

To one of the most consistent beggars of literature, Shelley's father-in-law William Godwin, the political philosopher, he was a generous supporter with his Whig colleagues. This did not prevent him from receiving a letter from the philosopher which opened 'the use of two hundred pounds for five or six days would very probably give tranquillity and competence to the remainder of my life'. It closed with the sentence 'The troubling you with a letter in this simple and direct style, you will, I think, regard as the strongest proof I can afford of my conviction of the liberality and rectitude of your character'. Whitbread has endorsed the letter 'W. Godwin — Money', and it is likely that it was one of those cases to which he did not contribute and to which he gave a blunt but courteous refusal generally ending with the phrase 'Trusting to your candour'.[13]

Another man to whom Whitbread was consistently kind was

the scholarly, gentlemanly lawyer — Francis Hargrave — of whom it was said by Lord Lyndhurst, who was not speaking lightly, 'no man ever lived who was more conversant with the law of his country'. He had appeared in the celebrated case of Somersett — the black who was set free on reaching English soil — and he had helped the Whig leaders and Whitbread with valuable advice on legal matters. His manuscripts are now an important part of the manuscript collections in the British Museum. Whitbread had helped him financially for some time. Brougham in 1814 gives a somewhat unfeeling picture of the distinguished lawyer. In a letter to Creevey he writes 'Just as I was going to begin a letter to you entered *old Hargrave*, as mad as bedlam, and I have been so completely bored to death by him that I can scarcely write at all. I have had him talking without any interruption for above an hour — part of the time raving. He had been at Whitbread's (who is one of his trustees) and he said he observed something very odd about him . . . he observed an appearance of somnolency in Sam.' And then poor Hargrave's madness took a more tangible turn. He published *Jurisconsult Exercitations*, an important legal textbook, and when, as was perhaps likely, the sale did not go briskly he put down Whitbread's name as the purchaser of 350 copies. The House of Commons petitioned the Regent to instruct the Treasury to purchase Hargrave's library and Whitbread, the prince's man of business William Adam and Edward Jerningham a barrister were the trustees of the purchase money for the family.[14]

A study of Whitbread's papers at Bedford shows that every crank, oddity, beggar and victim of man's inhumanity to man wrote to him. He paid and distributed over the eighteen years after his father's death an average of £2,000 a year in gifts and presents. But it was perhaps not so much the money as the time and care which he devoted to all these people — an attention which shows how keenly he felt the injustice of imprisoning people for debt, and he had for mankind in general that goodness of heart which the perceptive Mr. Creevey had noticed. These and kindred matters engrossed much of his time at Southill.

CHAPTER TWENTY

A Bedfordshire Doctor

SOUTHILL catches up and reflects all the sides of Whitbread's character. Here he is the family-man, the farmer, the magistrate, the sportsman, the benefactor and the politician. He was indulgent to Lady Elizabeth, generous with time and thought to his children but with politics and his country never far below the surface of his mind. England it has been said was governed from its country houses; of Southill that could not be said; rather it was the place where opposition was sharpened, where established and complacent men in power were paraded before the company as pantaloons and drooling idiots.

At Southill, following the advice of his father, who, long ago inveighed against the dangers of lying abed, Whitbread was up at six. At that uncomfortable moment he wrote letters and dictated to his secretary. He then went to see his children, planning what they might be able to do together through the day. 'His children always looked forward to this time of the day with the greatest delight. He was alone with them.'* At half past eight he was in the justice-room, attending to his duties as magistrate. Breakfast followed and he then generally rode out, going either to his farm or round the estate and attended to county business. He did not meet his family again till dinner, and he sat with them and his guests till ten, when he went to bed. Although no evidence survives, dinner at Southill was probably at half past four or at five. From Jane Austen we learn that Mr. Woodhouse in *Emma* dined at four, and General Tilney in *Northanger Abbey* at five 'even in the country'.¹ On his first visit to Southill, which was in the autumn of 1809, Creevey

* From a short memoir at Chewton, probably by Captain Waldegrave.

gives the outline of political Southill: 'Nothing but politics between Whitbread and me from the moment we meet just before dinner till bedtime.'[2]

It was, for example, in discussions at Southill that the rising figure of Sir Arthur Wellesley came under fire from these convivial Radicals. Whitbread had incurred the displeasure of Wellesley at the time of the latter's victorious crossing of the Douro in 1809 by saying that in reporting to the Government at home Wellesley had exaggerated his success. To a mutual friend of his own and Whitbread's Wellesley wrote that he was disturbed by Whitbread's statement because it meant 'that I had lyed'. Whitbread, writing direct to Wellesley, excused himself 'You know full well that the newspapers very commonly misrepresent what falls from Members of Parliament, and that it is impossible to answer for what is put in by the reporters'.[3] But in spite of the civilities of the correspondence the radical coterie at Southill were not unqualified admirers of my Lord Wellington as Whitbread generally called him in the Commons. Creevey was shown the correspondence when he was at Southill, and at the beginning of the following year he wrote to Whitbread, after Wellesley had been rewarded with a viscountcy, complaining that Whitbread was determined to think well of him 'without an atom of anything like reason for your so doing, except his private letter to you'. Creevey went on to describe Wellington as 'an ordinary, rash soldier' but 'no ordinary intriguer' who had fought for his peerage 'at so fatal and useless expenditure of our brave troops'.[4] These words were not without effect on Whitbread who spoke against the vote of thanks to Wellington after Talavera in 1810 and he voted against the grant of any annuity to him 'It appears to me that Lord Wellington had got his army into a prodigious scrape, and that they had brought him out of it most wonderfully'.[5] At the close of his life Whitbread trounced Wellington for signing, with representatives of the other powers assembled at Vienna, a statement that Napoleon, by the escape from Elba, 'had placed himself without the pale of civil and social relations' and had rendered himself 'liable to public vengeance'. Whitbread said that 'the name of Wellington was disgraced by being included in such a paper'. Later in the House of Commons, Wellesley Pole (a very foolish and insignificant brother of Wellington whose voice grated on the human ear as horribly as five fiddles)[6] said that he happened to be with his brother when a report of Whitbread's speech reached him. 'Never was a man so shocked as he then was.' Such outbursts were unpleasantly frequent and the truth was that Whitbread, though always a man of firm decision, was too readily influenced by the agreeable pressures of political-social life. Himself absent for long stretches from London he was perhaps too attentive to the light persiflage of Creevey and later of Brougham, who both seemed to him to bring the sharp sense of metropolitan life to those long Bedfordshire evenings.

Across Whitbread's life of bounding vigour there lurked the pitfall of advancing years, the danger that nature might rebel against a life superabundant energies and that with Matthew Arnold he might be brought to say :

I feel her finger light
Laid pausefully upon life's headlong train;

From 1809 he began to suffer from what he called 'listlessness and dejection'. Complaining of this to Grey two years later, he said 'The root of it I do not know. I live temperately and do nothing which can injure my health. I believe a good, active week in the House of Commons would do me more good than harm.'[7] So does the patient often turn with relish to the chalice which is poisoning his system.

No doubt from the point of view of his physique it was a thousand pities that he had to abandon the hunting-field. In the last year of his life Whitbread had a letter from his old hunting friend, Peter Payne; sportsmen are perhaps too readily dismissed by those who sit at desks as hard, unfeeling brutes their minds filled with little more uplifting than the kill. But Payne succeeded in putting on paper sentiments which must have

moved Whitbread and which were indubitably shared by him.
After saying how difficult it was for man to imagine that any of
his pleasures are gone for ever he asks 'shall I never with you
see Keysoe Park* again?' Then he goes on 'Yet but a little
while and I shall never see the sun rise again over those hills —
yet a little while and from those fields I shall never see the lark
rise again — yet a little while and I shall never see the shade and
hear the voice or the *silence* of those deep woods again — yet a
little while and I shall never see the storm-enduring shepherd
and his flock again. Is not the worn-out sportsman to be pitied?'⁸

In the case of Whitbread, those who loved him may have
pitied him for having to abandon the chase, but they also had
grounds for concern. Although it need not have been cause and
effect — such conclusions belong to the consulting-room — the
abandonment of hunting coincided with the obvious symptoms
of what then was called 'a plethoric constitution'. In 1812
Creevey, staying at Southill, wrote to his wife 'there is some
unfortunate defect in his constitution, his tendency to manufac-
ture blood and fat is beyond everything I ever heard of. . . . I
was struck beyond measure just now at the prodigious Gills and
Collops in his neck'.⁹ Eighteen months later Whitbread himself
was writing to Mrs. Creevey 'Do not be surprised to find me
doubled in size'.¹⁰

Whitbread was in admirable medical care. He saw the royal
doctor, Sir Henry Halford — but his chief medical confidant
was the Bedford doctor, G. D. Yeats. Born in Florida before
America was separated from Great Britain, this remarkable man
was educated at Oxford, practised in Bedford, where he was
mayor, and moved to London in 1814. When he started practice
in Bedfordshire Whitbread told him that he would have to pay
particular attention to croup and hydrocephalus. Parts of the
long letter which he wrote to Whitbread in August 1810
deserve to be quoted partly for the light they throw on Whitbread's health and partly for the wisdom of a country-doctor at
the dawn of the nineteenth century — wisdom not wholly upset

* In the Oakley country north of Bedford.

by the wonders of medical science in the years which separate our world from his.

After a general disquisition on the dangers of a plethoric condition (which is more or less in line with the views of twentieth-century doctoring) Dr. Yeats goes on:

So much for the general question you put to me. With respect to yourself more especially, allow me to say something to which the above observations may be considered as preliminary. You possess a constitution, I may say desirable, provided the person possessing it has sufficient resolution not to yield to the prejudices or to give way to the indulgences of conviviality, and the world knows enough of you for me safely to say that this may be predicated of you — as the logicians speak. There can be no doubt that there is a great tendency in your habit to accumulation with a direction of it more particularly towards the head — termed an apoplectic disposition — there is also a state of stomach both from a good appetite and a strong digestion highly favourable, if indulged in, to the increase and maintenance of this disposition by inducing a succulency of the constitution in the accumulation of fluid and fat particularly in the viscera of the abdomen between which (but chiefly the liver) and the head there is a particular sympathy. . . . no fat has ever been discovered in the brain, whenever therefore it is collected in the body, it must in proportion to its quantity, make a considerable pressure on the blood vessels (the blood will of course flow where there is the least resistance) it will consequently be directed towards and be accumulated in the head where there is not a proportionate increase of fat to produce equal pressure and resistance as in other parts of the body — hence apoplexy most commonly occurs in bulky people. You will be good enough to observe that the remarks I make on this complaint are solely applicable to your constitution and to those like yours for I have known a tendency to this disease in thin people and subdued by different means. I would make it a rule to live always with a diet restricted both in quality and quantity, avoiding such, not wholly but in a great measure, as are highly stimulating whether from spices or rich sauces. I would sometimes omit meat altogether and substitute fish — completely exclude all malt liquors and spirits except good sound table or small beer; to an occasional indulgence in a glass of which there can be no objection. With respect to wine you will find it much to your advantage to take very little of it — it would be as well at times to omit altogether and take nothing beyond a glass of hock and water or claret and water. For common beverage, water is the best either plain or with toasted bread or lemon peel infused in it or lemonade — bottled spruce beer is not bad under the restriction of moderation. As to exercise the more you take the better with the exception of sudden great exertions or continued exercise in the heat of sun as the head must at all times be kept cool by every means; indeed the diet and regimen enjoined will do that and will render great exercise not only not injurious but advantageous. The shower bath, *but not bathing generally in any other way* will be found of considerable use every morning during the summer. With respect to medicine recourse should be had to cooling salts in some shape or another — how frequently will depend upon circumstances. As a rule I may say that when the weather is hot or you feel heated or uneasy it would be wise to resort to their aid twice a week. Cheltenham salts are very well but in the summer months I prefer as more cooling a solution of four, six or eight drams of Epsom Salts (as much I mean as will produce three good evacuations) in a glass of lemonade or two ounces of the Effusion of Roses in a half glass of water taken in the morning fasting; and as aloes have the effect of irritating the blood vessels in the lower intestines and thus directing the blood from the head it is useful at times to take about 5 grains in two pills at night previous to the salts in the morning. The cooling and opening plan of diet however will after a time render it less necessary to take opening physic often by altering the constitutional disposition to apoplexy. Should there take place at any time, notwithstanding this, much pain and throbbing in the head, cupping in the nape of the neck should be immediately resorted to, (and the quantity of blood taken should not be small) followed up by a dose of opening physic in such quantity as you know from experience will produce copious evacuations.[11]

Whitbread's neighbour, Lord Ongley — never the most perceptive of mortals — wrote lamenting his own ill health and wrote to Whitbread: 'I wish I was as stout a fellow as you are. I can not help envying you.'[12] So perhaps the world saw him. The true picture was different. On one of the rare occasions when he was separated from his wife he wrote saying that he was going to have his dinner at Brooks's, but he promised her that he would eat and drink in accordance with Dr. Yeats's advice.

CHAPTER TWENTY-ONE

Independence at Westminster

In the last four or five years of his political life Whitbread's political power, unlike a pear past its prime, did not grow sleepy. The Government under Perceval, on countless occasions, gave an impression of that abject humility shown by a sinner detected in his sin. Whitbread was their flagellant. Over the whole range of current events his vigilance was unceasing. There were nearly 50,000 French prisoners-of-war in England and some Danes, Russians and Dutch. Was there anxiety over their treatment? Whitbread raised the question after personally inspecting the depots for these luckless men at Portsmouth. And what of English prisoners-of-war in France? Whitbread was determined that these men should not be forgotten, and above all that the Government should help with the education of their children. He was — inevitably — with the minority of forty-four in 1814 who thought that Lord Cochrane, who was accused of spreading the rumour that Napoleon had been killed in order to influence the stock exchange, was innocent. 'I firmly believe the possibility of his innocence.'[1] He was one of the promoters of the 1808 Act for the better care of pauper-lunatics. He took immense pains to find out and reveal the horrible conditions in which convicts had to serve in the hulks : in pursuit of truth he had a convict's dinner sent to Dover Street for his inspection. Petitions about the treatment of newspaper men, who were supposedly guilty of spreading sedition — and one in particular who was serving sentence in Dorchester Gaol — were laid before Parliament by Whitbread. He devoted much attention to the sad state of debtors in prison in the Channel Islands, of the Maltese struggling for a constitution, and of the naval officer

R

who punished a troublesome seaman by landing him and leaving him on the then uninhabited island of Sombrero. He did not eschew the trivial, and took up Parliamentary time by enquiring about a charger, which had carried Prince Platov, the victorious Cossack general, and had been given to the Regent. He thought this horse ought to have been allowed to pass the remainder of life in 'riotous felicity'. Instead of this, he had been informed that the brave horse of the hetman of the Cossacks was drawing a dung cart at Hampton Court.[2]

But Whitbread was fundamentally serious-minded, and it was on the graver issues of the day that he was most powerfully felt. His voice was, from the very first, loud in warning the House of Commons of the drift to war with the United States. In June 1812 the American President declared that a state of war existed between America and Great Britain. For two years Whitbread had been in the closest touch with the representatives of the American Government in London, trying to avert this calamity. A few weeks before war began he declared in the House of Commons that 'I look back to the contest in which she [America] had been engaged with this country, with reverence and admiration for America . . . I feel no jealousy of the prosperity of America, convinced as I am, that with proper management here, the more she flourished the more would this country flourish.'[3] The former Lord Chancellor, Erskine, a wayward, but independent-minded Whig, who was well described by Lord John Russell as having the tongue of Cicero and the soul of Hampden, wrote to Whitbread in vigorous praise of his efforts to stave off the war with America 'I well remember your exertions last session on the subject of America : I was present and afterwards in Dover Street told you what (with everybody else) I thought of them.' He continued in reference to Perceval's Government 'What men sow that shall they reap : and never to be sure was there such a harvest of wickedness and folly since men congregated and formed the nations of the earth as our Rascals and Blockheads are now getting in in its abundance'.[4] Whitbread was the leader of the critics of the futile and disastrous expedition against the Scheldt in 1809. On this topic his deepest thrusts were reserved for Canning, who was Foreign Minister at the time. He had done, as Whitbread pointed out, what in the whole history of England no other man could have been found to do. When the plans for the expedition were far advanced he had gone to the Prime Minister and also to the King to say that the Minister in charge (Castlereagh) 'was not competent to his situation'. Continuing, he said :

the Right Honourable Gentleman had no mercy for colleagues : in pursuit of his own views of personal ambition, he cared not what embarrassment he brought upon them or the country.

> Hot, cold, wet and dry
> All contend for mastery;
> But he threw chaos in.

He ended his speech by saying 'the memory of the dead and the honour of the Army call for vengeance upon the authors of this expedition. I trust in God that the House will attend to the call.'[5]

His personal relations with Wilberforce were never warm,* and he once said in the House of Commons that Wilberforce's mind always wavered in doubt. He would certainly have agreed with Hazlitt that the little Yorkshireman was forever playing the game of hawk and buzzard eager to do right but almost more eager to be popular. But for all these personal rubs Whitbread was inevitably an ardent advocate of the abolition of slavery. The slave trade only had been abolished by the Talents in 1807 : slavery, with its inevitable but illegal traffic in slaves, remained, and was constantly attacked by Whitbread in the Commons. Perhaps in all his political life he experienced only once the cold blast of disapproval from opinion on the Left. This centred round the proposals to encourage the exportation of corn in times of plenty and, by an import tariff to prevent the foreigner from

---

* Wilberforce was the originator of the remark about Whitbread's oratory — 'he spoke as if he had a pot of porter at his lips and all his words came through it' (R. I. and S. Wilberforce, *Life of William Wilberforce* (1839), v. 329).

underselling home-grown corn except in times of scarcity. During 1814 and 1815 there was much discussion over the figure to be reached for the cost of home-grown corn at which imported corn might be admitted duty-free. The figure varied between 70s. and 100s. The price of wheat on average in 1814 was 74s. 6d. and in 1815 64s. 6d. If the ardent protectionists, who were clamouring for 100s. had had their way no corn would have been admitted in either year duty-free. Dwellers in the towns saw the proposals as an attempt to pamper farmer, landlord and countryman at the expense of merchant, manufacturer and artisan. When the Corn Laws were finally passed in 1815 the Houses of Parliament had to be defended by troops and the slogan — 'No Corn Laws' was conspicuous among the banners at Peterloo.[6] Whitbread, with his farming and landowning interests, was plainly put in a position of difficulty not rendered easier by a forceful display of public opinion which on 6 March hooted and jeered those thought to be in favour of the Bill as they approached the Houses of Parliament. On the following day they attacked the Brewery in Chiswell Street destroying many of the windows with a shower of stones.[7]

Althought it is true that he publicly favoured a postponement of the Bill till passions were calmer his real feelings were made clear in a speech at the end of February 1815. He defended the rise in agricultural rents, arguing that they stimulated the tenant making him in reality richer. He would have agreed with the Member of Parliament for Taunton (Mr. Alexander Baring), who spoke just before him that visitors to farmhouses once refreshed with ale were now offered port or madeira, that farmers' sons instead of following the plough followed the hounds, and that farmers' daughters, instead of milking, used cosmetics on their hands so that they should look delicate when they were strumming on the harpsichord. He was outspoken in condemning high wages arguing that more human misery was caused by overpayment than by underpayment. He then indulged in what he would have regarded as playfulness, but which his more fastidious listeners must have regarded as unbearably coarse. He foretold a rapid increase in agricultural production and argued (with Malthus) that if there were an increase of production 'some little brat or other would always be found to eat the surplus corn'. He also thought that the wives of the returning soldiers and sailors would be very much more prolific than they were when they were 'kept' by the right honourable gentlemen opposite to him. Two days later Napoleon quitted Elba and Whitbread was engrossed by the themes of war and peace — more familiar to him and less likely to provoke his admirers out of doors.

On an earlier occasion when Whitbread spoke in the House of Commons on the Corn Laws the chairman of Ways and Means, Brogden a trimmer to the Right, who was once called by Creevey 'a cursèd, rum touch', wrote to tell Whitbread that 'it was one of the best speeches I ever heard in or out of that chair'.[8] But against praise from this quarter Whitbread had to face criticism from urban Radicals. He was sent a cleverly drafted pamphlet headed 'No! Not One!' This included the information that 'Samuel Whitbread Esq has been present every day since the Corn Bills have been agitated. He has made all kinds of speeches upon all manner of topics. He has advocated the cause of the people of Norway,* and of the people of America, and of Random de Berenger.† But has he uttered one syllable against the Corn Laws and in favour of the People of England? No. Not One.'[9]

Whitbread did not resent such pasquinades. Brougham placed high among Whitbread's virtues that he possessed a masculine understanding : hand in hand with that quality went a masculine rejection of trivialities and a masculine refusal to take umbrage. This was well illustrated by an episode in the House of Commons. His old sparring partner in the House of Commons, Charles Yorke, became a supporter of Perceval and lost his seat for Cambridgeshire at a by-election in 1810. In this enforced absence from the House of Commons Whitbread made

---

* Ceded to Sweden by Denmark in 1814.
† Cochrane's accomplice in the Stock Exchange fraud.

merry at his discomfiture. Yorke's brother, Sir Joseph, a
courageous man on a quarterdeck but not at ease in the House
of Commons, immediately rose and said that whatever legacy his
brother had bequeathed to the House of Commons it would be
remembered with respect. 'Certain I am that it must be as good
as any that proceeded from a brewer of bad porter.' There was,
in those days, always apprehension lest such personal attacks
should lead to a challenge. There was a general cry of 'Order!
Order! Chair! Chair!' which lasted for several minutes. When
he could make himself heard, Whitbread rose and said : 'I can
assure the House that I am in no other way affected by it than
as a tradesman.' He then asked Sir Joseph to make a trial of his
porter : 'I will undertake to furnish him with the best, and all I
ask in return is that he will give it to the electors of Cambridgeshire to drink the health of their late member.' Whitbread's
friends continued to demand that the words should be taken
down with a view to apology. Whitbread rose again : 'I wish, as
I am sure I feel perfect good humour on this subject and the
honourable gentleman (as I perceive by his countenance) is
restored to tranquillity, the House would not call for any
apology. I require none.'[10]

To one man, 'that damned, perfidious charlatan, Canning' — the words are Creevey's — Whitbread was less
accommodating. He loathed him. They constantly clashed in
debate, and Whitbread once said of him 'the Right Honourable
Gentleman's eloquence is of a stormy description, full of bursts
of genius and coruscatious of talent, but it has all the other
ingredients of the storm — vapour, cloud and wind.' William
Hazlitt said something the same when he wrote of Canning :
'Truth, liberty, justice, humanity, war or peace, civilisation or
barbarism are things of little consequence except for him to
make speeches upon them.'[11] That was true. He was the precise
opposite of Whitbread who felt those things to the depths of his
heart's being. To Canning a Parliamentary occasion was a
challenge to him to shine : to Whitbread such an occasion was a
chance for truth to shine.

'An annual exhibition.' With these unfeeling words Canning described Whitbread's painstaking arguments in favour of a negotiated peace which he invariably brought forward at the beginning of each Parliamentary session. He never wavered in his belief that negotiations with Napoleon ought to be attempted. But he would not have echoed the comment on Waterloo made by his friend, Lord Sefton, 'Horrible news! They have gained a great victory.'[12] When Napoleon was defeated in 1814 Whitbread wrote to Sheridan's son: 'there is no heart more fully satisfied than mine'.[13] But he was absolutely opposed to a renewal of the war after Napoleon's escape from Elba, to starting — as he put it — a new Crusade to decide who should fill the throne of France. Although Whitbread's opinions on this subject were never popular, they were respected. The House of Commons accepted them though without agreeing with them, and the only evidence of their stirring animosity was when the landlord of the 'Black Swan' at Hertford wrote to Whitbread to complain that his clients were saying that 'Mr. Whitbread said in the House of Commons "God send Bonaparte ships, colonies and commerce".' He had said something of the kind, and a Leicester journal seized on this to assert that his feelings towards England were in consonance with those of the French Emperor. But political feeling, on the whole, rose above the prejudices of the Hertford bar-parlour or of the Leicester journalists. Indeed nothing illustrates the drive downwards of political sanity more emphatically than a contrast between the fate of him who opposed a popular war at the beginning of the nineteenth century and those who trod the same path in the twentieth century. Even by the middle of the nineteenth century the change was apparent. As G. M. Trevelyan writes in his life of John Bright (the outspoken critic of the Crimean War): 'To attack the justice and wisdom of a popular war when it is still in progress requires more courage than any other act in a political society that has outgrown the assassin's dagger and the executioner's block.'

The sturdy figure of Whitbread, wearing on most occasions

a blue frockcoat with blue vest and blue trousers,[14] seemed to repel loose charges that Whitbread was 'unpatriotic'. 'I am not the partisan of Napoleon', he often said, 'I am the partisan of England.' 'He is the Representative of the English People — an epitome of the national character.' So wrote the editor of *The Times*.[15] There was also about Whitbread an unmistakable authority, shown clearly on the occasion of Perceval's murder in the lobby of the House of Commons by the madman, Bellingham. Immediately after the murder, Bellingham was brought to the Bar of the Commons, which was sitting in committee. The Speaker was sent for. The Speaker committed Bellingham to the prison-room, suggesting that Members should proceed first, as the immediate reaction of most Members to the news was that it might be part of a general attack on the nation's leaders. Whitbread then rose and, in a tone which betrayed the difficulty he felt in commanding his feelings, asked the Speaker, in order to avoid undignified confusion, to name the Members who should go to the prison-room. The Speaker named Mr. Long, Mr. Bootle and Mr. Whitbread. The three Members preceded the messenger of the House of Commons, who followed with Bellingham. We may picture Whitbread solemn, heavy-footed, weighed down with the emotion of the moment, recalling his many brushes with the little lawyer: 'I see that his silences are as dexterous as his eloquence', 'On the wings of "No Popery" he flew into power', 'an adventurer from the Bar raised by his talent for debate to a great situation', but — as he was to say in formal tribute to the statesman's memory — he never carried a feeling of resentment against any Member of the House of Commons beyond the door 'and in the case of the Right Honourable Gentleman I have ever found it impossible to carry such a feeling even so far as the door'. That was true but — more to the point — it was known to be true.

CHAPTER TWENTY-TWO
Chances of Office

ALL his life Whitbread would have proudly claimed that he was a member of the historic Whig Party; but with his strong, independent turn of mind he would have claimed to be a nonconformist member. There were two matters in particular where Whitbread was unadaptable. The first (though it was of much less consequence than the second) was the patent contempt which he, Creevey and their like showed for their leader in the Commons — Ponsonby. Poor Snouch, we feel almost sorry for him, the plodding leader of a wayward team, and try to excuse that 'deplorable incapacity' which all men noted.[1]

Much more serious in Whig eyes, because it was really calling in question the constitution, was Whitbread's inclination to appeal to the public over the head of Parliament. As we have seen, Whitbread was possibly too attentive to opinions outside the House of Commons, and Creevey was constantly stoking the fire on this subject — 'You are not sufficiently aware of the perfect apathy and indifference with which all reasonable men look on the proceedings of the House of Commons.'* Brougham also noticed that Whitbread in the House of Commons was too apt to speak to the newspapers rather than to his fellow Members. Such things and — more particularly — inflammatory political action outside the House of Commons alarmed Lord Grenville and his followers. On 22 April 1809 Whitbread attended a dinner of the livery of the City at the London Tavern

---

* Bedford, 11 December 1808. The feelings of Whitbread and his friends, which were shared by advanced reformers outside Parliament, that the House of Commons was out of touch with the nation are convincingly set out in *The Whig Opposition* (1939), by Professor Michael Roberts, 235 ff.

— ostensibly to celebrate the triumph of Colonel Wardle but in reality to sing a more militant song over the arrest of Sir Francis Burdett for issuing to the public a report of his speech in the Commons on a question of parliamentary privilege. He had been arrested on the Speaker's warrant, and the rabble of the town had taken advantage of the excitement to stage some formidable riots. One of the toasts at the livery dinner which caused the maximum of offence was 'House-breakers by Analogy'. Though it is a little difficult to follow the meaning of this toast, it was presumably directed at the serjeant-at-arms who entered Sir Francis's house to arrest him. Whitbread received a long letter from Grenville, pained and shocked at his attending the dinner but writing with some reason and much dignity. He began : 'I have no pretensions to control or question your opinions : but my friends have a right to know from me my own sentiments on proceedings which attract so much attention and what I must say to others on this point I ought not after our late conversations to withhold from yourself.' On the particular toast he suggested that the obstruction to a legal warrant which wantonly endangers the lives of innocent men 'approaches much nearer to murder than its execution can to housebreaking'. The burden of his letter was that Parliament was the proper setting for the discussion of these topics. In reply, Whitbread justified himself as best he could, and was able to prove that he had contested the toast about housebreaking. He firmly added, 'It will not do for me to abstain from public meetings — in principle I think it right to attend them upon certain occasions. In such meetings you can not meet the current of public opinion "bluff" — according to an expression of poor Fox — but you may guide, moderate and with proper management divert it.'[2] The trouble was that Whitbread and his associates made it too obvious that they thought that the main stream of opinion was flowing outside Parliament and that only a reluctant trickle found its way to St. Stephen's.

Continuing his argument about the wisdom of meeting public opinion 'bluff', Whitbread told Lord Grenville : 'In pursuit of the same line of conduct I shall attend the Whig Club on Tuesday sennight when Lord Holland has placed me in the chair.'* At this, the Whig hierarchy fired a shot from their most effective gun — the Duke of Bedford intervened. He thought that by attending the Whig Club, Whitbread would proclaim himself to the world as one with those whose 'only object seems to be to degrade and vilify all public men. . . . I fear you may have reason to think with me on Tuesday next — Messrs. Waithman,† Clifford (junior)‡ will I have no doubt attend'. And with enviable aristocratic severity the duke added 'from the hands of such men God send you a good deliverance'. In reply, Whitbread pointed out how Fox's friends, in his lifetime, had always lamented his attendance at popular meetings and at the Whig Club. He ended, 'I am always ready to listen to those who approach me as you do with kindness and reason, but I must consult my own understanding and decide for myself. . . . Suspend your judgment and do not cast me off.'³ He attended the dinner.

In a letter written in 1809 the Duke of Bedford told Whitbread that the union of Fox's friends with the Grenvillites had been urged by Fox 'as his dying hope' and that he had left this as 'his last legacy to his surviving friends'.⁴ The pull of party, expressed thus clearly by an adored leader, was strong: it muted some of the warlike fervour of the Grenvilles: it restrained some of the provocatively radical outbursts of Whitbread and his circle: it even drew Grey from his Northumberland fastness to take his part in the leadership. But no party in English political history can exist on the testament of a dying leader nor can it exist with the ideal of being a perpetual Opposition, a plight which would reduce a political party to the level of the lemmings which, having mustered themselves in strength, determine to rush headlong to the sea

* A chairman was chosen for each dinner, and presumably had the right of naming the chairman for the next dinner.
† Robert Waithman, a linen-draper at Ludgate Circus. Active on the radical side in City politics and later as Member for the City.
‡ Henry Clifford, a Roman Catholic barrister of very advanced opinions.

and destruction. Although office was in fact not to come to the Whig party for a quarter of a century, it was a real possibility especially during the three years of Perceval's premiership. Perceval and his cabinet were constantly seeking to furbish themselves with new men. He made overtures to the Whig Party in 1809, when he succeeded to the premiership, throughout 1811 when the Prince of Wales became Regent and in 1812 after the limitations on the Regent's powers expired.* They were made again later in the same year when Perceval was assassinated. Naturally it was always possible to coax individual Whigs on to the Government side: Lord Wellesley, a Whig, 'that broken-down scamp and bankrupt'[5] as Creevey called him, was a member of Perceval's Cabinet. But the value of such piecemeal enrichments to the Government was negligible compared with men who brought a following, leaders who brought their party with them. The possibility of office, more than any other single cause, kept the Whig Party in being and — strange as it may seem — Whitbread for all his waywardness was as eager for office as he had been when the Talents was formed in 1806.†

In 1809 he wrote to Tierney that he would be ready for office because 'in these times of danger and difficulty, which are so great as to make hope almost forlorn' he would like to feel that he was useful.[6] In 1811 Creevey had a long talk with Whitbread in Dover Street and described himself as 'penetrated with Sam's desire to be in office'.[7] In 1812 this desire became

---

* One of the difficulties within the Whig Party was the objection, which was strongly held by Whitbread and his circle, to serving under Grenville — if he was to hold, as he had held when he was Prime Minister of the Talents, the comfortable sinecure post of auditor to the Exchequer as well as First Lord of the Treasury. This objection was well founded. During 1811 Whitbread wrote to Grey that he could not serve under Grenville if he was going to keep both places. If he attempted to defend any such arrangement 'I should lose by the attempt all I have to depend upon, character: and having lost my character I could be of no use to my friends or to the world' (Letter to Grey, 19 January 1811).

† Professor Michael Roberts in *The Whig Opposition* argues that the hope of office diminished Whitbread's support for parliamentary reform. An equally strong factor was his recollection of the troubles which the reformers drew upon themselves in the 1790's.

more conspicuous. The Prince Regent, not unreasonably, became tired of trying to coax the Whig lords, Grey and Grenville, into the Government pen, for he lacked the traditional patience of a shepherd in similar circumstances. He burst out: 'They want to tie me hand and foot. Lord Grenville with his pomp and consistency. Lord Grey with his dam'd cocked-up nose.'[8] After the assassination of Perceval the Regent attempted first to entrust the formation of a Government to Lord Wellesley and then to a personal friend Lord Moira, afterwards Marquis of Hastings and Governor-General of India. At this juncture the negotiations with the Whig grandees were particularly difficult because they were insisting that if they were to form part of the Government, the Regent must show his confidence in them by changing his courtiers. An early biographer of the Prince asked a sensible question when he wrote 'what was to be thought of the patriotism of men who postponed the preservation of the Empire to the childish vanity of making chamberlains and vice-chamberlains?'[9] Yet there was something more than vanity involved. The chamberlain was Lord Hertford, the vice-chamberlain was his son Lord Yarmouth, and Lady Hertford — the inamorata of the Prince — was believed to have swung that passionate man away from the Whigs into the coils of the Tories. There is evidence that Hertford and his son had agreed to resign and that Sheridan was deputed to tell this to the Whig leaders. Instead of delivering his message that unpredictable man told the Whigs that he was prepared to bet £500 that the Hertfords had no intention of resigning. His biographer, Thomas Moore, reasonably calls this villainy 'the only indefensible part of his whole public life'. During this impasse Whitbread, who was less punctilious about the courtiers than his brother Whigs, saw Lord Moira and was impressed to find him prepared to agree that, if he was able to form a Government, the Orders in Council should be revoked, that every means should be attempted to conciliate the Americans, that there should be rigid economy and that even parliamentary reform should not be ruled out. At a meeting of

the Whig Party while these negotiations were in train Lord
John Townshend made a drunken effusion in favour of Whitbread 'as a man much too lightly thought of by the Party' —
sentiments, which were received with boisterous acclamation
from Coke of Norfolk. But Creevey had scarcely time to retail
all this to Mrs. Creevey when he had to add, 'But here is such
devil of new matter pressing upon me that I must be off.'
Moira's powers were revoked: Perceval's followers, under
Liverpool, were installed in office.[10]

When all this began Whitbread was in camp at Cardington,
where the overture from Moira reached him. His letters arrived
at five in the morning, and he immediately set off for London.
He agreed to serve and then drove back to Cardington through
the night — attending the review of his regiment as though
Moira, the Whig lords and court chamberlains were in another
world from the march and counter-march of the gallant
Bedfordshire soldiers. On the following Sunday he was back in
London much chagrined to find that his colleagues were standing
firm over the dismissal of the courtiers.[11] If Moira's Government had really come to pass and had been formed with the
policy detailed by Creevey it would have been a triumph for the
Foxites and for Whitbread in particular. But such triumphs have
their hazards and in attempting this one Whitbread attracted his
critics. 'He sunk a great way in my estimation' wrote a respected
Whig Member of the House of Commons.[12] But in those wild
days of crisis, reverberating with the chatter of excited men,
voices were heard above the hubbub saying that Whitbread
might go to the Exchequer and even to the head of the
Government: 'this triumph for the sturdy, honest brewer'
purred Creevey.[13]

In these last years of his life Whitbread stood out as a
political force in the country beyond the House of Commons: if
there had been mass meetings then he would have been in
demand as a speaker. To begin with he was recognised throughout the land as one of the handful of leaders of those who were
struggling for the establishment of schools. During the political

reaction which stalked across the country hand in hand with the war governments of Pitt, Perceval and Liverpool, there were signs that one side of a nobler life was struggling to emerge despite the baneful glances of authority. This was education. At the end of the 1790's a Quaker, Joseph Lancaster, started to teach a few poor boys in the Borough Road. The school, which (for all its origins in a shed) prospered famously, was based on the ideal of the elder children teaching in the school. The pupil-teacher rather than the usher — that pitiful flotsam of the world of learning — was the foundation of Lancaster's success. The education was limited to reading, writing and summing and the cost for each pupil was three half-crowns a year.

The services of aristocracy to education could never be a popular or acceptable theme among twentieth-century historians, yet this is a song which awaits its singer. The great liberal Duke of Bedford (that is Francis the fifth duke) and his friend Lord Somerville, the now-forgotten but enlightened west-country lord (who sent the present of merino mutton to Whitbread), were quick to visit Lancaster in the Borough Road and to give him their support and encouragement. The sixth duke followed his brother's example; he opened a Lancaster school at Woburn and told Whitbread : 'I have no object nearer to my heart than to see this cheap and expeditious mode . . . widely and generally diffused.'[14] Whitbread became a powerful and enthusiastic supporter of Lancaster.

Support was necessary. In 1805 Lancaster was summoned to Weymouth to meet King George III and his family. The kind words of royalty fall on the minds of some persons with the force of the strongest intoxicant. One of these was Lancaster. With the words of the good old King ringing in his ears he began a course of the most fanciful and utterly improvident schemes and schools. In 1808 Whitbread, with others, extricated him from his financial embarrassments and set his schools on a firmer foundation as the Royal Lancasterian Society. During the interview at Weymouth George III let fall these words : 'it is my wish that every poor child in my dominions should be taught to read the Bible'. But there was many a gaitered divine to whom this wish was disgracefully inadequate. Where was the Prayer Book to stay the wandering, infant mind? And where the catechism? In pursuit of these the National Society was formed in 1811 to carry forward education on the principles of the Church of England. Though a churchman, Whitbread was one of those who liked the influence of the clergy confined to the pews and pulpits of the parish church on Sunday; to him anything approaching an Anglican polity was intolerable.* In the face of this challenge from the Church he and his friends redoubled their efforts on behalf of the Lancaster system. English education, freed from the shackles of an insular Church, was — these pioneers hoped — to spread through a pacified Europe *urbi et orbe*. Progressive royal dukes — those of Kent and Sussex — lent the light of their large Hanoverian countenances to the project, and the Duke of Kent, never conspicuous for tact, dropped a heavy hint that only one man could manage Lancaster and that was Whitbread. But this proved too optimistic. As Lancaster was always impossible his supporters decided to form a society — the British and Foreign School Society — on his principles but without his awkward presence. Whitbread was an extremely generous benefactor to the society and in 1813 was one of the finance committee who appealed to the public for funds. In the absence of the Duke of Bedford Whitbread wrote to the Prince Regent asking him to become 'the patron and protector of the society'; he added that with such support he was confident that the benefits of the Lancasterian system 'will be rapidly diffused over every part of the Extensive Empire of His Majesty, and at no remote period throughout the world'. After a fortnight during which he had no doubt consulted the princes of the Church the Regent declined the proposal, though making plain that he would

* In his proposals for Poor Law reform in 1807 (see page 176 ff) Whitbread urged that it should be made compulsory for parochial vestries (then the foundation of all local government) to levy rates for the support of schools to teach reading, writing and arithmetic. The absence of religion from the syllabus was one of the reasons why the House of Lords summarily rejected his Bill.

continue his subscription to the society.* With another wayward celebrity of the time Whitbread was more fortunate. The poet Byron replied as follows to the appeal from Whitbread, which has not survived, but which was evidently a suggestion that the poet should attend and speak at one of the meetings of the Society.

Albany May 20th. 1814

MY DEAR SIR,

Ever since I was honoured with your letter I have been trying to nerve myself into attending you and saying something upon the subject of the meeting to whose object I am a sincere friend — but the recollection of the pain which my former attempts at public speaking have always occasioned to myself without giving any pleasure to others — must deter me now and ever from all further efforts to express my opinions before a large assembly.† You will oblige me if you will have the goodness to put down my name as a subscriber to the Institution for one hundred guineas and inform me to whom it should be paid; or — if you will permit me — I will send a draft on my Bankers for the amount.

To yourself I can only say that I am highly honoured and gratified by the contents of your letter — and ever most proud of being

Very respectfully and sincerely yours

BYRON[15]

Brougham said that it was Whitbread's uniform adherence to principle and his resolute independence which procured for him the undiminished confidence of his country.[16] There are countless examples among his papers of appeals to him for political help and advice from all parts of England and Scotland. Advanced politicians from Birmingham, the Potteries, Liverpool, Leeds and Manchester were in regular correspondence with him. From Barnstaple it was reported to him that the Tories, always a trifle desperate in that progressive setting, tried to discredit their opponent by saying that 'he was of Mr. Whitbread's

---

* *Letters of George IV 1812–30*, (1938), ed. A. Aspinall. Later, as King, he became a patron of the society.

† Alluding to his speeches in the House of Lords in the previous year which were generally regarded as unsuccessful, Lord Holland said that as a speaker in the House of Lords his style was 'not suited to our common notions of Parliamentary eloquence'.

S

politics'. A friend travelling in the west country wrote to
Whitbread : 'I noticed several instances of your popularity upon
the walls of Bristol.'[17] John Manby, an old friend who was
Vicar of Lancaster, wrote to complain that 'the Member for
Bedford stands much higher in estimation among the merchants
and freemen of Lancaster than their own vicar does'.[18] And
perhaps the standing of Whitbread is most clearly and luridly
revealed by the experience of a member of the committee
thought to be responsible for riots in the cotton town of Bolton.
He was arrested, and letters from Whitbread were found on
him. At Lancaster Gaol he was interrogated by someone on
behalf of the Government, who asked : 'Did Mr. Whitbread
write to you first? Why did you write to him and not to your
own Member of Parliament?' The prisoner explained that he
had written first, and that he had done so 'because Mr. Whitbread studied the true interest of the country'.[19]

CHAPTER TWENTY-THREE

Tribulations of a Princess

ONE summer's day in 1811, at the time of year when London begins to grow tired, when heat seems to bounce off the pavement so that smells, once tempting and fragrant, strike the passer-by as redolent of greasy cooks, Thomas Creevey, M.P., was strolling through Downing Street. Suddenly all his senses were alerted by exertions in the kitchen of Number 10. Four chefs and eight maids were busy preparing a great dinner for that highly particular and most fastidious guest the Prince Regent. And indeed this rich July dinner marked a political change of magnitude. The Regent was in the process of deserting the Foxite Whigs 'persons with whom the early habits of my public life were formed' and throwing the royal authority behind Spencer Perceval and his Tory Government. Writing to his wife while the scene was fresh in his mind Creevey burst out 'by God, this is too much. The folly and villainy of this Prinny is certainly beyond anything.'[1] Whether the Regent was either so villainous or so foolish as Creevey and the Whigs imagined is a matter of opinion: for the Regent to introduce a Government of squabbling Whigs, with the possibility that the King might recover, in the middle of a long-fought war would have needed courage and — it has to be confessed — more confidence in the Whigs than they felt in themselves. But one thing was certain — a section of the Whig Party — the *enragés* — was calling for retribution on the Regent: they were as vociferous as a pack of hounds round the stag at bay; they were determined to punish the Regent and put

down that mighty man. Unhappily for him he was protected by
nothing more substantial than the trappings of power and was
mercilessly exposed to the teeth of his enemies.

So much has been written about the relations between the
Regent and his wife that the essential has become hopelessly
entangled in the trivial. The sins of the husband have been used
as a screen for the follies of the wife. The Princess of Wales
was a member of the historic house of Brunswick which
was famous for its fighting princes and for its frivolous
princesses. Her great-aunt had been the wife of Frederick
the Great — possibly not a wholly satisfactory husband,
but husband and wife speedily separated. Her aunt married
Frederick the Great's successor: after four years they were
divorced. Their only child was the Duchess of York, who
preferred the society of a vast companionage of lap dogs to that
of her martial husband. Happily not everyone with eccentric
aunts necessarily shares their eccentricity. But even the
warmest advocate of the Princess could not pretend that the
oddity of the Brunswick ladies had passed her by. When the
marriage was contemplated she had a powerful advocate in
England — George III. (She was the daughter of his eldest
sister who had been greeted at birth by her illustrious grandmother Queen Caroline with those prophetic words: *'vous
voilà arrivée dans un désagréable monde'*.) As George III was
paying his son's debts in exchange for marriage he was in a
position to dictate who the bride should be. Some of the blame
for all the unhappiness of bride and bridegroom must belong to
the father who chose the bride. And when all has been argued
on both sides of the question some words of the bride's mother
hang in the memory: 'Her excuse is, poor thing, that she is not
right here', tapping her forehead.

They were married in 1795 and after a year of marriage
Princess Charlotte was born; the result, according to informed
opinion outside the nuptial chamber, of a single connexion; a
few weeks after the birth parted for ever. No doubt in normal
circumstances the princess might have gone back to Germany,

living a solitary if not wholly intolerable life as had her aunt and great-aunt. But Europe was being rapidly overrun by Napoleon, and was scarcely safe for a princess linked with England; in fact her mother, who fled to England after Jena, was convinced that her capture was the prime object of the Emperor's ambition. Such are the innocent vanities of royal persons.

The case of the Princess of Wales during Whitbread's lifetime was primarily political, secondarily personal. Historically this importance has become transposed and the personal has elbowed out the political. Moreover twentieth-century morality fastens on the peccadilloes of the husband as a justification for the vagaries of the wife. Such factors were lightweights in the scale of regency morality. Even English public opinion and the English royal family did not spring to the defence of George III's youngest sister when she was imprisoned by her husband, whose flagrant practice of abominable crimes was widely known. For the masculine there was one law, for the feminine another.

In politics the poor princess became an issue, and in the game of party became not unlike a football. One side 'had the ball', played with it, controlled it and used it as a means of thwarting their opponents: then the other side took the ball and played the same tricks on their rivals. In 1806 the Talents, anxious to strengthen their ties with the Prince of Wales, set up a commission to enquire into the princess's conduct. The members were Lord Grenville (the Prime Minister), Erskine (the Lord Chancellor), Ellenborough (the Lord Chief Justice) and Lord Spencer (Home Secretary) and their labours were known familiarly as The Delicate Investigation. In the result these lords did not think that the evidence and witnesses examined by them proved 'criminality' in the princess's conduct, but they felt obliged to add that her behaviour gave rise to 'very unfavourable interpretations'. With that, the Tories who were out of office 'seized the ball'. Spencer Perceval, crying 'to the scaffold or the Tower in such a cause', assumed the legal championship of the princess, and drafted for his client what has been called 'an incomparable letter of defence' which was addressed to George III. Throughout the closing months of the existence of the Talents, Perceval was eager that the evidence given at The Delicate Investigation should be published. Some 2,000 copies of 'The Book', as it was called, were printed, and stored in Perceval's house in Lincoln's Inn Fields. Then the Talents fell, and Perceval found himself Chancellor of the Exchequer. There was an immense conflagration of The Book in the midst of those comfortable, decorous private houses in Lincoln's Inn Fields and Perceval made desperate efforts to buy up any copies which the flames had missed. In that light-hearted century he was able to use secret-service funds for this innocent purpose. Grey, who had been Foreign Secretary, confided to a friend 'I don't know what this fund is'.* The princess showed her gratitude by entertaining the members of the new Cabinet to dinner, and there the matter rested.

Four years later the Whig *enragés* seized the ball and gave a brilliant display of tactics which, while they may not have been sufficient to upset the Government, gave them many a tense and uneasy moment. The full subtlety of that dinner in Downing Street, when the Regent supped with the former champion of his wife, was appreciated by Thomas Creevey : as a result he and his friends were bent on vengeance against the prince, determined to strike at him through the princess, and they picked up the ball dropped by the Tories. The principal players were Whitbread and Brougham. The latter, who was out of the House of Commons from the General Election of 1812 until 1815, was largely in the background though extremely influential with the princess because of his legal knowledge. Creevey, partly through his wife's health and partly through debt, was less in London. In consequence the parliamentary game was — if not played exclusively by Whitbread — at least captained by him. The official Whigs stood ostentatiously aloof, their attitude well epitomised by some words of Holland that they found the princess's business 'at all times degrading to the

* All these events are admirably described in Denis Gray's excellent biography *Spencer Perceval, 1762-1812*, published in 1963.

national character, disgusting and tiresome.'² But the *enragés* cared for none of these things, and Brougham told Whitbread that Snouch and 'Cole' had no more right to criticise him than the door-keeper at St. Stephens.³ But Whitbread himself summed up the matter for the princess in a letter — 'it is very difficult to steer in such seas as we navigate, and our course must at times be unintelligible, except to those who are accustomed to them'.⁴

The game opened playfully. In March 1812 the Regent applied to Parliament for a grant for his four surviving sisters living in England. At once the Opposition drew attention to the absence of any provision for the Princess of Wales. On her marriage her jointure was fixed at £50,000 a year: her debts in 1812 amounted to £49,000 which the Regent proposed to pay out of the funds allotted by Parliament for the payment of his own (very much larger) debt. In his speech in the Commons Whitbread called this 'One of the most complete juggles that ever was heard of.' But Perceval was the chief target for attack — the champion of the princess in 1806 and 1807 who, in 1812, had become the henchman of the prince. Whitbread attempted to draw him over the Book which — he said — had been prepared so that England and all Europe should be acquainted with the innocence of the Brunswick princess, then suddenly 'the Book had been suppressed, and the outstanding copies bought up at an enormous price, proceeding from what quarter I know not; I can not conceive that the Right Honourable Gentleman would now feel an inclination to be mute, when so recently he was supposed to have 10,000 tongues.'* At the end of the debate the Home Secretary said that the conduct of Whitbread and his friends in raising this question had created 'disgust and disapprobation'. There was little sign that this was true.

At the beginning of the following year the matter flared up once more. By this time Princess Charlotte was growing up —

* Two thousand copies of The Book were said to have been printed. With that capacity of public men to strengthen their own case Whitbread enlarged the figure somewhat.

she was 17; in consequence those two companions of the royal teens — an appropriate marriage and confirmation — were discussed and agitated. In 1813 the Princess of Wales wrote an enormous, turgid letter to her husband: it was not composed by herself and was a pompous recital of her wrongs (especially the fact that she was allowed to see her daughter, who was living at Windsor with her grandmother and aunts, only once a week designed for publication in the newspapers. The letter was comparable with those exchanged by Cabinet Ministers and the Prime Minister on a resignation: it was composed to justify action but to conceal both truth and feeling. One of the Princess of Wales's ladies-in-waiting called this correctly 'a letter in masquerade forced and unnatural'.[5] Almost certainly Whitbread had a hand in drafting this particular letter; if it was not his concoction, the letter was composed in close consultation between him and Brougham.

But Brougham was rightly alarmed lest the prince had some knowledge of the princess's behaviour. 'It all stands excellently *if he has no case* . . . the difficulty you see is this — He may have a case and yet be very averse to produce it.'[6] His case was — though at this stage the Regent only knew it in outline — that the princess had encouraged familiarities between her daughter and Captain Hesse, who was supposedly a royal bastard. These bedroom frivolities explained his reluctance for mother and daughter to meet. Had the mother's self-appointed champions and advisers known these facts they would hardly have raised the case with the reckless abandon which they showed in the following March. The publication of the letter reciting the mother's indignation at being kept apart from her daughter blew up the public excitement in a style comparable with a bonfire of straw. The public was not yet partisan: it was stirred, as it only can be stirred, by a royal *scompiglio*. When the question was known to be coming up for debate on 5 March the avenues to the House of Commons were crowded and the public galleries were filled at the instant the doors were opened. The Government supporters moved and carried that strangers should be excluded: this was done, and it meant that the reporters had to leave likewise. The record of what was said was kept by Creevey and another Whig member. 'I reported the first half of the debate and Parnell the second.'* Whitbread made unquestionably the speech of his life. As was said at the time he closed 'a most animated speech', 'amid shouts of applause'[7] and his leader, Ponsonby, referred to his eloquence as 'admirable, incomparable, resistless'. Creevey told Grey at Brooks's that it was the best speech I ever heard, and Grey laconically replied 'I'm damn'd glad of it'.[8] The debating strength of what Whitbread said lay in his attack on the ministers. Their advice was that the Regent should limit the meetings of the princess and her daughter not (as Brougham had feared) on any new facts but on the evidence of 1806. Yet these were the ministers who in distinction to the views expressed by the Talents had, in commenting on the evidence to the King, purposely left out the strictures on the general conduct of the princess which had formed an important part of the Talents' advice to the King. He asked rhetorically 'whether Ministers meant to escape from their own words. Were they to be permitted to pronounce on the old evidence a new verdict of guilty? Was ever woman so triumphant?' If Whitbread had allowed the matter to rest there posterity would have admired his chivalry but, as so often happened with him, his feelings — mounting higher with the excitement of the moment — carried him towards the rapids.

The witnesses who were examined at The Delicate Investigation in 1806 were for the most part representatives of the type embodied in the phrase 'what the butler saw'. There were Robert Bidgood, in the employment of the princess for twenty-three years; William Cole, who had been with her ever since she came to England; Frances Lloyd, the coffee-room maid; Mary Ann Wilson, the housemaid; Samuel Roberts, the footman; Thomas Stikeman, the page; John Sicard, the house-steward; and Betty Townley, the laundress. All would have felt comfortable and at ease in a modern divorce court. The general

* Otherwise the debate would have gone unrecorded.

impression from their evidence could be summed up by the
insular condemnation used by one of them about the princess 'she
was rather free in her conversation like foreign women in
general'.[9] But there were a few witnesses who were of a different
order, and these included Mrs. Lisle. She was the sister of
Lord Cholmondeley and was a member of the princess's household. Her evidence was favourable to the princess though she
said that Mr. Chester, whom the princess admired, was 'a pretty
young man' and that the princess was guilty of 'flirting conduct'.
A few days after his triumphant speech Whitbread proceeded to
arraign the legal members of the 1806 Commission — the Lord
Chancellor (Erskine) and the Lord Chief Justice (Ellenborough) for putting questions 'as though fishing for something
as if in a cross examination'. He then said that a friend of
'integrity and honour' had put in his hand a correct copy of Mrs.
Lisle's evidence. The correct copy was a private account which
Mrs. Lisle had written, after her examination, for the eyes of the
princess only. Whitbread must have been given this copy either
by Brougham or by the princess herself. This was of course an
outrageous attack on the integrity of the commissioners, who
were personal friends and political allies of Whitbread. On 22
March Whitbread's attack was raised in the House of Lords.
Erskine, who, it will be remembered, had warmly championed
Whitbread's handling of the Melville impeachment said 'my
professional character, my situation in life and the rank I hold
make it scarcely necessary to vindicate myself from such an
imputation as falsifying evidence'. The Lord Chief Justice was,
on the other hand, made of sterner stuff. Originally a Whig, he
had drifted to the Tory side and he was the first judge to move
from the working part of London and live in the fashionable
glory of the West End. Speaking in his unadorned Cumberland
accent he said that 'some person, with the most abandoned and
detestable slander, had dared to charge him with a gross act of
dishonesty . . . of me it was foully and slanderously alleged that
I had falsified the evidence. . . . This was all a lie — a vile
slander — *all false as hell*'.[10] As Lord Holland neatly said this

outburst diverted attention from the folly of the popular orator (Whitbread) 'and divided the censure and indignation of the Whig Party pretty equally between the two injudicious combatants'. J. W. Ward, then moving to the Whig side in politics — he was afterwards the first Earl of Dudley — and richly endowed with the acute and vigorous understanding of his family, wrote to a friend about the use which Whitbread had made of Mrs. Lisle's paper. He said that this had offended the aristocratic section of the Whigs 'mortally'. 'But the brewer regardeth them not. He stands firm upon a butt of his own entire.'[11]

The affair of the princess had one last, sordid twist for Whitbread. The most damaging witness against the princess in The Delicate Investigation was Lady Douglas, who had been her personal friend, and had remembered some unsavoury fragments of royal chat. Whitbread urged repeatedly in the House of Commons that Lady Douglas should be prosecuted for perjury. From the background the princess was constantly urging this on Whitbread. Lady Douglas's husband wrote to Whitbread 'as a Man of Honour' to demand whether he had declared in the House of Commons that his wife was 'a perjured person'. Replying, Whitbread said that the question was based on words attributed to him in Parliament. 'Mr. Whitbread is therefore under the necessity of declining all answer to the question.'[12] A decade later George IV enjoyed retailing this episode and hinting that Whitbread had shown discretion in the face of Douglas's challenge: and of Douglas the King slyly added 'he was a very determined man'.[13]

In the following year, 1814, Whitbread was to learn of the fickleness of royal personages. In that victory summer London was filled with sovereigns and princes: to many of them the princess was closely related, but out of courtesy to the Regent the visitors shunned the wife. Drawing-rooms, court functions and a great variety of metropolitan gaieties were held: but where the prince went he decreed that his wife should not go. 'Blasting to her character, fatal to her fame' was Whitbread's verdict in the House of Commons on this embargo. But in her wryly witty fashion the princess consoled herself by saying 'My dear — Punch's wife is nobody when Punch is present.'[14] And evidently she decided to leave the country now that Europe was freed from Napoleon and bid farewell to husband, troubles and self-appointed advisers. She embarked in August from Worthing on board the frigate *Jason* and comforted herself with a royal ball on board which she opened with Sir William Gell, a courtly and unmarried antiquarian. As she sailed away to a life of folly in the sunshine her parliamentary friends were left lamenting. In the House of Commons Whitbread had forcibly stated that she would not accept money from the Government — 'She will never consent to barter her rights to increase her income.'[15] Within days she had accepted £35,000 a year from the Government. The Government was ready to pay her £50,000 a year but on Whitbread's advice she asked for the lower figure. He explained to her that if she accepted £50,000 she would be expected to live — and spend it — in England. This was in addition to her jointure of £50,000. The fury of the *enragés* knew no bounds: Paul Methuen, who had originally raised the question of the princess's allowance in the House of Commons was 'an ass', 'a beast', and 'a fool'.[16] To Creevey the object of long months of devotion and attachment became 'this jade of a princess' and to Brougham she became 'the old B—'. While he could have intended something more vigorous, he probably meant nothing more alarming than 'the old Begum'. Just as the princess was leaving, she sent Whitbread a characteristically reckless and wounding and ungrateful letter. In his reply to Lady Charlotte Lindsay Whitbread wrote: 'A moment's reflection must convince Her Royal Highness that I, and the only other person who is supposed to be in the confidence of her Royal Highness,* have acted in defiance of all Party and Political considerations.' He ended, 'To the uncontrollable power of the House of Commons Her Royal Highness owes her salvation. She will not I am sure expect that

---

* Presumably Canning.

Power to cease, when it ceases to give her satisfaction. The House of Commons has interfered for Her Royal Highness : and when it sees proper will interfere.' Sensible and courageous words and the envelope is endorsed by Brougham 'An admirable answer to an abominable letter'. [17]

But the game had been fun while it lasted. It was delightful for Whitbread to draft pompous letters for the princess's signature and through her to give a knock to the wide-mouthed Queen Charlotte or a sharper blow to that renegade the Regent. 'If you can introduce the Regent with an appearance of *sarcasm* H.R.H. will be glad', wrote her lady-in-waiting. And it gave him a certain sly satisfaction, after attending a levee, to report for the princess's benefit that he had been received by the Regent with a very civil bow, and 'How do you do, Mr. Whitbread?' [18] It was pleasant to send a personal servant dashing on horseback to Blackheath with a letter from the brewer to the Princess of Wales and not to mind if the messenger was detained while the princess slept off a bad headache. [19] Nor was it disagreeable to know from many confidential letters of Lady Charlotte Lindsay (daughter of the Prime Minister, Lord North, and lady-in-waiting to the princess) that she and he were the steady, trusted advisers — barriers against the flood of foolish advice which poured in from less steady members of the royal circle. Lady Charlotte wrote to him at the time of the turmoil over Mrs. Lisle's evidence 'Mr. Fox,* Miss Berry† and myself have all of us been endeavouring to persuade the princess that she must leave it to you to act according to your judgment'. [20]

Then it was delightful for Whitbread to be consulted on points of royal etiquette. When the princess received a deputation from the citizens of Bristol — should the royal hand be kissed? [21] And far more delicate would he advise her Royal Highness to dress more decently? [22] And was there perhaps a certain joy in startling the respectable to whom the monarchy

---

* The statesman's nephew, Henry Stephen Fox.
† Horace Walpole's friend, Mary Berry.

was still something inviolable, sacred, linked with eternity? That dear old man, Francis Hargrave, deep in studies of seventeenth-century monarchical ideas, was alarmed to get a brusque letter from Whitbread demanding a speedy answer about the exact constitutional position of the wife of the heir to the throne. The barrister replied, 'The very reading of the points startles me.'[23]

Then there was the inevitable raggle-taggle of eccentrics who pester those reputed to have the ear of royal persons. He received an imperious letter from Mrs. Serres (who was also known, in her own eyes, as Princess Olive of Cumberland) asking him to go and see her in Abingdon Street explaining that she could not go to Dover Street because her eyes were inclined to inflammation and prevented her 'from meeting the cold air'. After the meeting she wrote to Whitbread about her daughter, who fifty years later was to disturb Victorian justice by her claims to royal blood: 'My daughter I have educated to be a Natural character. She is a Roman child. It would perhaps give you pleasure to see some of her writings.'[24]

'He has No Head', wrote Brougham to Creevey about Whitbread and the princess's case. 'He is good for execution but nothing for council, except indeed so far as his courage and honesty go.'[25] But was it not the courage and honesty which lifted the case of the unhappy Brunswick princess out of the privacy of family squabbles into the publicity of St. Stephen's, out of the clutches of family lawyers into the heroics of mob politics? An age which was gullible about royalty, which believed that several of George III's daughters were secretly married, which believed that the Duke of Cumberland had murdered his valet, which believed that the blood royal of England flowed in the bourgeois veins of Princess Olive of Cumberland was more than ready to believe in the wrongs of their future queen. They espoused her cause with the same unreasoning frenzy which had marked their support of Wilkes or Admiral Keppel. 'A very sorry and uninteresting heroine' thought Lord Holland. To the choicest blood of the Whig aristocracy that may well have seemed the case. But it was the courage, the honesty, the respectability and the popularity of Whitbread which turned this half-crazy and unlovely lady into a heroine, which threw her image as the wronged and injured wife of a sybaratic prince on to the minds of the inhabitants of even the meanest street in London. This may not have been wise; it was certainly not fair, but it was an achievement of a high order — possibly Whitbread's only positive, political triumph.

CHAPTER TWENTY-FOUR

Drury Lane

To Richard Brinsley Sheridan history has not been kind. The favourite of the Georgian theatre-goer was doomed after his famous years to swim in the deeps of politics — occasionally with grace, frequently with pathos and constantly with ineptitude. His relations with Whitbread reveal him at his worst — quarrelsome, tipsy, needy and seedy. But there was another Sheridan — never perhaps, even when Sheridan was at his most exasperating, forgotten by Whitbread and never more faithfully portrayed than in a passage from the diary of that severe critic — Byron.

Lord Holland told me a curious piece of sentimentality in Sheridan. The other night we were all delivering our respective and various opinions upon him and other *hommes marquants*, and mine was this : 'Whatever Sheridan has done or chosen to do has been *par excellence* always the *best* of its kind. He has written the best comedy (*School for Scandal*) the best drama* (in my mind far beyond that St. Giles lampoon, the *Beggar's Opera*) the best farce (*The Critic* — it is only too good for a farce) and the best address (Monologue on Garrick), and, to crown all, delivered the very best oration (the famous Begum speech) ever conceived or heard in this country.' Somebody told Sheridan this the next day, and, on hearing it, he burst into tears![1]

But politically — especially during the time that Whitbread was prominent — all these things were in the past and their author had become extremely difficult. He had — as Farington records — a brandy look,[2] and in politics the brandy look

---

* Presumably Byron means *The Duenna*, and according to some versions wrote 'opera', not 'drama'.

RICHARD BRINSLEY SHERIDAN

By Sir Joshua Reynolds

DRURY LANE THEATRE, 1812

should be as much a danger signal as the red light for mechanical transport. As early as 1802 at a convivial banquet at the Whig Club he referred to Grey as one of those who had been 'thrown by accident in the outset of life into situations for which they are not fitted, become Friends of the People for a time, and afterwards, finding their mistake, desert the popular cause'.[3] Grey was understandably furious and did not think that the attack was excused by brandy. Lord John Townshend, at the end of his long Whig life looking back on Sheridan the politician, called him 'a vapouring rogue'.[4] And even Fox, who loved him, described his anxiety to publish his differences with his political friends as 'an incurable itch'.[5] Throughout the time that he was associated with Whitbread he grew increasingly friendly with the Prince of Wales and was increasingly the counsellor at Carlton House. But some of the explanation for the difference between Sheridan and the Whig grandees was that the prospect of the rewards of office shone with a golden light for one encumbered by debt. The grandees could afford to wait; Sheridan could not.

Whitbread's relations with the playwright were of long standing, and were only partly political. Sheridan's second wife, Esther Ogle, daughter of the Dean of Winchester, was closely related to Charles Grey. Whitbread and Charles Grey were trustees for Mrs. Sheridan, and seldom can lawyers and mortgagees have enjoyed a more tangled and (for its size) more lucrative trust. It would be sad and profitless to recall the tribulations of the trustees: they are summed up by a sentence in a letter from Grey to Whitbread 'I wish to God we had never had anything to do with this business.'[6] The lawyer to the trust sadly confessed that Sheridan 'fairly sets all arrangements at defiance by never attending to any letter I write and never being at home when I call'.[7] Mrs. Sheridan brought with her a pleasant little fortune of £5,000, and Sheridan, by selling some of his Drury Lane shares made this up to £20,000, and bought the estate of Polesden near Box Hill. The Jacobean house was not grand enough for this debtor, and he pulled it down

T

intending to build something larger. Mrs. Sheridan's money was hopelessly entangled with his, and Whitbread and Charles Grey were troubled by such trifles as Mrs. Sheridan's pin-money. Then came a ray of light when it was heard that Sheridan had made a vague insinuation (the lawyer assured Whitbread that it could not possibly be called a concrete suggestion) that he might insure his life. Just occasionally the trustees were stern : once they ordered the timber to be felled at Polesden and on another occasion they decided to sequestrate the contents of Sheridan's London house. This was a disappointing venture as when the sequestrator arrived he found that nothing was the property of Sheridan since many other creditors were in possession.

And then in 1809 Sheridan's misfortunes were illumined by the disaster of the fire at Drury Lane. On 24 February the building was completely destroyed : the flames, at the height of the blaze, were 450 feet in breadth. The theatre had been built in 1794, and designed by Henry Holland : it carried below the roof a reservoir of water but this, which had been publicised as a great security against fire, fell on the flames with the effect of a fully loaded water-pistol. A literary gentleman, Mr. Kent, was first on the scene and with a professional eye rescued some books. These and a bureau of Mrs. Jordan's were all that was saved. 24 February was a Friday in Lent, and in that respectfully devout age there was, on that day, neither performance nor rehearsal. Within half an hour foot-guards and horse-guards were on duty at the fire, the glow of which startled and lit up the House of Commons. At the moment the House was discussing an effective attack by Ponsonby on the Government for the disaster of Corunna. Sheridan's remark to a friend, who found him enjoying a glass of wine close to Drury Lane, that a man might drink by his own fireside, is well known : less well known, but revealing his courage and composure, is his remark in the House of Commons in reply to the proposal that the House should adjourn, 'whatever might be the extent of the private calamity he hoped it would not interfere with the public business of the country'.[8] There were three reasons which each made the destruction of the theatre a calamity for Sheridan. First it was under-insured. It had cost £150,000 to build Holland's theatre : it was insured for only £35,000. Secondly there was a considerable sum owing on mortgage and, although the finances of the theatre were always uncertain, the mortgagees always had a glimmer of hope that they would be paid. They had none when the property lay in ashes. Thirdly the theatre gave him a standing in the world and an easy stage for the revival of his plays. After the disaster Whitbread evidently said to him 'though in a careless conversation only' at a chance meeting that he would 'not object to be one of a committee for rebuilding Drury Lane'. Thus emboldened, Sheridan wrote a skilful letter to Whitbread 'I say nothing, but what I sincerely think, when I say that, without comparison, you are the Man living, in my estimation, the most disposed and the most competent to bestow successfully a Portion of your time and ability in assisting the claim of Friendship. . . .' Then follows a pathetic sentence : 'It would not be easy to explain to you, or to anyone in prosperous and affluent plight, the private difficulties I have to struggle with.' He goes on to explain that he has never borrowed money from a private friend — election-subscriptions excepted. But there were perhaps two sentences which might have warned Whitbread of dangers to come. Sheridan alluded to his illness, and the fear that if his mind were tortured he might die and that others (Esther) might suffer by his death. The other sentence displayed that uniformly sanguine temperament which had led Sheridan astray so often in the past. 'Little more is necessary than resolution on my Part, and for a short time the superintending advice of a mind like yours.'*

---

* Thomas Moore's *Memoirs of the Life of Sheridan*, (1826), ii, 370. As Mr Quentin Skinner points out in his important contribution in *Theatre Notebook* (vol. xvii), the version of this letter printed in Moore's *Sheridan* is oddly different from the letter at Bedford which Sheridan wrote. As editor Moore evidently treated his material as a sub-editor in a newspaper, shortening passages and emphasising others. The quotations above are from the Bedford material. Possibly the most significant change is when Sheridan wrote : 'for a short time the superintending advice of a mind like yours'; Moore leaves out 'for a short time' and substitutes

Even a century and a half away we can hardly avoid blurting out 'For heaven's sake do not touch it'. A burned theatrical property, linked with the financial habits of Sheridan, had penury and worry stalking through the ruins. There was one personal consideration which weighed with Whitbread and did him honour. He had a sort of exasperated loyalty to Sheridan — part political and part an old association; he would also have been extremely anxious to help Esther to whom he and the Grey family were much attached. It is also probable that his banker Hammersley, who was involved in Holland's theatre, pressed him to help. But although these things cannot be proved, the guess may be made that what finally impelled him was the challenge, the feeling that he was indispensably the man and above all that it gave him the chance to show his full capacity — never really stretched in Chiswell Street — and now unlikely to be summoned by Government in Whitehall.

Lord Holland puts the same point more sharply (though correctly) when he writes 'he covets the applause that will come of managing so hazardous a business successfully.'[9] A close friend* of Whitbread's wrote that Drury Lane 'contributed more than other business to perplex, worry and fatigue a mind already sufficiently engaged'. The writer goes on 'his surviving friends have the melancholy satisfaction of knowing how strenuously they tried to prevent him — but in vain. He considered the rebuilding of Drury Lane Theatre as a vast, national object and that the metropolis of Great Britain ought not to be permitted to have only one large theatre, that it was of material consequence to rising authors and actors that their talents should not be left in judgment by one theatre, by which the world could never be the judge of their merits, and that a fair decision could only be obtained by having two theatres. With these opinions firmly fixed in his mind he considered it as

---

'active' before 'superintending advice'. His changes make the text correspond to what in fact happened but Moore's words are not Sheridan's.

* This is from the short memoir at Chewton, and was presumably written by his son-in-law, Captain Waldegrave.

a point of duty to attempt the undertaking thinking that he
could be enabled to give the various proprietors and creditors
of the old theatre some value for their shares or debts which at
that moment were worth nothing. . . .'[10]

Three tasks confronted Whitbread. The first was to disen-
tangle the finances of the old theatre, and to raise sufficient
money to rebuild, to equip and to maintain the house. The
second was to run the theatre as a paying concern. The third
was to keep on easy terms with Sheridan. The writer would be
rash who attempted to decide which was the most onerous of the
three. All were heavy, and in the life of a busy man one alone
would have been almost insupportable.

In his excellent biography of Sheridan, Thomas Moore is
careful to explain that although he had waded through the
details of the finances of the theatre 'it is by no means necessary
to inflict them on others'. This much can be said. The debts on
the old theatre were almost half a million — £436,971. The
Duke of Bedford was owed nearly £5,000 in rent and this,
with ducal generosity, he waived. His example was not followed
by the renters — these were the owners of the 150,000
debentures which Sheridan issued in 1794. It was only possible
to persuade these creditors not to oppose the rebuilding and not
to seize the insurance money by giving them an annuity in the
new theatre.[11] These negotiations took two years and, while
they were under discussion, an ominous cloud appeared. At the
beginning of 1811 a group of business men in the City petitioned
Parliament for the opening of a third patent theatre. Under Sir
Robert Walpole's Act of 1737 the rights of the crown to grant
patents for theatres in London was restricted, at the same time
as the responsibility of the Lord Chamberlain for the decorum of
the plays acted was confirmed. In fact there were only two
patent theatres — Drury Lane and Covent Garden, though the
Haymarket was open from May till the autumn when the other
two were closed. If the promoters of this third patent had
succeeded they must have made it uneconomic for Drury Lane to
be rebuilt. Whitbread said that if the third patent had been

sanctioned by Parliament 'Drury Lane would not have been worth one shilling'.[12] In a debate in the House of Commons, after Drury Lane was rebuilt and running, Whitbread made the point abundantly plain. He described how one evening in February (1813) after the House had risen early he visited the theatres.

There was performed in the King's theatre in the Haymarket, a favourite opera *Enrico IV*, in which was exhibited some of the greatest musical talent in the country: Mrs. Jordan played at Covent Garden: at Drury Lane a legitimate and well-acted opera was represented in which the principal part was sustained by Mr. Braham who had long been acknowledged to be the first English singer on the stage. It was a fine and favourable night: the opera was exceedingly thin — Covent Garden a little better — and Drury Lane still a little better: but in no one of them was an audience even to pay the expenses.

Another patent theatre must have been fatal to those already in being.[13] In a letter to the manager of Covent Garden Whitbread remonstrated against the tendency of that theatre to begin the season sooner and keep open longer thereby encroaching on the season of other theatres, and he confessed that this would greatly add to his difficulties when 'the theatrical warfare' opened in the House of Commons. But he was successful in thwarting the designs of the promoters of the third theatre and although a fierce General,* who sat for Liverpool, grumbled that it was an age of speculation in which honourable gentlemen were speculating in the theatres who never read the poets, and never entered a play-house Whitbread was able to say that £500 was the only extent of his personal interest and that he was active in Drury Lane 'solely through motives of friendship'.[14]

The committee formed for the rebuilding of the theatre, under Whitbread's chairmanship, was a strong one. It included Lord Holland and Lord Byron: the royal family was connected with it

---

* General Sir Banastre Tarleton.

through William Adam and Colonel MacMahon who were
attached to the Prince of Wales's court; the House of Commons
by Peter Moore the Radical Member for Coventry and by
'Dog' Dent; and the City of London by Alderman Harvey
Combe, a former Lord Mayor and reputed to be the best whist-
player in the metropolis. They were successful in raising a
subscription of £300,000* for the rebuilding and running of
Drury Lane. But on the reverse side of this sunlit picture there
was a cloud. Whitbread had persuaded his friends and dependents to hazard money in the venture. On 12 June 1811
Whitbread sent a circular letter to his friends asking them to
take shares of £100 each in the theatre. In his own hand on the
circular letter which is preserved at Chewton he has written
'Read it attentively and you will find you are quite safe. Pray
support me. For I have it much at heart.' He was successful in
persuading 134 people to subscribe. Among them were R. H. A.
Bennet, Robert Garrard, S. W. Reynolds, and Mr. Wilshere.
But Whitbread's list also included James Bellamy, a member of
a family which provided many doorkeepers and housekeepers in
the House of Commons; a don (George Caldwell) from Jesus
College, Cambridge; James Grant — the gardener at Southill;
John Weir, his butler; and Zaccheus Wright, another man-
servant from Dover Street. Now it is likely that, in his generous
way, Whitbread provided the £100 for some of these subscribers. But even when the cash was given, an expectation of
profit attached to the gift. Such thoughts were to weigh heavily
with Whitbread in the years ahead. And there were the inevitable bothers with the subscribers — especially those who
wanted, at an inconvenient time, to withdraw their money.
Happily few can have been quite so inconsiderate as the
Scotsman, William Adam, who clamoured for a return of his
share on the grounds 'I like money best'.[15]

The following figures[16] show that the committee was perhaps
more sanguine than a wider experience of theatrical management would have justified.

* Some authorities say £400,000. See *The Oxford Companion to the Theatre*.

*Statement of Receipts in the event of the Construction of a
New Theatre*

	£	s.	d.
Rent of Houses comprehended in leases but detached	500	–	–
Fruit office Let before the fire for . .	600	–	–
Vaults under the Theatre estimated at per ann. .	600	–	–
Ground Rent for Site of Tavern . . .	200	–	–
15 private Boxes at 300 £ . . .	4,500	–	–
6 Proscenium Boxes at 200 £ . .	1,200	–	–
Door Money on an average of years old prices .	52,000	–	–
Increased price estimated at . . .	5,000	–	–
Free admissions suppressed and frauds at doors .	2,000	–	–
	£66,600	–	–

*Statement of Outgoings in the event of the construction of a
New Theatre*

	£	s.	d.
Rent charge to New Renters on the Old Theatre .	3,750	–	–
Rent to the Duke of Bedford . . .	1,700	–	–
Insurance and taxes	1,800	–	–
Interest on Subscribers capital . . .	15,000	–	–
Annual Pay to Lord Chamberlain . .	350	–	–
Balance applicable to the annual expences of Representation and profit upon the Capital after the payment of 5 per cent Interest provided for above	44,000	–	–
	£66,600	–	–

These figures were well and good — but all turned on a
problematical figure — the capricious and incalculable fancy of
the public for the plays which were put on. The theatre was built
to hold about £630 a night.[17] Whitbread's own peregrination
through the theatres which he detailed in the House of Commons
when he saw the poor attendance was a pointer. For Edmund
Kean's first appearance at Drury Lane in 1814 his biographer
writes 'when the curtain drew up, there were but few persons
in the theatre'.

In the summer of 1813 when the Committee declared a dividend Lord Holland wrote to Whitbread, 'Your dividend sounds well, but I do hear it whispered that there is a flaw in the statement'. He possibly meant Sheridan here, but it is likely that he was alluding to the great imponderable — the fancy of the public.[18]

Once the financial background was settled, and once the threat from the third theatre was parried, the building went forward at remarkable speed. The first stone was laid on 29 October 1811 and the theatre was open on 10 October 1812. The architect, Benjamin Dean Wyatt, was a member (though not the most distinguished member) of the great architectural dynasty of Wyatt; he is perhaps remembered today as the architect of the Duke of York's column and of the old Londonderry House in Park Lane. The opportunity was tremendous and, coming in the middle of the Napoleonic War, was suggestive of that characteristic indifference to national emergencies which stamped the Regency mind. Much of Wyatt's interior survives and is, in fact, the only example of a Georgian theatre in London. But, as Sir John Summerson has pointed out,[19] 'the theatre was very far from successful' and the outside has the heaviness which Wyatt displayed in his St. James's Street clubs and indeed in the duke's column. More serious for those who had to manage the theatre was Wyatt's failure to grasp the practical needs of the stage end of the building.

But whatever defects Wyatt's design may have revealed, it fulfilled the first essential — it was built in time. And here the name of the builder, Mr. Rowles, deserves to be recalled — for some praise belongs to him. The feat of fulfilment was put into words by Lord Holland, who wrote, 'so rose within the compass of a year an age's work — a glorious theatre'. Its completion was marked by the curious episode of the Addresses, which showed the simplicity and unworldliness of Whitbread's character and — it has to be added — that over-weening confidence in himself which had certainly not been diminished by his success in getting the theatre finished. Conscious no doubt

that Johnson in 1747 had written the address beginning : 'When
learning's triumph o'er her barb'rous foes First rear'd the
Stage, immortal Shakespeare rose'; Whitbread was determined that the Address in 1812 should be worthy both of
the occasion and the precedent. He accordingly persuaded
the Committee to offer a prize of £100 for the best address.
The judges were Lord Holland, Whitbread and Harvey
Christian Combe. They were tersely described at the time
as 'one peer and two commoners, one poet [Holland] and
two prosers, one lord and two brewers'. Addresses fell in
showers on the desks of the Committee but as Lord Holland
said 'not one was tolerable'.* In this dilemma Lord Holland
turned to Byron, who gracefully replied that he would do his best
'to oblige you though I may offend 100 scribblers and the
discerning public'. Byron's Address was recited by Elliston and
as Lord Holland said this actor 'did it in a manner to drive an
author mad'.[20] The remarkable thing about Byron in this
connexion — though he was doubtless at that moment in
magnanimous mood at the tumultuous success of *Childe Harold*
— was his docile acceptance of criticism and suggestions for
alterations. 'If W. is inexorable — e'en let it go' is a sentence
from one of his letters to Holland. Whitbread insisted on the
removal of ten lines critical of contemporary taste in the theatre
which included the two lines :

> When Richard roars in Bosworth for a horse,
> If you command, the steed must come in course.

Accepting this, Byron wrote to Holland : 'Is Whitbread determined to castrate all my *cavalry* lines ?' He was.

---

* Horace Smith, who had with his brother James entered for the prize, published
Rejected Addresses — a series of skits on contemporary poets. The addresses
which were submitted were conspicuously feeble. They varied from the merely
pathetic — such as effusions from 'the poetess of nature', a music-seller, and a
painter and glazier — to lines bursting with classical allusions of which an elaborate
example was contributed by Mary Russell Mitford. Contributors included George
Lamb (the brother of the future Prime Minister, Melbourne) the Member of
Parliament for Sudbury, Joseph Hume, two relations of Sheridan and Philip
Martineau — presumably a connexion of Whitbread's partner, as well as the usual
poetasters prominent on all such occasions.

Here Whitbread may be divested of one barbed but witty story often told against him. This is to the effect that among the pedestrian addresses the very worst was one submitted by Whitbread himself. The authors of this story forget that he was one of the judges and could not possibly have submitted an entry. A study of all those sent in — including those sent anonymously — makes it clear that Whitbread was not a competitor. It is of course possible that realising the feebleness of the addresses he did attempt one of his own but this seems improbable because even "a poet" of his self-confidence would have sensed the danger if it had been publicly recited in a theatre for which he was responsible and after he had excluded all other competitors. At a dinner given by Samuel Rogers, the banker-poet, when the only guests were Byron, Thomas Moore and Sheridan the conversation turned on Whitbread's contribution. This was the setting for Sheridan's famous *mot* that Whitbread's contribution was a poulterer's description of a phoenix.[21] What Sheridan probably said was that if Whitbread had written an address it would have included an analytical dissection of the Phoenix. The story perhaps was based on the parody in *Rejected Addresses* of W. T. Fitzgerald's effusion. Fitzgerald was an Irish versifier whose contribution began :

> Hail, glorious edifice, stupendous work!
> God bless the Regent and the Duke of York!

Of this poet it was correctly said : 'On all public occasions his pen was ever ready'. In his favour it should be added that he never bore ill-will to the Smith brothers, whose parody of his address included the lines :

> In fair Arabia (happy once, now stony
> Since ruined by that arch apostate Boney),
> A phoenix late was caught : the Arab host
> Long ponder'd — part would boil it, part would roast;
> But while they ponder, up the pot-lid flies,
> Fledg'd, beak'd and claw'd, alive they see him rise
> To heaven, and caw defiance in the skies.

Afterwards Byron, describing the evening, said : 'Poor dear

Sherry! I shall never forget the day he and Rogers and Moore
and I passed together; when *he* talked and *we* listened, without
one yawn, from six till one in the morning.'[22] There is no
evidence that Whitbread knew of this pleasantry : he would not
have greatly minded if he had. He told Sheridan's son that he
had never been indignant with Sheridan — except so far as he
was difficult over business.

CHAPTER TWENTY-FIVE

Theatre Manager

AND now the second task which faced Whitbread was to run the theatre when it opened on 12 October 1812. In the previous March he had had the chance of leasing it to a manager for £20,000 a year but he preferred to cling to the dangers and the glittering prizes of management. There were, it is true, a few prizes, but for most of the time the storm-cone was flying. The absorption of time is what must horrify the humane. With much of his energy given to public life and to local affairs he had, as Mr. Skinner puts it 'to deal with the letters of dozens of hopeful playwrights, the demands of actors seeking parts, even the appeal of a doorkeeper against wrongful dismissal. . . . The stage-manager constantly invoked Whitbread's aid as backer, and even on one disastrous occasion as producer.'[1] He took on himself the arrangements for fitting up the Prince Regent's box and for protecting it from intruders 'who had proved offensive to His Royal Highness when he honoured the theatre with his presence'.[2] He sent the bill to the prince's secretary 'I will not state items but if the sum of £600 should not be thought too much, I will undertake to say the Committee will be satisfied with it'.[3] When there was a question of putting up a bust of Shakespeare in the theatre he made all the arrangements for Garrard to examine the bust then owned by Mrs. Garrick in her house at Hampton.

Like the Duke of Wellington, Whitbread was much exposed to authors. The greatest scourge of these was perhaps Mrs. Wilmot. Although much can be forgiven Mrs. Wilmot on account of her charm and wit, and although through the Ogles she could write to Whitbread as 'Dearest Cousin

Sam' and although Whitbread's closest political associate (Brand) was greatly enamoured of her and eventually married her, she was a shade too persistent over her play *Ina*. This was performed in the spring of 1815 — doubtless owing to the good offices of Whitbread — and it was a complete failure. She wrote him a long letter in December 1814, evidently with the casting for *Ina* in mind and full of barbed comments on the actors and actresses whom Whitbread had painfully collected.

Mrs. Bartley* was too detestable as Lady Macbeth. . . . I think marriage has disagreed with her and she looks old and stringy and frightful. Mrs. Glover's† bawling in the Queen‡ last night made me positively *perspire*. It is tenfold what it was last year. . . . I feel that Mrs. Bartley *is* the public aversion and I feel that Mrs. Glover is too vulgar and bawling and big to be a Princess in love.§ . . . Now then what you must do . . . is to get Mrs. Bartley into better looks and persuade people not to hate her and you must reduce Mrs. Glover within bounds both as to body and mind. I conjure Cousin Bess to undertake the front of her dress and prevent what never can be described — if Mrs. Weir‖ is a good packer she may furnish a hint or two concerning the stowing of luggage. Then you, Cousin Sam, must positively reduce the volume of voice (which like cannon would break the windows of the boxes if they had any) . . . Shakespeare alone can weather such disadvantages as these.4

She began her letter 'you can do everything' and ended it 'I expect you having built a house to build actors and audience too'.

Inevitably Whitbread, the business-man and politician, in the world of drama raised a smile. According to the lively authors, Horace and James Smith, of *Rejected Addresses* he was alleged to believe that an actor was like a portrait in a picture, and accordingly placed the green curtain in a gilded frame remote from the footlights; believing that no performer should mar the illusion by stepping out of the frame. And of all the inevitable

---

* Wife of George Bartley; she succeeded Mrs. Siddons as the outstanding tragic actress of the day, but the disparity between them was noticed.
† Julia Betterton. Mrs. Wilmot's strictures are perhaps here justified.
‡ Of *Richard III*.   § i.e. in *Ina*.
‖ Wife of the Whitbreads' butler.

bad jokes about his trade perhaps the least bad is to be found
in the same volume :

> Let us cheer our great commoner, but for whose aid
> We all should have gone with short commons to bed;
> And since he has saved all the fat from the fire,
> I move that the house be call'd Whitbread's Entire.

No doubt Whitbread sometimes imposed his views on the
management, but on the whole he seems to have acted in
accordance with the sense of this passage in a letter from him to
Thomas Dibdin, who was prompter at Drury Lane 'I do not
presume to give any direction; and I beg that my wishes may
be put quite out of the question when they clash with the
interests of the theatre or of the author'.[5]

Certainly there were compensations. The most notable of
them was the remarkable success of Edmund Kean : the credit
for his discovery belongs to Samuel James Arnold, the manager
under Whitbread. Kean was a young man of 27 when he was
fished out from Dorchester by Arnold. He appeared as Shylock
on 24 January 1814 and thereafter took the town by storm, filling
Drury Lane whenever he was billed. Mrs. Garrick, who was
nearly 90, came to see his Hamlet. Kean had a piercing, black
eye and Byron noticed that in *Othello* he showed a sort of Levant
fury of expression which 'we orientalists could appreciate'.[6] He
was under contract for a salary beginning at £8 a week.
Whitbread asked him to breakfast at Dover Street — not a meal
at which either politicians or stage celebrities are at their best —
tore up the contract and offered him a new agreement of £20 a
week.* Kean's health became a question of the first consequence
to the Committee and Sir Henry Halford, the royal doctor, was
called in. The young actor went down to Windsor Castle to be
overhauled, and Halford reported to Whitbread the dread
symptom of a little blood appearing after coughing. Socially

---

* Coleridge complained of an even worse experience. He was summoned to
Dover Street at 8.30 in the morning and Whitbread was shaving during their talk.
This concerned Coleridge's play *Remorse* successfully performed at Drury Lane at
the beginning of 1813 (*The Farington Diary*, (1922) vii, 164).

Kean was not at ease in Dover Street 'when they talk about parliament and so forth, I do not understand them : when they talk about acting it is *such* nonsense'. Whitbread told Mrs. Kean : 'We don't invite him because it seems so painful to him.' At the end of the 1814 season the Committee met at the Crown and Anchor and a dividend of 5 per cent was declared. After a great eulogy of Kean's talent, Whitbread concluded : 'It is to him that after one hundred and thirty five nights of continued loss and disappointment, the subscribers are indebted for the success of the season.'[7]

If it is true that Whitbread enjoyed dominating the minds of other mortals then at Drury Lane he found himself a big man in a smallish world, a grandee himself among the citizens. This was brought out clearly in an engaging letter, which was written in September 1812 to Whitbread by Arnold, who had to struggle all his life. 'To look at life through the medium of family, connections, fortune and liberal education is *one* view. To see it and to struggle with it; to contend with all the petty passions to which the mass of mankind is liable, without any of those advantages, is *another*. . . . With your rank, and other eminent advantages, it can scarcely ever be any man's *interest* to be ungrateful towards you.'[8] Whitbread kept the letter, and it may have crossed his mind that Arnold's sentiments could hardly be distinguished from those which he himself had formerly addressed to Charles Grey.

There was too a certain satisfaction, on the credit side, from a feeling of power. Even in 1812 there was a subtle enchantment in having a letter from the proprietor of *The Times* saying that he wished to include a paragraph in the paper about the rebuilding 'out of respect to you'.[9] Again it was pleasant to write to the Lord Chamberlain to enquire if it would be thought bad taste to play *King Lear* in view of George III's imbecility. The Lord Chamberlain did not feel able to pronounce on a question of that character and Whitbread was able to write back to assure him that with the King as he was, *Lear* would not be produced at Drury Lane. But there were possible disadvantages to the theatre in having at its head so warm a critic of the royal family and so notorious a political partisan. In the closing months of his life Whitbread had a letter from Sheridan warning him of the risk of playing *Richard II* and drawing his attention to the demagogic speeches of the gardeners in Act III.

7 March 1815
Leatherhead, Tuesday Evening

DEAR WHITBREAD,

I read Richard the second this morning — I see, beyond what I had recollected, infinite opportunity for Kean to make a great impression, but that is not my point in writing this. — How the play is altered I know not — but I find a number of passages in it, which if not *judiciously moderated*, are open to application which may produce the most inflammatory effect on the audience at this *peculiar* and perilous Crisis* — look at the scene between the Gardeners and others which I have marked. Beware, and listen to the wise. Keep politics out of the Theatre. Any mischief arising from the allusions I have stated will be laid at your Door. I will call on you when I get to Town on Thursday, if I find your house standing which I scarcely expect. I have a hatful of Polesden violets on the Table while I write and three samples of Lambs' wool. — God forgive you all in your curs'd City. R.B.S.[10]

Naturally enough politics went on in the auditorium. On one occasion Brougham wrote to Creevey asking him to arrange that Whitbread should be in his wife's box that evening 'I am anxious for a little serious consultation and there is no other way of meeting our commander-in-chief'.[11]

Finally there was undeniable satisfaction for Whitbread in the gratitude of his friends and associates on the Committee who commissioned that a bust of Whitbread by Nollekens should be placed in the theatre where it still stands. The words with which it is inscribed were written by Lord Holland — 'it is not joke but earnest when I say that it seems impossible to include your Drury Lane merits in so small a compass as in good taste an inscription should be'.† The amiable lord, when he

---

* Agitation over the Corn Laws.

† Bedford. Lord Holland's words record merely the basic facts of Whitbread's life. The bust was given to Lady Elizabeth; a copy is in the Upper Rotunda at Drury Lane.

wrote that letter to Whitbread, must have forgotten the busts
in the library at Southill with their flowery inscriptions composed by Whitbread.

The third task which Whitbread faced at Drury Lane was
most certainly without recompense or consolation. The weight
of this burden is revealed, in all the lurid light thrown on it by
a letter from Sheridan from Tooke's Court in the spring of 1814.
Tooke's Court was one of those places of restraint for debtors
used by bailiffs as a preliminary to more permanent place of
confinement. They were familiar to our forebears as 'sponging-
houses'. The relevant part of the letter ran :

I have done everything in my Power with the Solicitors . . . to obtain
my release . . . but in vain. Whitbread, putting all false professions of
Friendship and feeling out of the Question, you have no right to keep
me here. For it is in truth *your* act. If you had not forcibly withheld
from me the £12,000 in consequence of a threatening Letter from a
miserable swindler, whose claim *you* in particular knew to be *a lie* — I
should at least have been out of the reach of *this* state of miserable
insult — for that and that only lost me my seat in Parliament.* And I
assert that you can not find a Lawyer in the Land, that is not either a
natural born Fool or a corrupted Scoundrel, who will not declare that
your conduct in this respect was neither warrantable or legal. But let
that pass for the present. . . .

O God! with what mad confidence have I trusted your word — I
ask justice from you and no boon. I enclosed you yesterday three
different securities, which had you been disposed to have acted even as
a private Friend would have made it certain that you might have done
so without the smallest risk. These you discreetly offer'd to put into
the Fire, when you found the object of your humane visit satisfied by
seeing me safe in Prison.

I shall only add that, I think, if I know myself, had our Lots been
reversed, and had I seen you in my situation, and had left Lady E. in
that of my wife, I would have risked £600 rather than have left you
so although I had been in no way accessory to bringing you into that
condition.   R. B. SHERIDAN.†

* As a Member of Parliament he would have enjoyed freedom from arrest, and
deprived of the £12,000 he could not finance his re-election for Stafford in 1812.
This money was held back by Whitbread to cover claims against the previous theatre.

† This is taken from the letter at Bedford, from which some of the capitals and
underlinings (italics are used for underlined passages) used by Moore in his life
of Sheridan are absent.

Whitbread went round at once to Tooke's Court and made the necessary arrangements for Sheridan's release. That was but an act of common humanity. Whitbread's reputation has been damaged by this letter, but his defence rests on something more considerable than providing the cash for Sheridan's release.

After the publication of Moore's life of Sheridan Henry Burgess, who was Sheridan's solicitor, wrote to Moore: 'in Justice to the memory of Mr. Whitbread and to his family I deem it incumbent upon me to say that that letter ought not to have been given to you for publication, unless accompanied with the reasons why the sum mentioned in it has been withheld'. He went on to explain that Taylor, the proprietor of the Opera House, claimed £20,000 as a debt due to him from Sheridan and the owners of the theatre burned in 1809. Sheridan's description of this claim and of the man bringing it forward is not open to challenge. But Whitbread and the Committee took counsel's opinion and were advised that until Taylor's claim was established or dismissed they must not distribute money to Sheridan and others of the creditors of the theatre burned in 1809 as they would have been liable for any money paid out to Sheridan and the other creditors after receiving notice of Taylor's claim. 'Not the slightest blame ought to be imputed to Mr. Whitbread on this account', wrote Burgess.*

There are in existence many infinitely pathetic letters from Sheridan to Whitbread — not indignant but explosions of self-pity such as any fine-drawn human being might indulge at finding himself trapped by events. In 1811:

Lend me for six weeks two hundred or even one hundred pounds. I make this request with a degree of pain and mortification which it can not be possible for you to conceive. I can say from the sincerity of my soul that the most unobliged man on earth in this way, struggling with

* See his letter, *Letters of George IV*, (1938), iii, 194, ed. A. Aspinall. It is difficult to say now how Moore came by the letter from Sheridan to Whitbread. It is possible — though not in accord with Sheridan's natural practice — that Sheridan kept a copy. It is again possible that Whitbread's son, who was not wise, allowed Moore to use it. The letter at Bedford is the original.

distress through his life, is myself.[12] [Then in November 1814 he once again tries to borrow money and adds that he intends to sell his pictures.] 'What will you give me for my heavenly piping faun? I shall grieve to see them pass into strange hands — for I part with them at all most reluctantly.'

He calculated his pictures at £660 — Two upright Gainsboroughs £300, Landscape with cows £200, Two Morlands £120, Boys robbing an apple-stall £40. Whitbread took the trouble to write to his friend, the distinguished picture collector Sir George Beaumont, but that baronet of taste replied 'I certainly do not want inclination, but alas another want interferes.' Occasionally anger and playfulness were intermixed. In November 1814 he wrote,

You thought fit to tie up £12,000 of my property, by which I *lost my seat in Parliament*, God forgive you; and more than £4000 besides God d—n you! But as these form the 79th and 86th articles of the impeachment no more on the subject now truly yours notwithstanding

R. B. S.[13]

And to the last he could write playfully to Lady Elizabeth starting his letter 'Good and Lovely' and ending it 'Your Highness's faithful servant R.B.S.'.[14] Possibly less bearable even than the humiliation and badinage of Sheridan are two letters to Whitbread from Esther, scribbled in pencil at the time of the arrest 'Something is amiss — if you know anything I beg you will tell me — Uncertainty is always worse than anything'. And 'Sheridan's state of mind kills me — all I can say seems to him poison in his mind. Above all do not go to him yourself'.[15] In one of his franker moments Sheridan told a friend that if he ever got back to the House of Commons 'I could squeeze Whitbread to death'.[16]

It is perhaps in relation with Sheridan that Whitbread's faults are most conspicuous. The sensitiveness of a man of genius, with his feelings about himself more exposed than is the case with ordinary mortals, is patent. In March 1815 Sheridan is complaining 'they have never once asked me to Dinner tho they knew I was alone and had no recourse but a chop house'.

When Whitbread resigned from the chairmanship of the Drury Lane Committee Sheridan scornfully referred to his position as 'his Dictatorship'. Although allowance should be made for the circumstances in which Sheridan said this — he was writing a private letter to his wife — he was voicing an opinion which he truly felt, an opinion of which even those who most admire Whitbread must be at times conscious, 'I grievously doubt him. His Vanity is infinitely stronger than his regard for Truth or Justice'.[17]

The true explanation for Sheridan's feelings is that he felt that he had been prised out of money and — which was more grievous — of all connexion with the theatre. The Committee offered to give him a box — a fairly valuable concession — and though he took it he refused to acknowledge the generosity of the Committee. On the other hand the harsh truth has to be told. The Committee felt that they could never hope to win the confidence of the public so long as Sheridan was in any way connected with the finances or management of Drury Lane. Whitbread could, of course, be excessively blunt. That was the John Bullish streak in his character. He wrote to Sheridan's eldest son, Tom, explaining exactly how things stood. He thought that Sheridan threw his opportunity away by procrastination after the fire when public sympathy was at its height. 'The week after the fire your father could have done anything. The month after the fire he could do nothing. Nor you either in my judgment.' He went on that it was 'hard and galling' that there should be 'a sort of proscription on the name of Sheridan'. He frankly stated that if either Tom or his father had been known to be connected with Drury Lane 'the devil a subscription would we get'.[18] The payment of an interest to Sheridan as one of the creditors from the old theatre was of course a totally different question from including him among the promoters of the new theatre. And could any fair-minded person say that Whitbread was either wrong or unjust when he wrote to Tom Sheridan in 1812? 'If your father would devote one single day to the rational investigation of his private affairs and be guided by common sense in the adjustment of them they might be so arranged as to rescue him from the horrible state of misery in which he and all about him exist.'[19]

Earlier in the same letter Whitbread had written: 'I have devoted more than a whole year of the most active and uninterrupted exertion to the refounding of Drury Lane.' Two years later Whitbread's friend Pascoe Grenfell, a merchant and Member of Parliament, wrote on hearing that Whitbread had retired from the chairmanship of the Drury Lane Committee, 'I don't wonder at it, but what will become of the concern without you?'[20] Sometimes (though in this case mistakenly) concerns are greater objects for anxiety than human beings.

CHAPTER TWENTY-SIX

Death in Dover Street

IN the early nineteenth century the faces of human beings were possibly more revealing of character than, with the development of the race, they have become. Villainy showed in a man's face: benevolence shone out. In the great novel, which was published a year after Whitbread's death, Jane Austen makes Emma say 'You might not see one in a hundred, with *gentleman* so plainly written as in Mr. Knightley.' Though Dickens was portraying human character some years after this period the transparent faces of Uriah Heep, Nicholas Nickleby, Jonas Chuzzlewit, Mr. Dick or the brothers Cheeryble reflect their inmost being. And when Thackeray wished to describe a club-man he did it by saying 'he had billiards written all over his face'. Perhaps more affluent days have softened and standardised the physiognomy of the human race so that it becomes more difficult, at a glance, to distinguish the rogue from the angel. In Regency days such deductions were easier and people set store by what are known as first impressions. The Regent himself was a clear case in point; with his portly form, clear complexion, roving eye and ageless wig, he looked voluptuous — therefore he was a voluptuary. In exactly the same way — though at the opposite poles of character — Whitbread's exterior was expressive. What this revealed has been listed in a sympathetic portrait of him by Thomas Barnes — the editor of *The Times*.[1] He summed up his exterior by saying that it was as English as his mind: he noticed 'the steady eye', the countenance 'deeply marked with thoughtfulness, but fluctuating with feeling' the 'sober gait', the 'unaffected gestures', 'the vigorous cast of his person'; to Barnes they all gave assurance of the man 'where the naked soul may yet walk abroad and feel no shame'. Everyone would have agreed that as Whitbread moved through life he left in men's minds an impression of strength and of the authority which goes with it. Even in the most trifling things this was apparent. In the last year of his life — a few days before his death — he was noticed in the soda-water room in the corner of Exeter Change in the Strand. Soda-water was much drunk at this period as a supposed remedy against growing too fat. The waiter placed a tumbler in front of him, which was not full. He simply looked sternly and significantly at the waiter without saying a word. The fault was at once remedied. A fellow Member of Parliament, Francis Horner — who always viewed Whitbread with discriminating admiration — voiced the feelings of thousands when he said, on hearing of Whitbread's death that it was difficult to believe that all that rectitude of mind had been overthrown by 'a speck morbid' in the body.[2]

In the House of Commons, as the session of 1815 opened, there was no sign whatever of the 'speck morbid'. Whitbread was as active as ever, his mind ranging over such subjects as the effect of the property tax on auction marts, on the treaty between Great Britain and Naples, on false weights and measures, on the imprisonment of Lovell, the proprietor of the newspaper *The Statesman*. America was constantly in his thoughts and he was extremely critical of the conduct of the fighting because he maintained that in the naval engagement on Lake Erie, where the British had been overwhelmingly defeated, their vessels had been under-gunned. Poor Sir Joseph Yorke was so nettled by this attack on the Royal Navy in which he served then as Lord of the Admiralty that he burst out 'I would not exchange my feelings for his, nor my talent, nor my situation, nor my exertions, nor my patience, nor any one thing that belonged to me, for anything belonging to the Honourable Gentleman'.[3]

His severest pronouncements were made on the folly of continuing the war with France after the return of Napoleon, to which allusion has already been made, but he showed quite as much force in an attack on General Whittingham. This

English general had fought with the Spaniards in the Peninsula, was much in the confidence of that devout and miserable Bourbon, King Ferdinand VII, and he had supported him back to Madrid in triumph in 1814, trampling, according to Whitbread, on certain infant Spanish liberties in the process. He described General Whittingham as having helped to establish a tyranny 'more horrible and ferocious than the bloody reign of Robespierre'. He accused the general of being 'coupled with money transactions' and having been largely influenced by Spanish gold. He ended with an entertaining picture of King Ferdinand before restoration 'he was embroidering a muslin gown for the Virgin Mary who, in return for this present worked by the royal hand, had intimated that one day he would be restored'. Loud laughter greeted this sally, and Whitbread added 'Would to God he had continued all his life to work gowns and petticoats for the Virgin Mary'. After this speech a noisy connexion of the general's, Hart Davis, a banker, the reactionary Member for Colchester, allowed himself with much warmth to attack Whitbread, who vindicated himself with spirit. He argued that Whitbread had no right to vilify a meritorious officer who was his relation. Hart Davis was perhaps more resolute as a parliamentarian than as a lover. In the scandalous chronicles of Harriette Wilson he is described as paying out bank-notes for the privilege of patting ladies on the arm tenderly enquiring, as he did this, whether it felt 'nice'. Both were reported to the Speaker by a third Member, apprehensive lest the dispute should go further. Hart Davis told the Speaker that he 'reluctantly' submitted : Whitbread said that he would certainly do so.

This was in the spring. By the summer, when Waterloo had come and gone, the fire seemed to vanish from his speeches. He spread a thin but unaccustomed layer of praise over every department of Government which he said 'had exerted itself to the uttermost to secure the wonderful victory'. He even praised the zeal and competence of the Duke of York. But what alarmed his friends was the droning style of speaking and his general appearance of sluggishness which was totally at variance with the exuberance of his ordinary parliamentary manner.[4]

His friends believed that his trouble arose from a too full-blooded and too plethoric constitution which affected his brain and threatened a paralytic seizure. Brougham expressed this in a letter which he wrote to Creevey after Whitbread's death 'it was too plain that he could not live, and I expected every day to hear of his falling down, or becoming paralytic'.* Yet it could perhaps be argued that, all his life long, he had overdriven a brain, too tightly harnessed to a tense nervous system. Evidently Lady Elizabeth thought that his trouble lay there. In the autumn following his death she turned to Whitbread's first edition of Boswell's *Life of Johnson*, her Whiggish mind spurning more conventional comforters. She has heavily scored the passage where Johnson discusses constitutional melancholy : 'A man so afflicted, sir, must divert distressing thoughts. . . .' Boswell then asks, 'May not he attempt to think them down, sir ?' 'No, sir, to attempt to think them down is madness.'

As early as October 1814 Lady Elizabeth noticed a perfectly unreasonable outburst by Whitbread in answer to her request that her garden at Southill should be slightly enlarged by extending the boundary to include a large tree and 'a bee-hive seat'. After his sudden outburst she wrote to Whitbread and told him that she was ashamed of herself and could only excuse herself 'by saying that I became young for the moment, and was carried beyond myself by being pleased with what I saw looking so pretty'. This letter was found by Lady Elizabeth on the day Whitbread took his life and, endorsing it, she said that she had been surprised and alarmed by the earnestness of his manner.[5]

This trifling episode could be explained by the sudden realisation by a very wealthy man that he was spending too much money. Whitbread's friends believed that his expenses in the last year of his life outran his income by £14,000. This

---

* When he heard of Whitbread's death Byron characteristically wrote that all full-blooded hypochondriacs would be rushing to see their doctors on learning the news. He added of Whitbread, 'but surely he was a great and very good man' (Moore's *Byron*, ii. 625).

was certainly correct for 1813, but the full figures for 1814 have not survived. The figures for his expenditure and income will be found in Appendix 1 (pp. 309–16), giving an interesting light on the generosity and habit of life of a wealthy, Regency man. It will be seen that although his income fluctuated with the fortunes of Chiswell Street his expenditure remained tolerably constant at around £40,000. The books show that the value of his assets in 1813, after deducting his liabilities, was over £600,000, largely explained by his estates in Bedfordshire which are included at more than half as much again as when he inherited them two decades earlier. It is perfectly true that his property and his trade were not — to speak strictly — liquid assets. It is true that the most frequent cause of suicide in the early nineteenth century was that a man's circumstances were embarrassed. It is also true that a testator who makes eleven codicils to his will suggests a certain degree of fluster over his financial affairs.

His original will was drawn in the autumn of 1810 evidently after the illness for which his friend Dr. Yeats prescribed. It was a long, professionally-drawn document providing, in the Whitbread style, for a great diversity of legatees, and here and there showing the natural inclination of a strong character to rule from the grave. This was noticeable in the case of a provision for his second son, Samuel Charles, who, 'if he shall take holy orders' it is 'my desire and injunction' that he should be presented to the combined benefices of Southill and Old Warden and he urged that effectual measures should be taken to secure the resignation of any incumbent blocking this desirable preferment from Samuel Charles. The boy grew up to run the Brewery and to be a Fellow of the Royal Society, a scientist, astronomer and Master of the Oakley Hounds. The eleven codicils which followed were less formal, and four of them had to be proved by evidence that they were in Whitbread's writing. They increased legacies, and catalogued debts. The eleventh codicil listed a debt of £20,000 to Sangster in the Brewery, £15,000 to his bankers in Bedford and £10,000 to his son-in-law William Waldegrave. But even here he was giving larger legacies to Sam Reynolds and to Harman at the Brewery. The document is somewhat oddly endorsed in his own handwriting — '22 June 1815!' On the same day he wrote to his confidential clerk at the Brewery: 'I have communicated somewhat to the nearest and dearest and am the lighter. But 'tis a fearful load still.' A day or two later the confidential clerk (Harman), Whitbread and Lady Elizabeth had a discussion. Afterwards Whitbread wrote to Harman: 'Last night's conversation produced everything that could be wished consolatory and relieving, but the one thing needful is still wanting.'[6] There is also evidence that he asked Martin's Bank for a loan in the summer of 1815. The Bank wished to join his sons in the transaction, but Whitbread said it was difficult to explain this to them, and the Bank then asked that the security should be strengthened by life insurance. The first premium of £255 was due 10 days after Whitbread took his life. All this could of course be taken to mean that he was in financial difficulties, but it could equally mean that the difficulties were in his mind rather than in reality. While there may be nothing to imply financial embarrassment, the several codicils betray a rather haphazard attitude to business matters — possibly unexpected in a businessman.

But it scarcely accords with human nature that a man apparently worth more than £600,000 should allow financial anxieties to bustle him into the grave. Frederick Neve, who taught Whitbread's sons at Sunninghill, saw him five days before he killed himself and referred to lamentable proof of aberration when his mind could only dwell on the single subject of his pecuniary concerns. But who shall say whether those concerns were the reality or merely the symptom of the aberration?[7]

Searching for explanations the world naturally pointed in the direction of Drury Lane: 'it was the damned theatre' wrote H. G. Bennet — the son of Lord Tankerville and one of Whitbread's most faithful political comrades during the closing months of his life.[8] But before the damned theatre is accepted as the villain of the piece the matter warrants closer attention. It is perfectly true that Whitbread was acutely sensible of the friends and dependants whose expectations he had encouraged by making them shareholders in that anxious venture. Possibly it could even be argued that Drury Lane, for the first time in his life, brought home to him that even his wealth was limited and that it could not be stretched to rescue the theatre and those who had invested money in it. But it is inconceivable that in the normal poise and balance of his mortal life Whitbread would, as H. G. Bennet put it, 'have vexed himself to death about Drury Lane'.[9] Theatrical investment has never been other than highly speculative, and the particular financial history of Drury Lane was only too familiar to Whitbread's circle from Wilshere the agent to Weir the butler. In their heart of hearts they must have known that their shares in the theatre had no more likelihood of profitable employment than the talent buried in the earth by the man in the parable. Men reasonably reproach themselves when by chicanery they induce others to part with money or extract a personal profit from a venture in which others flounder. Of such things there was nothing whatever in the tangled story of Drury Lane. All was open, honourable, adventurous but disappointing. The affairs and chagrin of Drury Lane were a burden for any man; they were not sufficient to break the spirit of a vigorous personality. Such things oppress but do not destroy the character of a human being. In a passage which is difficult to decipher and has been severely but accidentally mutilated, Lord Ossulston, the elder brother of H. G. Bennet and close in Whitbread's councils, wrote to Creevey under the immediate impact of shock and sorrow. After emphasising to Creevey, who was in Brussels at the time, partly in flight from his creditors and partly on account of his wife's health, that the reason for Whitbread's death 'arose so obviously from disease' he put the question which on that summer's day was uppermost in the mind of all Whitbread's friends. 'How it cd. ever enter into the scheme of Providence that a man like Whitbread . . . the best man in all the relations of life and the most valuable person as well as the most esteemed in our time, shd. put an end to his impartial* life because the affairs of Drury Lane was going on ill is what it wd. be difficult to explain except' as a sign that Providence was determined 'to give a striking proof to all the world of the insufficiency of human reason and of human virtue'.[10] As ever the perceptive pen of Lord Holland put the matter fairly and squarely — 'His whole appearance indicated strongly that he would die suddenly, but he was the last man whom I would have apprehended to die as he did.'[11]

Perhaps for Whitbread himself the tragedy did not rest in the event of that July morning in Dover Street but in the fact that the medical profession could diagnose but not alleviate symptoms of this kind, so that he was left to betray them to all the world. The only remedy suggested by his friends was 'For God's sake get Lady Elizabeth to take him to Southill'.

Three weeks before his death he attended a meeting of the British and Foreign School Society : he was asked to speak, but had to decline explaining : 'I am oppressed with an intolerable headache which almost drives me out of my senses.'[12] To a partner in the Brewery whose son was killed at Quatre Bras he ended his letter of sympathy 'How I envy your son'.[13] Going to enquire for the daughter-in-law of his old friend Lambton — she was married to the renowned statesman, Lord Durham and was dying — he asked 'How is poor Mrs. Lambton?' Immediately he corrected himself 'Poor Lambton I mean. The survivor only is to be regretted'.[14] The week before his death he drove Lady Elizabeth to the pleasure gardens at Vauxhall : just as they were leaving there was a disturbance among the footmen at the door and, turning to Lady Elizabeth, Whitbread said 'They are hissing me. I am become an object of universal abhorrence.' Such were the stories of the town circulating to explain what had happened. Three more direct pieces of evidence as to his mind have survived. He suddenly was seized with the idea that Cambridge, which he had known and loved

* Presumably Ossulston really wrote 'immortal'.

since his youth, was unhealthy — a truth suspected by all except the long-lived inhabitants of that draughty city. During the Easter vacation he sent a friend from Hitchin to investigate the facts and report back to him. In consequence he wrote to his sons telling them that he could not allow them to return to Cambridge because of the impossibility of 'my risking your health'. In that princely age, when universities had to consult the convenience and the apprehensions of those who patronised them, it was agreed that the young brothers Whitbread should withdraw themselves for a term and endure the harsher but safer climate of Edinburgh University, Brougham making all the arrangements. Though trifling, this episode does suggest a mind agitated by trifles beyond reason.

In an undated letter, which was written shortly before his death, he expressed his feelings to his sister, Lady St. John.

MY DEAREST EMMA. I answer your kind enquiries by sending Sam Reynolds who can give you a faithful account of me. I am not ill but I am not well, and I feel the sort of depression which you have often felt. . . . I shall soon be well I have no doubt. Give Sam Reynolds something to eat and a glass of ale.

And then in a furtive, scrawling hand unlike himself he adds a postscript: 'Tell me what Sam Reynolds says of me. I should like to know what observations he makes.'[15]

The last letter of Whitbread's which has survived was written to Lady Elizabeth from the House of Commons on 3 July.

MY DEAREST BESS, I want to say that I would come and eat a mutton chop with you and then accompany you wherever you are going. I was quite grieved that you should have so much to bear with. And would to the gracious God I had [not] brought such a burden upon you, but in vain are wishes now and I will support myself as well as I can. Yours as ever and forever. Most affectionately

S. WHITBREAD.[16]

That letter was written on the Monday of the last week of

Whitbread's life. He spoke in the House of Commons that evening, and again on the following day. His friends who were present at the debate on the Tuesday were somewhat comforted because he spoke 'more in his usual style than of late'.[17] On the Wednesday he attended a meeting at Drury Lane, without inviting particular comment except as he walked along Piccadilly with a friend, after it was over, he said: 'The world will point and scoff at me. The populace will pull down my house.'[18] And as he turned off Piccadilly into the quiet and splendour of Dover Street, he may have vividly imagined the rabble roaring for retribution against him. He went into the house — his home for nearly two decades and the centre from which radiated the politics and benevolence of his active mind — and dined quietly at eight with Lady Elizabeth and Mr. Wilshere. He was called by Weir the butler in the morning and he told him 'I am very well'. At ten o'clock Weir found the dressing-room door locked, and young Sam Reynolds told him that he had been knocking several times. They forced the door, and found Whitbread lying dead on the ground before a looking-glass, his arms and legs extended, his throat cut by a razor.

The news that he had been found dead — though not the manner of his death — sped through the town. His political friends, as their letters to Creevey show, were shattered — 'the day was one of general mourning among all of us'.[19] Friends and foes were silenced, though — as one of his intimates remarked — after the stunned silence, his enemies — in their heart of hearts — would rejoice. As by magic, bills, with deep-black borders were posted outside Drury Lane 'The public are respectfully informed that in consequence of the sudden and much lamented death of Mr. Whitbread . . . there will be no performance this evening.' The Duke of Devonshire was giving one of those formidable meat breakfasts, beloved by Whig magnates, at Chiswick House: on hearing the news he immediately sent off servants with cards postponing the gathering. A generous whisper came from Carlton House, whose owner had endured many of Whitbread's sharpest thrusts, 'Whitbread was an honest man'.

The greatest European of the day, embarking on H.M.S. *Northumberland* for St. Helena, had a long talk about Whitbread with W. H. Lyttelton, the Whig Member for Worcestershire and asked minutely about the manner of his death. With the instinctive politeness of the foreigner he gave to Whitbread the position which he had coveted but never held. 'Will Ponsonby succeed Whitbread as leader of the Opposition?' asked the fallen Emperor.

The boys were in Scotland : Lady Elizabeth and her younger daughter drove away from Dover Street to Osterley to the aristocratic stiffness but unexpected kindness of Lord and Lady Jersey. Tom Adkin, good-natured, but bewildered, attended Lady Elizabeth with the fidelity of a spaniel : the learned and saintly Howley, Bishop of London, called to comfort her. But she bore her affliction with the fortitude of her Whig mind without, as her companion Julia Grant said, giving way to make-believe or what was worse the dreaded enthusiasm of the Evangelicals.

Could the manner of dying be concealed? Grey was in London, and he and the other Whig leaders, flustered no doubt and desperately anxious to spare Lady Elizabeth, attempted to suppress the facts. The inquest was held on 6 July — the evening of Whitbread's death — and when three newspaper-men arrived at Dover Street the Whig chieftains attempted to exclude them from the house. It was explained that this could not be done because an inquest was an open court. Whitbread's friends felt keenly that, far from shunning publicity, Grey might have done more to bring out the stress of mind under which Whitbread had plainly been labouring for the last weeks of his life. Of the twelve honest men and true, one, McNaughton, was of Irish origins the others carried English, peasant names — Ashmead, Hanson, Peacock, Smith, Tombling, Atkins, Doggett, Brown, Wood, Walker and Turner. These simple, honest men seemed to reflect those unhurried, English qualities of openness

x

and fairness which had stamped the character within the body
over which they were called to pronounce their verdict. Preceded by Weir, the butler, carrying lighted wax candles and
remembering no doubt the countless occasions on which he had
led a distinguished company into his master's dining-room, the
members of the jury moved awkwardly forward through the
hall with its busts and portraits of the illustrious, political
comrades of the dead man, to the room where he was lying,
untouched since he had been found that morning. Their
unanimous verdict was that 'he died by his own hand — but in a
deranged state of mind'. He was buried on 12 July and lies in
the family vault at Cardington Church. Countless were the
lamentations and ephemeral tributes to the dead man. His
sincerity, his benevolence, his concern for justice and for the
dignity of human beings were all well known to his contemporaries, but no lasting memorials — no statues, no biographies
carried his fame in his own day, forward to posterity. For
Whitbread's life was not one of achievement: it was a life of
endeavour.

APPENDIX 1

Samuel Whitbread's Accounts

MR. PETER WRIGHT has written the following explanation of the accounts, and he has also provided the explanatory notes on p. 314.

INTRODUCTORY NOTE

The following statements were extracted from the Account Books, kept by Abraham Harman clerk to Whitbread. They show receipts and expenditure with details of the valuation at 31 December each year. Information is incomplete as some books are missing. Missing, too, is one very important step; the link between the receipts and expenditure account and the valuation. The surplus/deficiency shown by one account should be capable of reconciliation with the surplus/deficiency shown by the other. Only in 1799 and 1803 are they the same. This may be due to items being revalued in the valuation account each year instead of representing actual expenditure. There are also instances of capital expenditure being written off to receipts and expenditure accounts, although it is clear that not all capital expenditure was dealt with in this way.

There is little financial information on the last year of Whitbread's life. As far as can be seen there was no reason to worry over a loan (see author's comments on page 302). Although he was short of easily realisable assets the estates were worth a large sum. Was he trying to repay loans but finding it difficult to raise further sums to make the repayments? The incomplete correspondence in the private finance files at Bedford rather suggests this. There is evidence that £107,000 was still owing to his creditors in August 1818 and repayments of loans amounting to a further £92,000 can be traced in the Cash Book from 6 July 1815 to 31 December 1819.

309

Letters in brackets refer to notes on p. 314	Midsummer to Christmas 1796	1797	1798	1799	1800	1801	1802	1803
Receipts	£	£	£	£	£	£	£	£
Estates	..	..	..	..	..	10,351	9,213	7,37?
Trade Chiswell St.	14,634	42,121	33,000	30,153	7,727	3,822	15,773	15,43?
Trade Purfleet	..	291	576	1,172	2,593	2,310	4,533	3,60?
Trade Blackfriars	..	..	..	..	..	..	..	..
Farming	..	..	..	..	177	510	..	..
Interest Receivable	753	358	2,601	4,078	9,109(a)	3,641	2,373	2,36?
	15,387	42,770	36,177	35,403	19,606	20,634	31,892	28,79?
Expenditure								
Estates	6,825	5,210	7,709	13,026	4,908	..	..	..
Trade Purfleet	730	..	..	..	..	..	..	..
Trade Blackfriars	..	..	..	..	..	..	..	..
Interest and Annuities Payable	7,674	16,209	14,540	13,882	19,100(b)	13,617	19,663	17,20?
Farming	158	728	602	446	..	..	1,001	26?
House Rent	601	992	1,400	1,282	1,200	1,050	1,331	1,33?
Housekeeping	1,285	3,452	3,282	3,774	3,475	3,534	3,842	4,00?
Servants	662	686	573	1,321	1,233	1,166	1,010	1,30?
Horses	1,336	1,093	1,410	1,570	1,296	2,153	1,233	1,17?
Carriages	54	1,163	261	98	140	97	1,035	14?
Apparel	40	120	578	373	255	407	211	19?
Furniture	555	1,134	5,704	1,959	3,009	3,172	5,495	1,76?
Books	53	319	186	317	360	253	399	20?
Journeys	142	201	190	365	310	320	216	24?
Medicine	1,055	104	356	152	764	344	358	20?
Gifts	1,555	2,815	3,141	2,718	1,777	1,760	1,663	1,38?
Presents	1,515	1,749	2,259	2,786	1,249	668	861	30?
Elizabeth Whitbread	125	585	533	557	496	932	699	93?
Children	..	77	91	73	103	180	273	32?
Sundries (Income Tax, Wages, Election Expenses etc.)	3,859	3,127	2,414	6,109	5,107	5,516	4,619	2,24?
Petty Expenses	331	473	458	621	483	552	338	39?
	28,555	40,237	45,687	51,429	45,265	35,721	44,247	33,62?
Excess of Receipts over Expenditure	..	2,533	..	..	..	..	..	..
Excess of Expenditure over Receipts	13,168	..	9,510	16,026	25,659	15,087	12,355	4,83?

RECEIPTS AND EXPENDITURE ACCOUNT

1804 £	1805 £	1806 £	1807 £	1808 £	1809 £	1810 £	1811 £	1812 £	1813 £
11,999	12,256	13,879	15,519	14,070	13,026	9,467	14,430	10,223	6,971
10,301	7,158	11,340	14,377	14,453	13,422	9,833(e)	27,781(e)	22,156	12,753
1,842	3,179	3,831	4,160	3,618	3,493	3,115	5,366	4,238	3,630
..	..	..	..	8	465	20	264	537	..
216	131	754	319	1,028	750	387	829	808	294
2,004	1,710	1,240	3,495	1,013	1,137	1,064	1,879	985	1,525
26,362	24,434	31,044	37,870	34,190	32,293	23,886	50,549	38,947	25,173
..	..	..	..	..	..	..	..	..	..
..	..	..	..	..	..	..	..	..	..
..	..	..	..	..	..	..	..	..	115
17,256	16,294	16,967	17,541	17,475	17,422	15,149	21,305(c)	18,686	17,394
..	..	..	..	..	..	..	..	..	..
1,341	1,352	1,359	1,365	1,364	1,346	1,362	1,366	1,446	1,446
3,845	3,927	3,627	4,005	4,426	4,316	4,577	4,529	4,543	4,456
1,214	1,105	1,122	1,125	1,253	1,111	1,264	1,383	1,337	1,335
1,099	870	860	692	1,032	1,115	989	1,277	1,559	1,803
353	541	196	541	570	188	351	482	297	266
304	282	222	256	218	209	239	328	221	207
1,084	1,856	1,285	581	1,244	1,446	1,839	2,293	2,103	2,107
197	430	257	258	296	338	446	251	373	314
397	479	407	712	548	344	348	409	512	582
441	254	454	153	319	108	717	118	130	232
1,176	1,432	1,189	1,086	857	961	750	990	880	972
458	983	638	651	894	421	432	465	934	500
557	454	564	703	601	673	971	531	587	508
361	724	409	653	837	856	1,116	705	14,335(d)	1,475
2,535	5,378	3,640	5,089	4,127	2,635	3,427	7,511	6,218	6,965
479	670	797	722	620	652	677	622	411	365
33,097	37,031	33,993	36,133	36,681	34,141	34,654	44,565	54,572	41,042
..	..	..	1,737	..	..	..	5,984	..	..
6,735	12,597	2,949	..	2,491	1,848	10,768	..	15,625	15,869

Letters in brackets refer to notes on p. 314	31st Dec. 1796	1797	1798	1799	1800	1801	1802	1803
Assets	£	£	£	£	£	£	£	£
Estates	412,780	417,780	371,760	378,850	357,411	350,626	470,100	464,60
Trade Chiswell St. (f)	250,000	250,000	133,333	66,667	66,667	66,667	100,000	116,66
Trade Purfleet	9,696	9,026	7,937	7,695	9,016	8,544	11,889	13,03
Trade Blackfriars	..	..	..	..	..	..	..	..
Farm Stocks	2,666	2,757	2,690	2,577	2,727	2,803	2,891	3,26
Insurance unexpired	120	215	213	200	200	200	200	20
Wine Cellar	1,000	1,000	1,000	1,000	3,000	3,000	3,000	3,76
Horses & Carriages	1,500	1,500	1,500	1,500	1,500	1,500	1,500	1,50
Apparel	100	100	100	100	100	100	100	10
Furniture	5,000	5,000	5,000	5,000	25,000	25,000	25,000	25,00
Books	500	500	500	500	800	800	800	80
Cash Balance	222	171	117	19,640	1,400	5,186	1,574	3,01
Debts Receivable (f) (including investments)	81,922	65,670	126,287	115,311	108,853	122,782	100,044	80,49
	765,506	753,719	650,437	599,040	576,674	587,208	717,098	712,43
Liabilities								
Debts Payable (g) (including overdrafts)	270,670	260,301	270,811	235,440	217,482	247,879	256,187	256,35
Net Assets	494,836	493,418	379,626	363,600	359,192	339,329	460,911	456,07
Increase in net assets	..	..	..	..	..	..	121,582	..
Decrease in net assets		1,418	113,792	16,026	4,408	19,863	..	4,83

ALUATION

	1804 £	1805 £	1806 £	1807 £	1808 £	1809 £	1810 £	1811 £	1812 £	1813 £
	64,600	462,500	462,505	440,205	440,850	440,850	457,670	457,670	457,670	690,900
	16,667	116,667	116,667	116,667	116,667	116,667	116,667	116,667	112,500	112,500
	10,910	14,189	14,857	14,677	14,630	16,326	16,658	20,607	22,278	23,519
		..	..	..	2,572	2,827	2,817	2,781	3,233	3,048
	3,173	3,328	3,878	4,083	3,735	3,850	3,842	4,149	4,375	4,293
	200	200	200	200	200	200	200	200	200	200
	3,871	3,678	3,597	3,382	3,315	3,044	3,209	3,094	3,279	3,094
	1,500	1,500	1,500	1,500	1,500	1,500	1,500	1,500	1,500	1,500
	100	100	100	100	100	100	100	100	100	100
	25,000	25,000	25,000	25,000	25,000	25,000	25,000	25,000	25,000	25,000
	800	800	800	800	800	800	800	800	800	800
	6,955	7,371	6,402	6,094	7,366	7,681	6,341	6,918	8,356	10,934
	35,832	74,395	59,788	116,248	116,878	120,737	63,919	59,705	66,812	39,333

	1804	1805	1806	1807	1808	1809	1810	1811	1812	1813
	9,608	709,728	695,294	728,956	733,613	739,582	698,723	699,191	706,103	915,221

	1804	1805	1806	1807	1808	1809	1810	1811	1812	1813
	69,454	272,072	270,907	306,392	313,327	322,020	290,267	246,224	266,514	286,363

	1804	1805	1806	1807	1808	1809	1810	1811	1812	1813
	50,154	437,656	424,387	422,564	420,286	417,562	408,456	452,967	439,589	628,858
	..	..	..	..	..	..	..	44,511	..	189,269
	5,922	12,498	13,269	1,823	2,278	2,724	9,106	..	13,378	..

Explanatory Notes

(a) In May 1800 General Fitzpatrick agreed to purchase an annuity of £1,000 from Whitbread and paid him

£ 9,925

In November 1800 Whitbread agreed to reduce the annuity by one-half as the only security Whitbread could offer was defective in title and want of proper landed security would make it impossible for Gen. Fitzpatrick to sell any part of the annuity. Whitbread repaid

4,963

Credit to Receipts and Expenditure Account

£4,962

(b) £19,100 includes two items totalling £4,833 described as 'Loss by Stock'. This appears to be a reference to the purchase and sale of Consols. Whitbread on occasion promised to replace money borrowed by the purchase of a stated nominal amount of Consols at a later date.

(c) £21,305 includes two years share of profits from the Brewery due to Wilshere and Webb, i.e. about £3,000 of the charge relates to the previous year.

(d) Includes a marriage portion, gifts and wedding expenses of £13,546 on the marriage of his daughter Elizabeth to Captain Waldegrave, R.N.

(e) In 1810 a dispute occurred between the partners at the Brewery which resulted in Timothy Brown retiring. Because of this only £4,000 was brought into these Accounts as the trade profit for 1810, and a further £9,397 was brought into the 1811 Accounts when the dispute was settled. This also affected the charge for Interest Payable (see (c) above). 1810 and 1811 should, therefore, be taken together, the excess of expenditure over income being £4,784.

(f) In the valuation table Whitbread's share in the partnership capital is shown gross; the loans made to him by Wilshere and R. H. Webb in return for a share of the profits are included in Debts Payable. In 1798 Whitbread lent Yallowley and Sangster £30,000 each to take up their share in the partnership.

Yallowley's death in 1801 is reflected in the Accounts in 1802. Sangster gradually reduced the debt due, i.e. the amount stood at £24,000 in 1802, £17,000 in 1803, £13,000 in 1805, £5,150 in 1809 and was finally cleared in 1812. In 1813 the position was reversed and £4,045 was included in Debts Payable as owing to Sangster. There is an entry in the Cash Book, 9 July 1818, Payment 'Sangster — in full of Principal and Interest £20,791'.

In 1807 a new amount appears, I. A. Herman £51,798 which is reduced to £769 by 1810. The increase in 1809 was due to a larger holding of Public Funds. The reduction in 1813 is mainly accounted for by a reduction of £19,000 in the amount due from the firm of Whitbreads.

(g) Included under this heading in 1796 is £60,000 being certain (but not all) legacies payable under the Will of his Father. In later years some of the legacies were paid and others treated as loans to Whitbread.

314

ACCOUNTS FOR 1814 AND 1815

Unfortunately, the General Account Books and Ledgers for 1814 and 1815 are missing but two Cash Books remain, one in respect of cash kept by A. Harman and the other dealing with the Bank Account at Hammersley & Co. It is not possible to prepare Receipts and Expenditure Accounts or Valuations but the following is a summary of the Cash Books. The reader will notice that the figures for 1815 are from 1 January to 6 July only.

		£	£
Balance in hand 1 Jan. 1814 — Cash		3,620	
— Bank		7,314	
			10,934

	£
1814 — *Receipts*	
Income	38,162
Received on loan	19,773
Received on loan or possible repayments of money borrowed from Whitbread	5,382
Apparently a sale of land	154
Bedford Road Subscription	270
	£63,741

	£
Payments	
Purchase of Investments	597
Sundry drafts	54,157
Expenses — i.e. living expenses, gifts, donations, interest payable, annuities, taxes etc.	12,740
	£67,494

	£
Excess of payments over receipts	3,753

		£	£
Balance in hand 1 Jan. 1815 — Cash		2,780	
— Bank		4,401	
			7,181

1815 — *Receipts*	£	£
Income	15,274	
Received on loan	16,608	
Received on loan or possible repayments of money borrowed from Whitbread	703	
Bedford Road Subscription	144	
Drury Lane Theatre	73	
Sale of Consols	6,052	
	£38,854	

Payments		
Repayment of loans	9,085	
Sundry Drafts	22,650	
1 Drury Lane Share	100	
Expenses — i.e. living expenses, gifts, donations, interest payable, annuities, taxes etc.	6,341	
	£38,176	

Excess of receipts over payments		678

Balance in hand 6 July 1815 — Cash	2,939	
— Bank	4,920	
		£7,859

There is a note on the last page of Hammersley's Cash Book :

	£	s.	d.
'Balance per Cash Book 6 July 1815	4,919	17	–
Drafts outstanding	907	5	8
Balance per Hammersley & Co.	5,827	2	8
retained by them as part of debt due on £6,000 notes	6,000	–	–
Due to Hammersley & Co.	£ 172	17	4

The drafts outstanding Hammersley's have refused to pay'.*

* As, of course, was usual after a death (P. R. Wright).

APPENDIX 2

1802 Samuel Whitbread Esqr.
Election Expenses at Swan Inn Bedford.

July 1

		£	s	d
Butchers Bill of meat		9	8	3
2 pieces Boyld. Beef			10	0
8 Boild. Fowls with Sauce		1	0	0
8 Roast Ducks		1		
2 Ham 49 lb		1	10	5
4 Tounges		1	4	0
2 Pigs Faces			7	0
6 Plum Pudding			15	0
8 Large Fruit Pyes	2/6	1	0	0
vegetables & butter @ 4 each		1	0	8
bread & cheese @ 2 each			10	4
86 bottles of port		17	4	0
23 Sherry		5	15	0
Punch		3	13	6
33 Suppers		2	9	6
Punch		1	10	0
Tobacco			4	0
Lemons Nutmegs & Sugar			7	6
Rum, Brandy & Hollands			16	0

July 2

		£	s	d
Butchers Bill of Meat		8	3	8
Ham 24½ lbs		1	14	8½
8 Boild. Fowls with Sauce		1	0	0
8 Ducks		1	0	0
2 Tounges			12	0
2 pigs Faces			7	0
6 Plum Puddings			15	0
8 Large Fruit Pies		1	0	0
vegetables & butter			13	8
Bread & Cheese			6	10
97 Bottles Port		19	8	0
16 Sherry		4	0	0
Punch 7 Bowls		2	12	6
Cyder 9 Bowls			9	0
Lemons Nutmegs & Sugar			8	0
Tobacco			7	6
Tea 3/9 Brandy 6			4	3
		93	7	4

		£	s	d
Brought up		93	7	4
14 Suppers 1/6		1	1	0
cyder			4	0
Punch			15	0
Mr. Lilburne's Breakfast			1	0
horse hay & corn			2	6

July 5

		£	s	d
2 Breakfasts			2	0
6 Dinners 6/0 Brandy 2/0			8	0
Port 7/0 7 Suppers 10/6			7	6
Brandy 4/0 Punch 3/6			7	6

6

		£	s	d
Brandy & water			3	0
Cold eating etc for servants			15	0
Gin to Biggleswade & Shefford Lads			5	0
Sherry Nigus			10	0
Smiths Bill of meat		13	16	3½
12 Puddings		1	10	0
16 Large Fruit Pies	2/6	2	0	0
16 Fowls		2	0	0
16 Ducks	2/6	2	0	0
3 Hams 73½ lbs.	1/5	5	4	1½
3 Tounges			18	0
3 Pig's Faces			10	6
vegetables and butter Bread & cheese				
122 Gentin*	@6d	3	1	0
331 Bottles of Port		66	4	0
32 Do Sherry		8	0	0
7 Do Lisbon		1	8	0
25 Bowls Punch	7/6	9	7	6
Cyder		2	3	0
Lemons, Nutmegs & Sugar		1	0	0
Tea & Coffee 30		1	10	0
Glasses broke the 3 days				
81 wine glasses	7	2	7	3
9 Small Tumblers	9		6	9
5 Large Do	1/6		5	0
3 Decanters	3/6		10	6
33 glass bottles	4		11	0
1 window broke			4	9
1 chair spoild			8	0
Bar & Porter for the 3 days				
136 Gallons	2/0	13	12	0
		£237	16	3

* Presumably bitters.

317

References

In the preparation of this book I have consulted the following manuscript sources : Samuel Whitbread's papers at Bedford in the county record office, his family letters at Southill Park, the collection of papers acquired by his eldest daughter, Lady Waldegrave, and now at Chewton, his letters to Lord Grey at Durham, typescripts of his unpublished letters to Creevey at Whitfield, his private account books in the possession of Mr. Humphrey Whitbread, Lord Brougham's papers at University College, London, and a few letters in the Public Record Office and British Museum. In the list of authorities which follows I have referred to each collection simply by the place where it is lodged, except in the case of the account books which are described as such. At Bedford there is a full and helpful index to the collection, but in one or two instances I have added a further indication e.g. the Stocks papers, Bedford. (These are the family papers from Stocks House, the home of Whitbread's sister.)

As will be plain from the text I have leant heavily on the *Dictionary of National Biography*, Hansard's *Parliamentary Debates*, the *Annual Register* and Mr. Steven Watson's volume in the Oxford history on the reign of George III. I have not always given a reference to these when it seemed obvious without one.

In giving the reference to secondary authorities, where there is no index to the book in question or where some general statement seems difficult to trace I have given the page references. Otherwise I have not done this. To some readers the list of secondary authorities may seem largely compiled from the older books and biographies. That was deliberate. Since no biography of Whitbread was written after his death the comments and opinions about him by his contemporaries had to be collected. No doubt several of these will have escaped me.

CHAPTER ONE: FAMILY BACKGROUND

1. Sir Gilbert Elliot, Earl of Minto, *Life and Letters*, (1874) i, 301.
2. Edward FitzGerald, *Letters And Literary Remains*, (1902) i, 67.
3. Thomas Fuller, *History of Worthies of England*, (1811) i, 122.
4. Stocks papers at Bedford.
5. Ibid.
6. Chewton.
7. E. Phipps, *Memoirs of R. P. Ward*, (1850).
8. Stocks papers at Bedford.
9. Ibid.
10. Southill.
11. Bedford.
12. Stocks papers at Bedford.
13. Joseph Farington, *The Farington Diary*, (1922) vol. i.
14. Horace Walpole, *Letters*, (1903) xii, 210.
15. Stocks papers at Bedford.
16. G. M. Trevelyan, *Lord Grey of the Reform Bill*, (1952).
17. Henry Gunning, *Reminiscences of the University Town and County of Cambridge*, (1855).
18. Chewton.

CHAPTER TWO: ABROAD WITH THE ARCHDEACON

1. Bedford.
2. Chewton.
3. Chewton.
4. Chewton.
5. *The Pembroke Papers, 1780–94*, ed. Lord Herbert, (1950).
6. H. A. L. Fisher, *A History of Europe*, (1936), 793.
7. W. Coxe, *Travels into Poland, Russia, Sweden and Denmark*, (1792) iv, 73 and iv and v generally.
8. Earl of Malmesbury, *Diaries and Correspondence*, ed. 3rd Lord Malmesbury, (1844).
9. Southill.
10. Bedford.
11. Bedford.
12. Coxe, *Travels into Poland*.
13. Southill.
14. Southill.
15. Southill.
16. Chewton.
17. Chewton.
18. Chewton.
19. Bedford.

CHAPTER THREE: ELIZABETH GREY

1. Chewton.
2. Southill.
3. Iris Leveson Gower, *The Face without a Frown*, 5th ed., (1947).
4. Bedford.
5. Bedford.
6. Southill.
7. Peter Pindar, *Works*, (1797) i, 322.
8. Southill.
9. Chewton.
10. Chewton.
11. Chewton.
12. Southill.
13. Chewton.
14. Southill.
15. Southill.

CHAPTER FOUR: A RECRUIT FOR FOX

1. Charles James Fox, *Memorials and Correspondence*, ed. Lord John Russel, (1853) i, 221.
2. J. Steven Watson, *Reign of George III*, (1960).
3. Charles Whibley, *Political Portraits*, (1917).
4. Edmund Burke, *Works*, (1826) viii, 10.

5. Elliot, *Life and Letters*, (1874).
6. Chewton.
7. Chewton.
8. Chewton.
9. *Correspondence of George, Prince of Wales*, ed. A. Aspinall, ii (1789–1794), (1964).
10. Bedford.

CHAPTER FIVE: FRIEND OF THE PEOPLE

1. Duff Cooper, *Talleyrand*, (1932) 19.
2. Lord Rosebery's Introduction to *The Windham Papers* (1913).
3. Charles Pigott, *The Whig Club or a Sketch of Modern Patriotism*, (1794).
4. Chewton.
5. Bedford.
6. Mrs. Sandford, *Thomas Poole and his Friends*, (1888).
7. William Hazlitt, *Lectures on the English Poets: The Spirit of the Age*, (1910) 203.
8. Bedford.
9. *Annual Register*, (1792) 75–90.
10. Edward Thompson, *Making of the English Working-Class*, (1963).
11. Watson, *Reign of George III*, (1960).

12. E. J. Payne in *Encylopaedia Britannica*, 11th ed.
13. Bedford.
14. Whitfield.
15. Fox, *Memorials and Correspondence*, (1853) iii, 60.
16. See Mr. Baker Short's interesting article in the *Transactions of the Unitarian Historical Society*, (Oct. 1964).
17. Bedford.
18. Bedford.
19. *Farington Diary*, (1922) i, 109.
20. Bedford.
21. Bedford.
22. Durham.
23. Bedford.
24. Stocks papers at Bedford.
25. Bedford.

CHAPTER SIX: COUNTRY LIFE AND NEIGHBOURS

1. Chewton.
2. Chewton.
3. *Southill, A Regency House*, (1951).
4. *Country Life* (1930), vol. lxviii.
5. Bedford.
6. Bedford.
7. Fox, *Memorials and Correspondence*, (1853) iii, 317.
8. Bedford.

9. Lord Colchester, *Diary and Correspondence*, ed. 2nd Lord Colchester, (1861) i, 15.
10. Bedford.
11. Bedford.
12. Bedford.
13. General Grey, *Some Account of the Life and Opinions of Charles, 2nd Earl Grey*, (1861).

CHAPTER SEVEN: WITH THE OAKLEY HUNT

1. Bedford.
2. Bedford.
3. Bedford.
4. Bedford.
5. Bedford.
6. Bedford.
7. British Museum, Add. MSS. 26055 f86.
8. *Annual Register*, (1796) 24.
9. Quoted by W. E. H. Lecky in *A History of England in the Eighteenth Century*, (1892) vii, 352.
10. Bedford.
11. Chewton.
12. Bedford.
13. Bedford.
14. Durham.

CHAPTER EIGHT: CARES OF CHISWELL STREET

1. Quoted by Peter Mathias in *The Brewing Industry in England (1700–1830)*, (1959) 273.
2. Durham.
3. Mathias, *The Brewing Industry*, 301.
4. *The Story of Whitbread's*, (1964).
5. Ibid.

CHAPTER NINE: ENTOURAGE AT SOUTHILL

1. Bedford.
2. *The Journal of Elizabeth, Lady Holland*, ed. Lord Ilchester, (1908).
3. *Gentleman's Magazine*, vol. 98 (1828) 274–5.
4. Bedford.
5. Private Account Books.
6. *Southill, A Regency House* (1951).
7. Bedford.
8. *Southill, A Regency House* (1951).
9. Bedford.
10. *Southill, A Regency House* (1951).
11. Sir Lionel Cust in *The Dictionary of National Biography*.
12. Bedford.
13. Bedford.
14. Gertrude Lyster, *Family Chronicle* selected by Barberina, Lady Grey, (1908) 17.
15. Bedford.
16. Facts on pages 102–4 from Reynolds papers at Bedford.
17. The Earl of Ilchester, *The Home of the Hollands, 1605–1820* (1937).
18. Chewton.
19. Chewton.

CHAPTER TEN: JOYS OF OPPOSITION

1. Bedford.
2. Trevelyan, *Lord Grey*, (1952).
3. Ibid.
4. Watson, *Reign of George III* (1960).
5. Durham.
6. Fox, *Memorials and Correspondence*, (1853) ii, 360.
7. Ibid. iii, 35.
8. Bedford.
9. Thomas Campbell, *Life and Letters* ed. W. Beattie, (1850) ii, 84.
10. Durham.
11. Bedford.
12. Fox, *Memorials and Correspondence*, (1853) iii, 465.
13. Bedford.
14. Chewton.

CHAPTER ELEVEN: IMPEACHMENT OF MELVILLE

The Melville papers at Bedford have been used generally throughout this chapter.

1. Lord Macaulay, 'Warren Hastings' in *Critical and Historical Essays*, (1878) iii, 333
2. Duke of Buckingham and Chandos, *Memoirs of the Courts and Cabinets of George III*, (1855) iii, 355.

3. *The Grenville Papers*, ed. W. J. Smith, (1852–3).
4. Lord Campbell, *Lives of the Lord Chancellors*, (1846) viii, 23.
5. H. Furber, *Henry Dundas, First Viscount Melville*, (1931).
6. *Windham Papers*, (1913) ii, 252
7. Public Record Office, 30/58/6.
8. *Gentleman's Magazine*, (1806) vol. 76, 462ff.
9. *Dictionary of National Biography*.
10. C. Matheson, *Life of Henry Dundas, First Viscount Melville*, (1933).
11. *Hansard*.
12. Speech on pages 124–5 from *Hansard*.
13. *Hansard*.

14. Malmesbury, *Diaries and Correspondence* (1844).
15. *Gentleman's Magazine*, (1806).
16. *Historical MSS. Commission* (Fortescue MS.) viii, 79.
17. *Letters of C. K. Sharpe*, ed. W. K. R. Bedford, (1888).
18. George Rose, *Diaries and Correspondence*, ed. L. V. Harcourt, (1860) ii, 297.
19. *Letters of C. K. Sharpe*, (1888).
20. Fox, *Memorials and Correspondence*, (1853) iv, 134.
21. See generally W. J. Fitzpatrick, *Secret Service Under Pitt*, (1892).
22. *George Canning and his Friends*, ed. Josceline Bagot, (1909) i, 221.

CHAPTER TWELVE: NO PLACE FOR WHITBREAD

1. Lord Holland, *Memoirs of the Whig Party*, (1852) ii, 48.
2. *The Complete Peerage*, ed. Vicary Gibbs (1929–49).
3. Durham.
4. Holland, *Memoirs of the Whig Party*, (1852) i, 219.
5. Durham.
6. Lord Holland, *Further Memoirs of the Whig Party, 1807–21*, (1905) 354.
7. Bedford.
8. Holland, *Memoirs of the Whig Party*, (1852) ii, 90.

9. These particulars are in the correspondence at Durham.
10. *The Creevey Papers*, ed. Sir H. Maxwell, (1904) i, 80.
11. Durham.
12. *Farington Diary*, (1922) iv, 32.
13. *H.M.C.* (Fortescue) viii, 347; *Farington Diary*, (1922) iv, 25.
14. *Creevey Papers*, (1904) i, 183.
15. Bedford.
16. Colchester, *Diary and Correspondence*, (1861) ii, 102.
17. Whitfield.

CHAPTER THIRTEEN: ELECTIONS AND TEMPER

1. Bedford.
2. Hazlitt, *Spirit of The Age*, (1910) 218.
3. Bedford.
4. *History of the Westminster and Middlesex Elections* (1807).
5. Bedford.
6. *H.M.C.* (Fortescue) viii, 439.

7. Bedford.
8. Bedford.
9. Bedford.
10. Bedford.
11. Bedford.
12. Bedford.
13. Bedford.

CHAPTER FOURTEEN: THE REBELLIOUS WHIG

1. Edward Gibbon, *The History of The Decline and Fall of the Roman Empire*, (1905) chap. xxxv.

2. Bedford.
3. Lord E. Fitzmaurice, *Life of William Earl of Shelburne*, (1875) iii, 527.

4. Fox, *Memorials and Correspondence*, (1853) iii, 67.
5. Durham.
6. Bedford.
7. *Farington Diary*, (1922) iv, 87.
8. J. L. and Barbara Hammond, *The Village Labourer, 1760–1832*, (1911) 180.
9. Durham.
10. Bedford.
11. Whitfield.

12. Public Record Office.
13. Buckingham, *Memoirs of Courts and Cabinets*, (1853) vii, 147. The confusion over the Ministry's proposals makes a tangled page of history. Professor Michael Roberts gives the clearest account of it in *The Whig Party 1807–12*, (1939).
14. Bedford.
15. Bedford.
16. Bedford.

CHAPTER FIFTEEN : CREEVEY AND NUM-NUM

1. Trevelyan, *Lord Grey*, (1952) 163.
2. *H.M.C.* (Fortescue) ix, 149.
3. Buckingham, *Memoirs of Courts and Cabinets*, (1853) viii, 210.
4. *Parliamentary Portraits*, reprinted from *The Examiner*, (1815) (Thomas Barnes) 31.
5. Holland, *Memoirs of the Whig Party*, (1852) ii, 238.
6. Bedford.
7. *Creevey's Life and Times*, ed. John Gore (1934).
8. Buckingham, *Memoirs of Courts and Cabinets*, (1853) iv, 216.
9. Bedford.
10. Bedford.
11. Lord Brougham, *Contributions to the Edinburgh Review*, (1856) i, 337.
12. Bedford.
13. Quoted from Roberts, *The Whig Party*, (1939). As this letter is not

at Bedford, it was possibly among those which were destroyed by Grey.
14. Bedford.
15. Chewton.
16. Chewton.
17. *The Greville Memoirs 1814–60*, ed. Strachey and Fulford (1938).
18. *Journals of Lady Holland*, (1908) and Lady Seymour, *The Pope of Holland House* (1906).
19. Whitfield.
20. Bedford.
21. Bedford.
22. Bedford.
23. Bedford.
24. Whitfield.
25. *Creevey Papers*, (1904) i, 91.
26. Bedford.
27. Bedford.
28. Whitfield.

CHAPTER SIXTEEN : A ROYAL MISTRESS

1. Quoted in article in *Dictionary of National Biography* on Col. G. L. Wardle.
2. D. M. Stuart, *Dearest Bess*, (1955).
3. S. H. Romilly, *Letters to Ivy from the First Earl of Dudley*, (1905).
4. Holland, *Further Memoirs*, (1905) 28.

5. Bedford.
6. Denis Gray, *Spencer Perceval*, (1963).
7. Chewton.
8. Bedford.
9. Buckingham, *Memoirs of Courts and Cabinets*, (1853) iv, 156.
10. Bedford.

CHAPTER SEVENTEEN : THE RADICAL IN BEDFORDSHIRE

1. *H.M.C.* (Fortescue) ix, 269.
2. *Farington Diary*, (1922) vii, 230.
3. Glamorgan Record Office (Bute Papers).

4. Bedford.
5. Bedford.
6. Bedford.
7. Bedford.

8. Bedford.
9. Bedford.
10. Bedford.

11. Bedford.
12. Hansard.
13. Bedford.

CHAPTER EIGHTEEN: FARMER AND SOLDIER

1. Bedford.
2. Whitfield.
3. Creevey Papers, (1904) i, 94 and Whitfield.
4. Bedford.
5. Bedford.
6. Bedford.
7. Bedford.

8. Bedford.
9. Bedford.
10. Bedford.
11. Whitfield.
12. Bedford.
13. Bedford.
14. Bedford.

CHAPTER NINETEEN: HOSPITALITY AT SOUTHILL

1. Southill.
2. Bedford.
3. Bedford.
4. Bedford.
5. Journals of Lady Holland, (1908).
6. Bedford.
7. Whitfield and Bedford.
8. Bedford.
9. Lord Broughton, Recollections of a

Long Life, ed. Lady Dorchester, (1909) i, 92.
10. Bedford.
11. Bedford.
12. Farington Diary, (1922) vol. v and Bedford.
13. Bedford.
14. Bedford.

CHAPTER TWENTY: A BEDFORDSHIRE DOCTOR

1. Arnold Palmer, Movable Feasts (1952).
2. Creevey Papers, (1904) i, 109.
3. Ibid. i, 101ff.
4. Bedford.
5. Hansard.
6. Parliamentary Portraits, (1815) 122.

7. Bedford.
8. Bedford.
9. Creevey's Life and Times, ed. Gore, (1934).
10. Whitfield.
11. Bedford.
12. Bedford.

CHAPTER TWENTY-ONE: INDEPENDENCE AT WESTMINSTER

1. Hansard.
2. Hansard.
3. Hansard.
4. Bedford.
5. Hansard.
6. Thompson, Making of the English Working-Class, (1963).
7. Annual Register (1815), 23.
8. Bedford.
9. Bedford.
10. Hansard.

11. Hazlitt, Spirit of the Age, (1910) 320.
12. Lord Stanhope, Notes of Conversations with the Duke of Wellington, 1831–51, (1888) 122.
13. Creevey Papers, (1904) i, 191.
14. The bill of Messrs. Winter & Shee (1810) is at Bedford.
15. Parliamentary Portraits, (1815) 226.

CHAPTER TWENTY-TWO: CHANCES OF OFFICE

1. Romilly, *Letters to Ivy*, (1905).
2. Chewton.
3. Chewton.
4. Bedford.
5. Bedford.
6. Bedford.
7. *Creevey Papers*, (1904) i, 142.
8. Stuart, *Dearest Bess*, (1955).
9. George Croly, *Life and Times of George IV*, (1830) 386–7.
10. Whitfield.
11. Chewton.
12. Leonard Horner, *Memoirs and Correspondence of Francis Horner*, (1843) ii, 114.
13. Whitfield.
14. Bedford.
15. Bedford.
16. Brougham, *Contributions to the Edinburgh Review*, (1856) i, 472.
17. Bedford.
18. Bedford.
19. Bedford.

CHAPTER TWENTY-THREE: TRIBULATIONS OF A PRINCESS

1. *Creevey Papers*, (1904) i, 145.
2. Holland, *Further Memoirs*, (1905) 174–5.
3. Bedford.
4. University College, London (Brougham papers).
5. [Lady Charlotte Bury], *Diary Illustrative of the Times of George IV*, (1838) i, 218.
6. Bedford.
7. Robert Huish, *Memoirs of Caroline, Queen-Consort of England*, (1821) i, 480.
8. Whitfield.
9. *The Genuine Book. An Enquiry or Delicate Investigation into the conduct of the Princess of Wales*, (1813) Bidgood's evidence.
10. Huish, *Memoirs of Caroline*, (1821) i, 513–14.
11. Romilly, *Letters to Ivy*, (1905).
12. Bedford.
13. *Correspondence and Diaries of J. W. Croker*, ed. L. J. Jennings, (1884) i, 304.
14. John Doran, *Lives of The Queens of England of the House of Hanover*, (1875) i, 288.
15. Huish, *Memoirs of Caroline*, (1821) i, 564.
16. Whitfield.
17. University College, London (Brougham papers).
18. Ibid.
19. Bedford.
20. Bedford.
21. Bedford.
22. *Memoirs of Courts and Cabinets During the Regency*, ed. Duke of Buckingham and Chandos, (1856) ii, 46.
23. Bedford.
24. Bedford.
25. *Creevey Papers*, (1904) i, 181.

CHAPTER TWENTY-FOUR: DRURY LANE

1. Lord Byron, *Poetical Works*, (1857) iv, 218.
2. *Farington Diary*, (1922) ii, 81.
3. Trevelyan, *Lord Grey*, (1952) 126.
4. Fox, *Memorials and Correspondence*, (1853) ii, 24.
5. Ibid. iii, 272.
6. Durham (Grey family correspondence).
7. Bedford.
8. Thomas Moore, *Memoirs of the Life of Sheridan*, (1826) vol. i, ch. xx.
9. Holland, *Further Memoirs*, (1905).
10. Chewton.
11. Report to the shareholders, Bedford.
12. British Museum, Add. MSS. 42721 ff79–81.

13. See Quentin Skinner's article in *Theatre Notebook*, vol. xvii.
14. *Hansard*, 20 March 1812.
15. Bedford.
16. British Museum, Add. MSS. 42721 f63–64.
17. Lord Chamberlain's Papers, Public Record Office.
18. Bedford.
19. Sir John Summerson, *Georgian London*, (1945).
20. Holland, *Further Memoirs*, (1905).
21. Thomas Moore, *Letters and Journals of Lord Byron*, (1830) i, 369.
22. Ibid.

CHAPTER TWENTY-FIVE: THEATRE MANAGER

1. Skinner in *Theatre Notebook*, vol. xvii.
2. *Letters of George IV, 1812–1830*, ed. A. Aspinall, (1938).
3. Ibid.
4. Bedford.
5. Thomas Dibdin, *Reminiscences*, (1827) ii, 21.
6. Broughton, *Recollections of a Long Life*, (1909) i, 125.
7. B. W. Procter, *The Life of Edmund Kean*, i, chaps. 2 & 3.
8. Bedford.
9. Bedford.
10. Cecil Price, *The Letters of Richard Brinsley Sheridan*, (1966).
11. Whitfield.
12. Bedford.
13. Bedford.
14. Chewton.
15. Bedford.
16. Price, *Letters of Sheridan*, (1966).
17. Broughton, *Recollections of a Long Life*, (1909).
18. British Museum, Add. MS. 42721 ff79–81.
19. British Museum, Add. MS. 42721 ff122–125.
20. Bedford.

CHAPTER TWENTY-SIX: DEATH IN DOVER STREET

1. *Parliamentary Portraits*, (1815).
2. Horner, *Memoirs . . . of Francis Horner*, (1843) 261.
3. *Hansard*.
4. Whitfield.
5. Chewton.
6. Chewton.
7. Chewton.
8. *Creevey's Life and Times*, ed. Gore, (1934).
9. Whitfield.
10. Whitfield.
11. Ilchester, *Home of the Hollands*, (1937) 266.
12. F. Phippen, *Authentic Account of the late Mr. Whitbread*, (1815).
13. Broughton, *Recollections of a Long Life*, (1909).
14. Whitfield.
15. Chewton.
16. Chewton.
17. Whitfield.
18. Phippen, *Authentic Account*, (1815).
19. Whitfield.

Index

PRINTED IN GREAT BRITAIN BY ROBERT MACLEHOSE AND CO. LTD
THE UNIVERSITY PRESS, GLASGOW

Universitas
BIBLIOTHECA
Ottaviensis